PRAISE FOR REPORTING THE TR~

'The Irish journalist who never reporte~
those who did, and welcomes this m
journalists and what they did '
in their line of work – livii.
Raymond Sno~

~ss

..

'A compelling account of one ,   ~st turbulent
periods in Northern Irela..~ s history.'
Suzanne McGonagle, *Irish News*

'The tales coalesce into a magnificent overview of Northern Ireland during a
conflict which claimed over 3,600 lives ...
The cumulative effect is somehow of hope in adversity.'
John Mullin, *Daily Telegraph*

'*Reporting the Troubles* is a gripping, prismatic account of half a century of
fear, tragedy, hatred, loss, grief, bewilderment, and hope ... [It] will stand, as
its editors assert, as "an epitaph, of sorts" for three decades of suffering.'
Kevin Power, *Sunday Business Post*

'An important and welcome contribution to the collective recording of our
recent past ... This is a book everyone should read – in fact,
I urge everyone to do so.'
Paul Harron, *Ulster Tatler*

'*Reporting the Troubles* is a remarkable, unique and invaluable
insight into the darkest days of our history.'
Lindy McDowell, *Belfast Telegraph*

'Even in the belly of pain and chaos, come surprising, revelatory
moments of humanity and unexpected kindness.'
Gail Bell, *Irish News*

'This Blackstaff Press book is an essential and important
one because reporters saw the raw, unvarnished truth before
the alchemy of "understanding", of putting deaths into a so-called
"hierarchy" of tragedy, of mythologising, of politicians explaining
it away or "placing it in a wider context" ...'
Gail Walker, *Belfast Telegraph*

Reporting the Troubles 2

More journalists tell their stories of the Northern Ireland conflict

Compiled by DERIC HENDERSON and IVAN LITTLE
Foreword by Bertie Ahern and Sir Tony Blair

·THE·
BLACK
·STAFF
PRESS

To the memory of the men, women and children who died during the Troubles; and to their loved ones, who are still struggling with the massive gaps left in their lives.

For my baby grandson, Patrick Deric Jack Henderson. (DH)

In memory of my wonderful parents, William and Lola, and to the memory of my former teacher, Mr Sam Ross, who inspired me to believe. (IL)

First published in 2022 by Blackstaff Press
an imprint of Colourpoint Creative Ltd
Colourpoint House
Jubilee Business Park
21 Jubilee Road
Newtownards BT23 4YH

Printed and bound by CPI Group UK Ltd, Croydon CR0 4YY

A CIP catalogue for this book is available from the British Library

ISBN 978-1-78073-325-8

www.blackstaffpress.com

Contents

Foreword

Bertie Ahern

This collection from journalists is contemporary history, with all the freedoms and limitations that entails. It is a timely reminder to the generations of political leaders, community activists and people who live in Northern Ireland and beyond, that we can never again return to those days when suffering and devastation were stark and searing drumbeats for its people.

The turbulent history of Northern Ireland may seem an impossible landscape for the triumph of democracy over violence and yet, despite all-too-frequent examples of needless pain and suffering, which mark every page of this collection of news stories, nationalist and unionist communities somehow managed to forge a fragile and imperfect peace.

The greatest gift that we as a society can aspire to bequeath to future generations is to create safe democracies that are grounded in mutual respect and the acceptance of alternative views.

The history of our island is sadly chequered with stories of suffering inflicted upon families. But, unlike the fleeting news cycle, their pain, grief and suffering is enduring. It lives on in every moment of every day for them. They carry their history within, and for that reason, this book is a good way to give the rising generation a glimpse of the horror that we have thankfully left behind.

It proves that the real legacy of the Troubles is that violence solves nothing. It merely leaves behind a trail of destruction and devastates the lives of ordinary innocent people who become collateral damage. There are those who hold the view that without violence the democratic avenue would not have been possible, but hateful intimidation is not the precursor to democracy, it is its enemy. The proof is that violence had to be abandoned before peace could begin.

Journalists and correspondents from Ireland, the UK and all over the world have an enormously important role to play in exposing the truths and the criminals that lie behind the events designed to bully and intimidate communities in Northern Ireland.

I personally know many journalists who worked in Northern Ireland during the Troubles and who will never forget the horrors they witnessed.

Many will be affected in a lasting and real way for the rest of their lives. Memory will remain their wound. Bravery and profound empathy with a commitment to tell the truth, often in the face of deadly threat, is not always easy but is necessary to record the first draft of history through the press. In bringing together this collection of stories by journalists who worked in Northern Ireland during the height of the violence, Ivan Little and Deric Henderson have again served a raw, real-time reminder of the impacts of these devastating events, which we must all endeavour to ensure are never again repeated.

Sir Tony Blair

Behind all the news reports and television footage about the Troubles over too many years, this new collection of reminiscences lays bare the terrible toll of the tragedies, provides insight into what it was like to conduct sometimes dangerous and clandestine meetings with actors on both sides and offers a personal perspective on reporting in those times. It reveals the stoicism and bravery of those journalists, reporters and their colleagues who, faced with unimaginable pain and suffering, bore witness to the atrocities perpetrated and their aftermaths with admirable professionalism.

The golden thread running through this collection is humanity, as they witnessed first-hand the devastation caused to families and tried to come to terms with what they were seeing and hearing in order to report and reflect their stories.

No one can doubt the deep and lasting impact of these experiences.

It is, of course, important that we remember and reflect on life as it was then for so many, the transformative change from living in fear to thriving and with optimism for the future. The road to peace is long and sometimes hard, with setbacks to overcome, but the people of Northern Ireland have come so far and, as these recollections remind us, the advances made since the Good Friday Agreement and the continuing peace process remains precious and life-affirming.

Introduction

Deric Henderson and Ivan Little

Not long after *Reporting the Troubles* was published in 2018, we received a phone call from a relative of a Troubles victim. He rang us to say that he had been profoundly moved by the first book; that he believed it was important because it reminded people of what had happened in the conflict. He thought that people who were born after the Good Friday Agreement should know what it had been like to live through those years and our book gave them a sense of that. These comments were echoed by others, and by reviewers, and they became the catalyst for this second volume.

Our focus in the first book was mainly on reporters from newspapers, television and radio who, like us, had worked in Northern Ireland when the civil unrest first broke out in the late 1960s and through the worst years of the Troubles. We were enormously proud of the book and of the way it was received both at home and further afield. We also knew there were many significant stories still to be told. Although we had included contributions from sixty-six colleagues, we were aware that there were many others with compelling and powerful stories – contemporaries of ours who had worked during the early days of the conflict and beyond, and a new generation of journalists who had come up more recently, in the years leading to the Good Friday Agreement and later.

And so began another round of phone calls, emails and letters, in which we asked dozens of friends and colleagues if they would be interested in writing for the second book. They all said yes. As before, the contributors were free to decide for themselves what they would focus on. We didn't make any requests about events or eras to be covered. When the pieces came in, they covered many of the key events in Northern Ireland's troubled history, running from 1970 – when Conor Brady (future editor of the *Irish Times*) arrived in Belfast knowing 'next to nothing of the city' – to 2021, and Will Leitch's contribution about the inquest into the Ballymurphy Massacre and the meaning of the word 'legacy' here.

Legacy and the aftermath of the Troubles are key threads in this new book. 2023 marks twenty-five years since the signing of the Good Friday Agreement, so it's particularly fitting that we have forewords from Sir Tony Blair and Bertie Ahern, two of the architects of that agreement. This book extends the range of the first, covering not only the years before but also the years after this key moment in our history, and shows how we are still trying to realise the vision for peace set out in that document, as well as manage the legacies of our troubled past.

We dedicated the first volume of the book to the victims of the Troubles, and they and their families are still at the heart of this second book. We hope that both volumes stand as an enduring act of remembrance.

The books are also about the impact the violence had on the people who reported it. As Lance Price writes in his contribution, 'Reporting the Troubles … is never just a job. It changes you and the way you look at the world. It would be extraordinary if it didn't.' Many of the journalists here reflect on the toll their work took on them; how they coped and sometimes how they didn't; how the constant danger and risk and sadness affected them.

The way we access news has certainly changed in the years covered by this book, but a phrase quoted by contributor Gary Honeyford – 'We lived by the news' – is just as true today as it was throughout the Troubles. We depend on good journalists to inform us and help us to understand, but that work can be dangerous and high risk. In the first book, Jim McDowell wrote about the murder in 2001 in Lurgan, County Armagh, of the investigative journalist Martin O'Hagan. Jim Campbell also wrote powerfully about being shot, also by loyalist gunmen, at his home in Belfast in May 1984.

Since the publication of that book, tragically we have lost another journalist, Lyra McKee, who was murdered by dissident republicans in Derry in 2019. An emerging young writer born in 1990, she was one of the Ceasefire Babies, a generation who were children at the time of the Agreement, or born after it. Lyra was shot dead a week after the twenty-first anniversary of its signing; Donna Deeney's piece in this book pays tribute to her.

We believe passionately that good journalism can make a difference and we hope that this new volume of *Reporting the Troubles* has a part to play in helping all of us come to understand our past so that we can build a better future.

The town we didn't know so well
Belfast, 1970

Conor Brady

Five or six of us stood around the news desk in the old *Irish Times* building in Westmoreland Street. Our average age was probably twenty. All wet-behind-the-ears youngsters, for the most part straight out of university. The deputy news editor, Gerry Mulvey, a veteran of Enniskillen's *Impartial Reporter*, gave us our instructions and the necessary documentation: a book of railway vouchers; a green docket allowing each of us to draw £100 from the cashier downstairs; an AT&T code book that would enable us to use public telephone and telex services wherever we could get a line.

It was the autumn of 1970. The North had been swept by violence during the summer. The *Irish Times* had maintained a staff of seasoned journalists at its Belfast office. Fergus Pyle was northern editor. Henry Kelly was his deputy. Renagh Holohan was on temporary transfer from Dublin more or less permanently, it seemed. Dermot Mullane, who had covered *Les Évènements* – the student protests in Paris – was based in Derry.

We were to be rotated through the Belfast office, which was then located in Castle Street. For the most part we were billeted in a city centre hotel, although sometimes when it was fully booked with overseas press and broadcasters, the lucky ones got to stay at the Wellington Park. We worked around the clock, sometimes from the office, sometimes at Stormont, more often – especially at night – out on the streets. Down time was a few pints in McGlade's or The Crown. We worked two weeks and then got a week off, usually returning to Dublin by train or in a photographer's car.

We knew next to nothing of the city and such understanding as we had of the conflict and its causes was from history books. On my first night going out, Henry Kelly wrote 'S=P' and 'F=C' on my hand: Shankill equals Protestants, Falls equals Catholics. But we learned quickly. Belfast is a small city and there are easy points of reference for the stranger. Cave Hill, for example, always gives a reliable bearing. We had no transport but we had an open account with one of the taxi companies and we got to know the regular drivers. They knew how to get a reporter or photographer to the trouble spots

1

without getting into danger. More importantly, they knew how to get us out again. It was hazardous work. The press were generally treated with hostility, especially in loyalist areas.

Reporters had some anonymity. But photographers and camera crews with their equipment were easily identifiable targets. Often they had their cameras seized and smashed. Sometimes they were roughed up or threatened. Some chose to tag along with police or army patrols as a means of protection. But that could have the effect sometimes of drawing hostility from locals, notably in nationalist areas. Reporters were frequently required to produce their identification for vigilantes or 'community workers'. Happily, the NUJ card of the time did not state the organisation its holder worked for. Reporters from the 'southern' newspapers were particularly unwelcome in loyalist areas – one *Irish Press* reporter who could do a perfect Cockney accent succeeded in persuading a UDA patrol in Woodvale that he worked for the *Jewish Chronicle*.

Along with photographer Dermot O'Shea, I was assigned to cover the annual parade of the Royal Black Preceptory at Rathfriland in August that year. The 'blackmen' were in a resentful mood. Somebody pointed us out as press and a circle formed around us. There was pushing and jostling and shouted threats about putting us in the river. Just as it seemed to be about to turn ugly, the imperial grand master, Captain L.P.S. (Willie) Orr, resplendent in full Preceptory regalia, pushed through the crowd and put a hand on each of our shoulders. 'These gentlemen are our guests,' he announced solemnly. 'We will treat them as guests ought to be treated.' And with that he led us across the road to a refreshment tent where he poured us hot tea and insisted that we have currant buns with strawberry jam.

We lived with just enough danger to make the work exciting but probably not enough to leave most of us with long-term scars. A lot of the time we didn't fully apprehend the risks. I turned out to Flax Street off the Crumlin Road one September night to report on an incident involving a military patrol that had engaged with IRA snipers around the mill. The night was warm and balmy and I could hear a buzzing sound around my head. Odd that there should be bees about at night, I thought. Then a weighty NCO of the Green Howards barrelled into me and threw me flat on the ground as more sniper rounds buzzed through the air, more or less where my body had been.

The other major task was to cover proceedings at Stormont. The *Irish Times* had fully reported the Northern parliament for years, the only southern newspaper to do so. Some wag remarked that Fergus Pyle's 'Stormont Report' was actually longer than Hansard. Covering the chamber was generally pretty routine stuff. But one learned a lot about Northern Ireland – its skewed politics and its deep, historic divisions – in the bar or in conversations in the corridors in the long hours of the night. I experienced at first-hand the bullying, intimidatory tactics of Ian Paisley. But I also experienced the courtesy and gentlemanliness of Education Minister Phelim O'Neill; the calm, reasonableness of Roy Bradford; and indeed the good humour of the bête noire that was Bill Craig, then home affairs minister and later founder of Vanguard.

One learned that behind the stereotypes and the tribal slogans there was usually a human being who experienced much the same joys and sufferings as the rest of us. They had their own hopes and fears, and plans and ambitions for their families and communities. Yes, the unionists looked down on the nationalists and saw no reason why these people should expect any more than the share of the loaf that they had been allocated. But later, as one clocked up the years, one came to realise that the instinct to get on top and keep somebody else below is fairly universal. Only when that instinct is confronted and confounded can democracy succeed. And that is the ultimate triumph of politics. These were significant discoveries and revelations for young journalists from easy-going Dublin or peaceful, sleepy towns and villages in Connaught or Munster.

My coverage of the Troubles did not last very long, in the sense that my work as an on-the-ground reporter was time-limited. After two years I was assigned to the London office of the *Irish Times* and thereafter I held a sequence of editorial roles that kept me largely desk-bound.

But it was in my years as editor of the newspaper that the experience of those early times in Belfast proved their importance. The *Irish Times* played no insignificant role in facilitating the dialogue that eventually yielded the peace process and the Belfast Agreement of Good Friday 1998. In the frequent engagements with political and civic leaders that are part and parcel of an editor's role, I was enabled to go beyond theoretical abstractions, to relate to the realities that I had witnessed and, to some degree, experienced in the streets and in the towns and villages of the North in those early years.

I am sometimes asked by students and others to identify the most important story that I dealt with in more than a decade-and-a-half as editor of the *Irish Times*. I answer that the most important story was not published in a single day but over years. And it was not put together by any one journalist but by a whole cohort of reporters, photographers, feature writers and editors who, year in, year out, walked the streets and the estates, went down the country roads to bomb sites, sat through endless negotiations and listened to the countless stories of men, women and children from all sides and in all circumstances.

A few – some of the more highly profiled – got recognition in the form of awards and commendations. But for the most part they just got by-lines and the satisfaction of knowing that what they were doing was important, that the story had to be told, day by day, hour by hour. And that telling it could make a difference. It would be difficult to imagine that there could ever have been a peace process without that.

Conor Brady was editor of the *Irish Times* from 1986 to 2002.

How bombs stopped play during rooftop cricket matches
Belfast, 1970s

Sir Trevor McDonald

The rooftop of the old Ulster Television building in Belfast was the most unlikely setting for impromptu cricket matches but, nearly fifty years ago, it gave visiting ITN journalists like me the perfect vantage point to see where bombs were going off in the troubled city. I'd never heard a bomb explosion in real life before going to Northern Ireland as a reporter for ITN and I have to admit that, as a card-carrying coward, I was terrified, for myself and my crew. But Belfast was where I cut my teeth as a journalist. It was one of my first assignments for ITN and those cricketing encounters were light relief during dark times.

Journalists from UTV, including their redoubtable news editor Robin Walsh, used to pit their cricketing wits against crews and reporters from ITN. We sometimes had to use hurley sticks for bats, and we had to be careful about what shots we made because we couldn't risk a wayward stroke injuring someone on the streets below Havelock House. Frequently it was bombs and not rain that stopped play during those incongruous games. From our position on the roof, we could not only hear the blasts but we could also see the smoke rising from where the bombs were going off and we were able to get the crews on the road quickly.

My 'home' in Belfast in the 1970s was the Europa Hotel, which was reputed to be the most bombed hotel in the world at that time. Five or six bombs must have gone off at the Europa during my stays in the hotel. But I was never unduly worried. The bombers usually gave enough time for us to get out. It was the hotel they wanted to damage, not the guests (most of whom were journalists), and the terrorists knew that they would be guaranteed maximum publicity by targeting the Europa. In one picture, taken just after an explosion, I can be seen exiting the hotel across Great Victoria Street.

People often ask me why I was so keen to go to Belfast in the 1970s, but the answer is simple: Northern Ireland was at the top of the news every night. We were pretty obsessed with the place, and as a young reporter I wanted to be at the top of the news. I wanted to be noticed. There was a kind of symbiosis in it because the prominence of the news story there did give me some prominence early on in my career.

As well as hearing my first bomb blast in Belfast, I also heard my first shots from an AK-47 there. And there were riots nearly every day. The army used to say that news crews were perpetuating the violence because the rioters appeared on the streets in late afternoon to guarantee they would be seen on the teatime bulletins.

I have to say that I brought not an ounce of bravery to any of the disturbances on the streets. During the worst riots, I would tell my camera crews that I needed to find a house with a phone that I could use to contact our news desk in London – this was in the pre-mobile telephone era – and I would stay indoors while the crews filmed the onslaughts outside.

In my 2019 memoir, *An Improbable Life*, I made a point of praising the courage of the TV crews with whom I worked all around the globe. Some of them helped to keep me safe, especially in Northern Ireland. They knew instinctively how to conduct themselves in a tricky situation. I learnt from them.

Before Belfast, the closest I had been to violence was seeing the odd Friday night bust-up in rum shops in my native Trinidad. Nothing had prepared me for what I experienced in Northern Ireland.

Another question I am often asked is whether Northern Ireland was a good training ground for what was to come for me in trouble spots all around the world. I always reply that it taught me how to run. When I got to Beirut, I was an expert runner. But I found nothing elevating about violence. I thought that it always made us poorer.

One atrocity in Fermanagh still haunts me. I'd received a phone call at about 2 a.m. about a culvert bombing that had killed a number of soldiers. We got there before the security forces arrived to seal off the area and we found bits of bodies hanging off gorse bushes. I included the gruesome images in my report for the lunchtime news. My bosses in London were furious, saying I'd gone too far and ordering me to edit the harrowing pictures out of subsequent reports. But I have no regrets about the initial bulletin. We'd got into a sort of clichéd mode of saying that 'a bomb went off' without viewers ever realising what that meant. But that early report from Fermanagh showed exactly what had happened. Some time later, an army press officer thanked me for illustrating the reality of what soldiers were having to face so often in Northern Ireland.

During my regular visits to the province I developed an undying admiration for the people who lived there. They were genuine, they were real and they would talk to us. And I think the same goes for the politicians. Even though we may have disagreed, I enjoyed their company. I don't recall any personal hostility. The sight of a non-uniformed Black West Indian man on the streets of Belfast in the 1970s may have been unusual but there were only a few adverse comments.

I was always looking out for a sign of a breakthrough in Northern Ireland. And when the Peace People came along, I became a great friend of their leaders Betty Williams and Máiread Corrigan. They wanted to achieve something for people who definitely deserved better. I always had a feeling that peace was inevitable in Northern Ireland but I didn't know how or when it would come and I wouldn't have put any money on it.

One of the most uplifting things I saw was when Ireland produced outstanding results in the 2007 Cricket World Cup. A letter of congratulations to the team was signed by Ian Paisley and Martin McGuinness, the First and deputy First Ministers who were once sworn enemies. They also hosted a reception for the players.

In my book, I wrote about my sadness at seeing how the divisions in Northern Ireland and at the Assembly still resurfaced from time to time. But I live in hope for the province.

I still return to Northern Ireland occasionally. I was there not so long ago as a guest at a charity lunch that had a strong link to my beloved passion, cricket. Until 2020, I was the national president of the Lord's Taverners, which helps disadvantaged and disabled young people. My visit to Belfast in December 2018 was at the invitation of my aforementioned old friend Robin Walsh who was president of the local branch of the charity. Perhaps not surprisingly, those old UTV rooftop cricket games featured in our reminiscences at the lunch venue, which also took me back in time. It was the Europa, happily a very different and relaxed hotel in a very different and relaxed Belfast.

Sir Trevor McDonald OBE began his career in journalism in the 1960s. From 1973 to 2005, he worked for ITN, and in 1992, became a household name as the sole presenter of their flagship news programme, *News at Ten*. In 1999, he was knighted for his services to journalism.

Fighting the print industry's sectarian saboteurs
Lurgan, 1970s

Eric Villiers

For this piece I thought of revisiting Troubles-related stories I covered that were personal: the Reverend Ian Paisley rescuing me from cudgel-wielding loyalists; the Kingsmills massacre, when my football teammate Reggie Chapman was executed; the Provisional IRA murder of my cousin Trevor Elliott; or the 1980s car bombing (twice) of my newspaper offices and print works in Armagh. Instead, a striking phrase used by Jim McDowell, former northern editor of the *Sunday World*, in the first volume of *Reporting the Troubles*, reminded me that sectarianism is a first cousin of terrorism. His statement that you 'could almost bite the sectarianism' on Lurgan's streets brought back memories of my days editing the *Lurgan Mail*, trying to set a neutral course through bigotry that had produced generations of local Catholics who largely boycotted a paper they despised as the 'Lurgan Liar', and, conversely, generations of eagle-eyed Protestants sensitive to any sign of the paper surrendering ground to the 'enemy'.

The hands-off political philosophy of the paper's owner, Jim Morton, was 'a plague on both their houses', as he once told me. As bitterness intensified during the Troubles, the *Mail*'s circulation plummeted and I, along with several key editorial staff – David Stokes, John Bingham, Jim Gracey and the late Lindsay Kilpatrick – instigated changes. The mainstays of these were establishing contacts with long-disillusioned organisations, and weekly GAA coverage.

As it happened, the 1970s saw a flowering of excellent GAA footballers as the county enjoyed unprecedented, sustained success, challenging for Ulster county and club titles, and reaching an All-Ireland final. Historically, the *Mail*'s GAA coverage was abysmal. A fact of production meant that the large classified advertising section could encroach into the sports section to facilitate hundreds of small ads, and since these nearly always ran over, sport was cut. However, instead of losing minority sports like indoor bowls, darts, golf, and so on, the GAA columns were binned. Moving the GAA coverage away from the ads was the easy bit; for the first time, Gaelic sports fans could rely on weekly reports and analysis, which included contributions from All-Ireland star Jimmy Smyth, who would go on to provide live match analyses for the BBC.

While the bitterness in the air was almost visceral for Jim McDowell, it had been on public display on the pages of the *Lurgan Mail* for years due to lazy management and self-appointed censor-printers who conspired to 'lose' reports they did not like.

This blew up into something of an in-house contest, as loyalist content was sabotaged in retaliation. Had it only been political, cultural or religious bigotry that management faced, they might have disciplined one or two employees, and stood firm behind the new editorial line, but a secondary factor was the 1970s rise of trade union power within newspaper companies – threats of industrial action were never far from the surface.

During the Ulster Workers' Council strike the printers worked 'secretly' behind blacked-out windows directly across the street from a supermarket petrol station manned by masked men, an anarchy outside that encouraged the in-house extremists to feel connected, in support or opposition, to the strike. In my case, there was low-level bullying about my appearance, along with faux puzzlement about my credentials as a Protestant, what with my red hair, South Armagh 'haitches' and 'strange' surname. On one occasion it escalated into a fist fight with a printer.

Every perceived editorial 'misstep' was added up, nothing was forgotten and the bitterness was compounded. With the printers – from both sides of the political and religious divide – free from management sanctions, they were emboldened to create embarrassing 'misprints' and mischief, and crow about their tiny triumphs.

One compositor, a self-proclaimed Marxist-socialist-republican from the Falls Road, delighted in getting away with altering lines in loyalist adverts. His pet ploy was changing the line 'God Save the Queen' that signed off the notices to 'God Help the Queen'. When a front-page caption in the *Mail*'s sister paper, the *Portadown Times*, was sabotaged after one Twelfth of July, the Falls Road man became the prime suspect: with the nip of a scalpel and a couple of pokes of a printer's pen, an 'r' under a photo of a blonde majorette became a 't' in 'The Pride of the Birches Accordion Band'.

While, historically speaking, a new generation of Northern Ireland Catholics were asserting their civil rights, this petty nonsense in Lurgan became a weekly battle of one-upmanship, exacerbated by the town's evenly split population: I was once informed that a soccer match result was not 2–1, as reported, but 6–5 – a reference not to the scoreline but to the numbers of Catholics and Protestants on a visiting 'mixed' team. Outside on the street, as editor of a 'Fenian' paper, I was warned, 'I know where you live,' at the same time as supportive messages filtered through to the office from the Catholic community, where some people appreciated what was going on.

A young Catholic called Martin O'Hagan, an electrician, came into the office to see me because he had noticed the new inclusivity. He told me about his former involvement with the Republican Workers' Party, and asked for advice on getting into journalism. He started coming to the office regularly as I taught him 'journalese' and later I gave him a start as a part-timer. His freelance career blossomed and he eventually became a *Sunday World* reporter. Martin was passionate about his investigative work and years later I bumped into him with a photographer in a city centre bar in Cork. After increasing threats from loyalist and republican gunmen, the *Sunday World* had moved him to their Cork office as a temporary safety measure. We spent that day out together in Cork, and it did not surprise me to learn he was stalking a high-ranking paedophile priest – without paramilitaries to pursue he had pointed his investigative antenna elsewhere. Martin's contacts within republicanism were excellent, and one senior Special Branch officer, who'd known me growing up in Armagh, once queried the *Mail*'s sources for some interesting Troubles-related stories: his questions were basically rhetorical because the elephant in the room was Martin O'Hagan. Martin was murdered by paramilitaries in 2001.

Martin's 'republican' contributions exacerbated my problems with the in-house compositors, whose ruses to block or sabotage such content became increasingly bizarre. One morning at home, after a thirteen-hour day that had ended with me signing off on the last of the pages for printing, I got a frantic phone call from Seamus Lavery, a Lurgan secondary school teacher who, as our regular GAA correspondent, provided county match reports. The previous Sunday, Armagh had beaten Derry but a strapline over the *Mail*'s big match coverage read, 'GAA County Football: Londonderry v. Armagh', while in the body text the space before the word Derry had been used to squeeze in a one letter prefix and a single apostrophe – L' – to make it 'L'Derry'. With Seamus's byline prominent, he told me, 'I could get a hiding or a kneecapping.' After trying to assure Seamus that he was overreacting and that any reader would see that there was some skulduggery at work, I headed for a confrontation with sniggering union members who photographed pages and regarded themselves as the aristocrats of the printing unions.

Although there were only three members of that union among the company's two hundred employees, they regularly invoked the era's trade union buzzwords, 'work to rule' and 'demarcation': any sign of encroachment into their jealously guarded tasks had them bristling with indignation, and gave management the jitters. Their power to disrupt at the pinch point had long since cowed management and the bosses gave into wage demands so often that these men were earning three times an editor's salary.

My 'Stroke City' complaint to management saw me called to Jim Morton's office to discuss the paper's editorial line: apparently his wife had been accosted on the street and at the hairdressers about the 'Fenian Mail' and she had asked him to do something about it. The one-sided conversation went something like this: 'Now, as far as me, my wife and you are concerned, I've had a word with you, but between me and you, don't change a thing.' The latest circulation figures were on his desk, and the *Mail* now had over thirty-thousand readers, up from twenty thousand a couple of years earlier, which meant advertising rates could rise and revenue with them without an extra pound being spent. While the shift to a neutral editorial stance went unacknowledged in-house, there was an oblique reference with the announcement that the paper's staff could pick a hotel of their choice for a dinner and night out to celebrate the circulation figures.

Nearly thirty years separates my experience of Lurgan from McDowell's in 2001, which sadly suggests the problem is historical and immutable. So, if that little local realignment in the 1970s and 1980s means anything in historical terms, perhaps it's this: even universal wars are won by local battles. As the American historian Joseph A. Amato wrote, '… all history is local'.

Eric Villiers, a history researcher, was a reporter, editor and newspaper owner. His 2012 book, *Ireland's Forgotten Explorer: Australia's First Hero*, is about John King, sole survivor of the first crossing of Australia.

The Bloody Sunday line I wish I had not filed
Derry, 1972

Paddy Clancy

There are two quotes linked to the Troubles in Northern Ireland that remain indelible in my memory, although they date back to the early 1970s. One was a prediction that totally underrated how many lives would be lost. The second, seared in my memory forever, was a moment of congratulation for soldiers who killed thirteen innocent people and fatally wounded another.

The late, very-much-lamented Gerry Fitt seriously underestimated the toll the Troubles would take on his home territory when we had a drink in a London pub in 1970. I'm not sure if he was still the West Belfast MP for the Republican Labour Party or if he was already first leader of the SDLP (he started the year in one and ended it as leader and founder of the other). A couple of dozen people had already died in the Troubles since the start of 1969. 'There will be five hundred more before it's all over,' he predicted. It's rather chilling now to wish that Fitt's forecast had been accurate. Instead, more than 3,500 died in the conflict. Fitt's words have remained sharp in my memory. They actually prompted me to press the news desk of the *Daily Telegraph*, for which I worked, to send me on assignment to Northern Ireland. It took time, the reason for which I will explain later.

While in Northern Ireland, I heard on Bloody Sunday – when British paratroopers killed thirteen unarmed marchers – another comment that I remember more acutely than even Fitt's doom-laden prophecy. 'They shot well,' said the *Daily Telegraph* defence correspondent, Brigadier W.F.K. Thompson, in apparent praise of the British Army operation as he approached me at the bar of the City Hotel where most visiting journalists stayed on assignment in Derry. Thompson, a hero of the Battle of Arnhem in World War Two, became defence correspondent of the *Telegraph* after resigning from the British Army in 1960. Before joining the paper, he had no or very little experience of journalism but the then owner of the *Telegraph*, Lord Hartwell, had a preference for appointing high-ranking ex-security forces personnel to specialist expertise positions on his editorial staff.

On 30 January 1972, Thompson used his special relationship with the British Army to locate himself in the Derry army communications HQ. Among Thompson's contacts was General Robert Ford, Commander Land Forces (Northern Ireland). Ford was on William Street when the marchers were halted by soldiers with a deluge from water cannons. As the sodden marchers diverted towards the Rossville Flats, near what was known as Free Derry Corner in the Bogside, troops from 1st Battalion, Parachute Regiment, raced after them. Ford shouted loudly, 'Go on, 1 PARA; go get them.' Minutes later, there was the sound of gunfire. Shortly after that, I was one of many reporters peering from William Street into Rossville Street when we saw Father Edward Daly – later Bishop of Derry – step from a footpath and crouch as he waved a bloodstained handkerchief. He was seeking protection from fire for a group of men behind him who were carrying Jackie Duddy, one of the fatalities. Teenager Jackie was shot by a Para as he ran alongside the priest. Not long afterwards, a hastily organised press conference was held at the William Street/Rossville Street corner by Ford and Colonel Derek Wilford, the officer directly in charge of the Paras on the day. Both were emphatic the soldiers had been shot at from within the Bogside before opening fire.

That prompted copy for the early editions that there had been a gun battle. To this day, I regret filing that copy. Although I gathered local claims for later editions that unarmed civilians had been shot dead by the Paras and that there had been no gun battle, it was the early edition that reached Ireland the next day. Of course, my reporting attracted criticism in neighbouring Donegal, from where I had travelled to cover the march.

I filed the later copy from a payphone in the hallway of the City Hotel (no mobile phones or laptops in those days) before I stepped back into the adjoining bar. That was when *Telegraph* Defence Correspondent Thompson walked in with his 'they shot well' comment. The bar was fairly noisy and I managed to direct him to an unoccupied area along the counter so, luckily, he may not have been heard. When I told him of the local convictions that innocent unarmed civilians had been killed, he refused to accept there had been indiscriminate shooting by the Paras. It was one of the rare occasions in journalism that I 'made my excuses and left' – the cliché that *News of the World* reporters used when they exposed brothels. My excuse to Thompson was that I had more copy to file. I headed back to the phone and he departed the bar soon afterwards.

My brief conversation with him was an insight into the mindsets of former and current officers of the British Army when dealing with what they and Ted Heath's Tory government regarded as troublemakers in Northern Ireland. A later inquiry headed by Lord Saville unearthed a confidential memorandum from Ford prior to Bloody Sunday in which he stated: 'I am coming to the conclusion that the minimum force necessary to achieve a restoration of law and order is to shoot selected ringleaders amongst the DYH [Derry Young Hooligans] after clear warnings have been issued.' At the inquiry, Ford claimed not to remember having written the memo.

Thompson's view that the Paras did not shoot and kill innocent people may have been coloured by his experience at Arnhem. There, after gliding with the 1st Air Landing Light Regiment into a location near Arnhem in September 1944, the troops Thompson led combined with others, including Paras, in a battle to protect artillery positions and to block a German advance. Thompson was wounded and captured by the Nazis and was held as a POW until the end of the war. He died in 1980, four years after his retirement from the *Telegraph*. Despite their roles on Bloody Sunday, Ford was knighted five years later and Wilford was awarded the OBE by Queen Elizabeth within nine months. The Paras were found by Saville to have lied.

I was in Derry on Bloody Sunday almost as an afterthought! Until the middle of December 1971, my pleas to the *Telegraph* news desk to be assigned to the team covering Northern Ireland went unheeded. Nobody said it aloud, but there was a strong suspicion that an Irish Catholic might provide biased pro-nationalist reporting in the pro-Tory *Daily Telegraph*, which was firmly on the side of unionists in its opinion features and leader articles. Rank-and-file news reporters were proud that their copy on any story was rigidly unbiased and did not reflect opinion on other pages. Despite this, there was a mysterious mental attitude within the paper's senior management to writing about Ireland.

Finally, I won my argument that an Irish Catholic could capably produce a straight news report on his country, irrespective of the paper's politics on the issue. So, on 31 December 1971, I arrived in Belfast for my first assignment in Northern Ireland as a member of the *Daily Telegraph* team, which reported in shifts of several weeks. My copy must have been satisfactory because when I returned to London in mid-January there was a call for backup support from the newsroom staffer in Derry. He feared there might be trouble at the march against internment organised by civil rights leaders and which had been banned by Brian Faulkner's unionist government. First, I grabbed a few days leave in my wife's home county, Donegal, then a friend drove me from Donegal town to Derry. My wife and our first two children, who were then aged three and one, joined me on the journey, leaving me off at the City Hotel around the corner from William Street.

I thought the 'trouble' my Derry-based staffer feared was likely to be no more than a confrontation between soldiers and youths throwing stones at them from behind street barricades, a spectacle that was not unusual in Derry. How awfully wrong I was! My family was barely an hour out of town on the way back to Donegal when the march started and paratroopers killed thirteen people and injured fifteen, one of whom died some months later to bring the death toll to fourteen.

Paddy Clancy, following a Fleet Street career, returned to Ireland to freelance for newspapers and as a broadcaster. In 2019, he received the Lifetime Achievement Award at the NewsBrands Ireland journalism awards.

How my picture became Bloody Sunday's iconic image
Derry, 1972

Stanley Matchett

My *Daily Mirror* colleague Joe Gorrod and I were expecting to be back in Belfast from Derry in the early evening of that fateful Sunday but in the end we didn't return over the Glenshane Pass for three weeks.

No one could have predicted what would happen on that civil rights march in January 1972 and I certainly couldn't have known that a picture I would take would become THE iconic image of the Troubles in Northern Ireland, according to *The Sunday Times* no less. It is the photograph showing Father Edward Daly – later to become Bishop Daly – waving a bloodstained handkerchief and walking in front of a group of men carrying the body of a young man, Jackie Duddy, who was one of thirteen people shot dead by the Parachute Regiment.

I had been in Chamberlain Street and I have a sequence of photographs of the crowd coming towards me. Father Daly then administered the Last Rites. Another image I took that day was of a young medic with his head in his hands – he was in tears crouching over a body. It has often been said to me that the people in the area must have been going mad after all the shootings and the deaths, but it was quite the opposite. You could have heard a pin drop in the deathly silence because everyone was so shocked and didn't believe what was actually happening. It was one of the saddest days of my life.

My Bloody Sunday photograph went right around the world and it's remarkable how many people have claimed it was their picture and also put it on their own websites as their own work. I even know of one young man who brought the picture with him when he went to a newspaper office looking for work – he said he had taken it. When he filled in his age on a form the person dealing with him remarked that he must have shot the photo when he was eight months old!

A few years ago I went back to Chamberlain Street with a film crew who were making a documentary about the work of press photographers during the Troubles. Returning to that location was a strange experience. When I was in the museum in the Bogside with the same crew, the conversation turned to the massive Bloody Sunday picture on the wall and a woman said she would love to have met the man who had taken it. It was pointed out that I was that photographer; the woman said she was related to Jackie Duddy. It was very emotional for both of us. I still bitterly regret that I never got the chance to meet Bishop Daly before his death in August 2016. That's because I was usually rushing up to Derry and back to Belfast in the same day.

Several months after Bloody Sunday, I was on the scene of a no-warning car bomb in Belfast, which was said to have been the IRA's retaliation for the killings in Derry. It was on 20 March 1972. I heard the bomb exploding near the *Daily Mirror* office in Donegall Street so I grabbed the camera that was always on my desk. The whole facade of the *News Letter* building had been blown away. There were bodies and injured people all over the street. It was pure carnage but once the dust had settled I took a picture of which I am particularly proud. It shows a soldier, a Para, cradling a young Czech girl. It is extremely moving and a great contrast to the other horrible shots of that day. It was later confirmed that 7 people had been killed and 148 injured by the no-warning 250lb bomb.

The girl in my picture, Blanka Sochor (now Blanka Suehiro), was studying fashion design at the nearby art college and she sustained devastating leg injuries. She later returned to Belfast from her home in Canada to thank our wonderful surgeons in the Royal Victoria Hospital for saving her legs. It was only later that I discovered that I had walked past the car in which the bomb was planted on my way to work. I was lucky that I never sustained serious injuries there or anywhere else during the Troubles but the violence and what I saw definitely did have a massive impact on me.

There were many days that you thought things couldn't get any worse here but then they did. Another awful day in 1972 was in July, on the afternoon that became known as Bloody Friday. The attack at Oxford Street bus station was just one of a series of around twenty bombings by the IRA that claimed 9 lives and injured 130 people. As I made my way to the bus station, people were running away from it and I recall an ambulance man shouting at me. I thought he was telling me off for taking pictures of wounded people but in fact he wanted me to photograph an unrecognisable victim to show just how gruesome it all was.

I finally realised that I'd had enough of man's inhumanity to his fellow man in March 1988 after the appalling killings of the two army corporals Derek Wood and David Howes in West Belfast as they strayed into an IRA funeral. I had my film taken off me after the crowd attacked the soldiers. The month afterwards, the *Daily Mirror* closed its Belfast office saying the circulation of the paper dropped in England every time there was a story about Northern Ireland on the front page.

I look back now and wonder what the violence achieved. The politicians are still arguing and bickering and it frustrates me. I feel for all the people who have been bereaved by the Troubles and I think about the empty chairs at the dining tables. It must be awful for them to have to live with the memories and I don't believe we will ever know the half of the suffering. When I think back to the early days of the Troubles, if someone had told me that thirty-five years later 3,700 people would have died, I would have been in total disbelief.

Stanley Matchett was a staff photographer with the *Belfast Telegraph* in the 1960s and with the Mirror Group in the 1970s. He has presented a series on photography with UTV and, in 2003, was awarded an MBE for services to photojournalism.

The black-and-white print from 1972 that caught up with me
Belfast, 1972

Michael Denieffe

The British Army intelligence officer was polite but insistent. Across a table in a room in the depths of the sandbagged RUC station in Andersonstown, the game of wits had played out. We had painstakingly gone through my personal and professional history several times. My appraisal of the Dublin political situation had been queried and my opinions sought about the level of support in the Republic for the Provisional IRA campaign.

My increasingly assertive insistence that I was a journalist working for Independent Newspapers in Dublin, supplementing our Belfast staff and merely doing my job, was met with studied indifference. My flourished press card was examined, taken away and returned without comment. It was obvious that my interrogator did not believe me or chose not to believe me.

What was I doing in a taxi on the Falls Road in the middle of a shooting incident between the IRA and the British Army? Did I know in advance that such an incident was planned? Who was my source? Who were my contacts?

In fact, that night I had been making my way back to my base in the Hamill Hotel – near the old Great Northern Railway station and a haven for journalists on secondment from Dublin. The Hamill also housed the Belfast office of the *Daily Express* and was subsequently bombed by the IRA. On a dark, rainy Belfast night, I was returning by taxi from a community meeting when the street lights literally went out, just as we were halted by a roadblock mounted by the British Army.

An order was barked to the taxi driver to turn off his lights. As my eyes grew accustomed to the gloom, it became apparent that a number of soldiers' weapons were aimed directly at the taxi, its driver and its passenger. This silent, dark tableau was disturbed after a few minutes by the static crack of a single shot apparently fired from buildings overlooking the scene. Orders were shouted and soldiers hit the ground or took cover behind a 'Pig' armoured car, squatting in the middle of the road. More orders were barked out: 'Open the fucking doors.' Two soldiers opened the four doors of the taxi. The interior lights flooded the car. 'Stay there. Sit up straight.' Another bark: 'Headlights on. Open the windows.' Right. Doors and windows wide open. All lights on. We were illuminated targets defined by the surrounding darkness. The only visible figures in a frozen nightmare. For an hour we were compelled to sit there, grotesquely exposed and illuminated by the only lights in a street theatre of menace. The tension was palpable and steadily increased as the minutes ticked over. Would the IRA fire again? We appeared to be the only visible targets. Would they recognise that we were civilians? Would the soldiers respond? Instinctive and increasingly compelling urges, driven by fear and anger, to either jump out of the car or voice loud protest were stifled by the realisation that we could not predict the reaction of either side.

The hapless taxi driver and I were simply in the wrong place at the wrong time in the nightmare that was Belfast back then. We were, arguably, being used by the soldiers as visible bait for the IRA gunman. In those times, rules of engagement tended to be improvised. The ordeal eventually ended with soldiers ordering us out of the taxi. Personal restraint evaporated and remonstrations with the officer in charge were countered with the curt assurance that we were left in the illuminated taxi so that the IRA could clearly see we were not soldiers or 'legitimate targets'. It was for our safety. After further pleasantries were exchanged, we were ordered into the back of the armoured Pig. When the doors opened again, we were inside Andersonstown RUC station.

We were there to 'assist with further enquiries'. After several hours of questioning, my photograph was needed. Just head and shoulders would be fine. For the record. Then I could go. Okay then. One head on and two side images. After five hours as a reluctant guest of the British Army, I walked out of Andersonstown RUC station imbued with a mixture of anger, bemusement and sheer relief. Before I left, I was asked to sign the back of a print of my photograph. I came complete with a gingerish beard at the time. 'Bet you hope you never see that again,' was the farewell comment.

Dublin, 1978. It was the day before Christmas Eve six years later. I was now on the staff of the *Sunday Independent* under the editorship of the late, great Michael Hand. Pre-Christmas goodwill had just taken a decided turn for the worse. I'd had a home visit from two Special Branch detectives, not bearing greetings but rather an unseasonal invitation to accompany them to Store Street Garda station. To my shock and disbelief, I was required to assist with enquiries into the discovery of a loaded firearm in the drawer of my office desk. And to add sauce to the goose, initial ballistic tests indicated that the gun had recently been discharged. The detail of the incident in a Dublin newspaper office was sensational even in those fraught times.

The discovery of the .32 revolver in a tooled leather holster in the drawer of my desk in Middle Abbey Street was immediately regarded as a serious security incident, particularly as it contained two spent shells. It was also a deeply embarrassing and awkward situation for Independent Newspapers at the time. Once in Store Street, I was fingerprinted and taken to an interview room. My strenuous denials of any knowledge of the gun, how it had got into the desk and where the shots were fired were repeatedly challenged. The interrogation team included a senior Garda officer, who had himself featured in a recent *Sunday Independent* investigation. This involved the discovery of a fingerprint found on a helmet at the scene of the car-bomb assassination of British ambassador, Christopher Ewart-Biggs, in 1976.

Following the controversy over the identification of the fingerprint, that senior Garda officer, who was innocent of any wrongdoing, was transferred to Store Street station. He obviously still felt aggrieved about the controversy and the *Sunday Independent* story, and opined repeatedly that my predicament would not do any favours for my career with Independent Newspapers. I was privately arriving at the same conclusion.

After several hours of questioning, which sometimes became less than polite, I did actually get to use the line, 'Charge me or let me go.' Eventually, I was released into the late Christmas night. There was no offer of a lift home, no Christmas wishes, just a promise that this incident was not over. But it was virtually over. After a somewhat uneasy Christmas, the mystery of the gun and shots fired was resolved early in the New Year. Two junior employees who had been hunting seasonal cheer confessed to taking what they believed to be an imitation gun from an unoccupied desk. They then verified the gun's credentials by firing two shots into an innocent door in nearby Lotts Lane. The possible outcomes of such an incident were shocking. The perpetrators panicked and tried to return the gun but found the drawer had been locked. So, they hastily stuffed it into the nearest vacant desk, which was mine, unfortunately. It was then discovered by someone searching for the editorial for the next *Sunday Independent* edition. The phrase 'loaded editorial' stuck for months.

Incredibly, it eventually transpired that the gun was owned by my colleague, E.B. 'Ned' Murphy, a civil war army intelligence veteran who now happened to be the *Sunday Independent* political correspondent. He was a respected journalist of the old school who had retained close links to Fine Gael and had broken a number of major political stories during his career. Was the gun just a treasured souvenir of another bloody period in history or did Ned expect a visit from someone with as long a memory if a different historical perspective than his? Some unfinished business from the Civil War to be settled? Whatever the reason, the gun had remained in the desk drawer ready for action. It was never fully explained. What is certain is that a number of gardaí had initially believed they had uncovered a significant criminal incident within the hallowed portals of Independent House. They had also believed that I was a prime suspect.

There was a suggestion that the old warrior Ned should be arrested and charged. I personally contacted Ned and informed him that the 'jig was up' and that the possibility of Dan Breen or anyone from the Republican side of that era challenging him to a duel was now unlikely. He actually agreed with that suggestion and graciously apologised for any inconvenience.

I suggested he should make himself available to the gardaí in Store Street or face embarrassment and possible disgrace. I also expressed the hope that he had enjoyed a peaceful Christmas. Following an investigation, no charges were preferred against Ned. However, some months later, he called me into his office. He opened his desk drawer to reveal the .32 revolver nestling in its tooled holster. It had been returned to him, albeit spiked and rendered harmless. I wished them both a happy reunion.

Some weeks later, I met one of the detectives who had taken me into Store Street that day before Christmas Eve. 'Why were you so certain it was me?' I asked. 'Surely not just because the gun was found in my desk? That was too obviously a plant.' He had come prepared. He reached into his coat and produced a photograph. There I was, staring back from the black-and-white print taken in 1972 in Andersonstown RUC station. The years rolled back. The questions tumbled out: How? Why? Cross-border security co-operation in 1972?

'You haven't changed much,' he said. 'Bet you thought you'd never see that again.'

Michael Denieffe is a former group managing editor with Independent News and Media (now Mediahuis Ireland). On the company's editorial staff for over forty years, he was assigned for several stints to Northern Ireland in the early 1970s.

The day I asked the IRA, 'What the fuck was that all about?'
Belfast, 1972

Malachi O'Doherty

The problem for me at the start of the Troubles was that journalism seemed an inappropriate response. Ideally a reporter stands outside a story and observes it with some detachment. I was living inside a barricaded no-go area and travelling every day to the centre of town to work at the *Sunday News*. My ambition in life was to be a journalist and – after doing the pre-entry certificate at the College of Business Studies, as it was known then, in the same class as David McKittrick and Walter Ellis – I had arrived. I was a card-carrying member of the NUJ and I had more money than I had ever had before. In a normal world, I would have stuck at that. Others did. They were able to take advantage of having the biggest story in the country unfold around them and to progress through their careers.

I was having to keep secrets. I knew where IRA men who had escaped from the *Maidstone* prison ship moored in Belfast Lough in 1972 were staying. I could have broken that story. I saw men with guns cross my front garden to fire on passing army vehicles on Finaghy Road North. The worst of it was when some of these men asked my father if they could spend a few nights in our house. I moved out. My best effort at recreating life in a no-go area close to IRA safe houses was an article in which I pretended to be an anonymous housewife describing events around her. I hadn't needed to interview anyone to get the story.

My news editor Jim Campbell was later shot and wounded for annoying the loyalists.

I would drink with Martin O'Hagan in Lurgan and hear his enthusiasm for journalism and he later got shot dead. In recent years I did a story about a neighbour of mine called Terry Herdman who was murdered by the IRA as an 'informer'. His girlfriend, Libby Dornan, had urged the IRA to give her more information and they conceded in 2012 that he had not been an informer but a 'liability'. That made me reflect on how unsafe I had been among those men, as someone who knew more than it made sense for them to let me know.

Occasionally they tried to provide me with a story. Two IRA men asked to meet me one day and told me their intelligence people had uncovered a loyalist hit list. One of their names was on it. I didn't even pass the story on to Jim because I didn't believe it. At other times stories that annoyed them appeared in the *Sunday News* and the tone of their criticism of me was that I should have known better. And people would occasionally have genuine grievances with the paper because reporters and compositors made mistakes too, though none quite as tragic as terrorists leaving it too late to call in a warning that they'd just left a bomb in the Abercorn. Those were horrific times.

One time, Jim and I went to a bar on the Falls to talk to people about a story, and even as we sat there, others came to us with more stories. At one point I realised I was being followed about the bar by a young man with a horrific bullet wound, like a star, in his cheek. Something about me annoyed him. How could he even have been in a balanced state of mind anyway with such an injury?

On Bloody Friday, 21 July 1972, I walked through the city at lunchtime as the first bombs went off. When the IRA press officer, Gerry O'Hare, phoned the office after the last bomb I said, 'What the fuck was that all about?' Jim said I should know better than to talk like that to a contact.

I met the English reporters coming in and wondered if their matey way with army officers kept them any more detached from the big story than I was. I met some wonderful freebooting freelancers like the Black American reporter Marc Crawford.

I took Marc with me when the Official IRA, supposedly on ceasefire, drove around the Markets area in a jeep with rifles at the ready. On the day he left, Marc wanted to interview me about how it was impossible to get laid in Belfast at that time. I had told him too much. 'Och,' said Jim, 'don't be shy. Tell him how you can't get your end away.'

One of my stories made the national broadcast news. The local IRA had posted a notice in a shop window warning that they had mined the area between the M1 motorway and Riverdale. When my father saw my story in the paper he was angry: 'You want to be careful, writing up stuff like that.' A soldier called Harry Beaves has written about that in his book *Down Among the Weeds*. The 'weeds' were the people of Riverdale. He knew some of my neighbours in the safe houses better than I did and he described the blundering management of informants or 'Freds' who were coaxed into accompanying foot patrols. If I had been a good citizen I might have been one of those 'Freds' and wouldn't I have been stupid?

But the army was as careless with its own people. After the story about the minefield was reported, Beaves was sent out from Casement Park at night to patrol the area and crawl through a culvert. He was able to report back that there were no mines there after all. He wouldn't have been reporting back if there had been.

I went on to find a niche in journalism which was more comment than reportage, though often a mixture of both. And in recent years I have written in deeper detail, in articles and in books, about those early years, in part to make up for having managed so poorly as a journalist at the time.

Malachi O'Doherty started out in journalism with the *Sunday News* in Belfast in 1971 and has passed most of his career as a freelance writer and broadcaster.

Deadly secrets stashed in a wardrobe
Belfast, 1972

Johnny Watterson

During the school holidays, when his mother went shopping and no one was at home, we went to Eugene's house, where his dad kept weapons behind a false panel in a wardrobe in a back bedroom. That day we closed the front door quietly behind us, banged into the sitting room and walked across to the bottom of the stairs. We stopped and listened. Motionless, all we could hear was silence.

We bolted up the stairs so wildly and close together that our heads and hips and torsos touched, and our arms wrapped backwards around each other in a tangle as we tried to get to the top of the stairs first. Eugene, diving from behind, clutched my trailing ankle and pulled me down backwards on my belly with my pullover rolling up my chest and almost over my head. Then, standing on my back, he levered off in a lurch towards the top before I did the same, violently pulling him back. Smaller, thinner and weaker, he hit his chin off each stair.

Red and carpet-burned, laughing at the pain, it was Eugene who pulled his parents' clothes across the rail to one side and removed the wooden side boards. For an excited boy it was an act that required gentle precision. Eugene didn't want to scrape or chip the paint and show the soldiers that something had been moved. Inside were nests of bullets – shiny, with copper rims and brilliantly new – cartons of them, dense and heavy, row upon row, each one inside its own square of cardboard inner casing inside the larger box. The combination of the blunt dome of the lead noses and the brassy cylinder that held it in place; the dot on the flat golden bottom with a red ring around it and an indentation, where the gun hammer would hit and strike a spark to the gunpowder. I was enchanted by their colour, dazzling out from the dark as the light struck.

The rifles stood upright in the small space alongside a Thompson sub-machine gun, its magazine ugly and circular, hanging off the stock and bloated with bullets. Three or four hand grenades were scattered on the floor panel among the yellow and brown butts. I felt their threat as they sat there, half in shadow, half in light and glistening, tooled like jewellery. It was thrilling. But the danger of the weapons took me no closer to understanding what people in Belfast were doing to each other. It took me no closer to their causes or their risks or their threats to others. For those stolen few minutes we were hunkered down, quietly inhaling the spores of the inner wooden skeleton of Eugene's house – the ginger-coloured rough, dry, inner surface of the panel, the air shot with oil from the cloth-rubbed steel barrels.

The first time we looked – and we looked only once because they soon disappeared – we each took one bullet as a souvenir, turned the box around and pushed it deeper into shadow and the darkness at the back of the wall so that the space left by our trophies would not be instantly seen.

We were fearful, giddy and excited around the wardrobe and we were serious and sworn to say nothing. As children, our touching distance to the guns and grenades was a sacred glimpse into an adult world. The running of our fingers lightly down the barrels and the smooth, varnished wood elevated us briefly from our play world into a real one. We became in those moments co-conspirators.

For some minutes we stood in the bedroom equal with something or somebody and somehow also chosen to be there and blissfully uncaring. We left inflated, bearing a grown-up secret, one I knew I was incapable of keeping.

Like drunkards we began our run out of the house. With insane energy we bolted two at a time down the front steps, pumped and mighty with unspeakable knowledge. We assumed, for those minutes, a preposterous greatness and had little concept of the war that, in 1972, eleven-year-olds had already become used to: the constant, simmering menace on the street; the people's loathing of the military, their Saracens targets to stone; a war that we didn't then know was waiting for us.

I felt a strong sense of belonging with Eugene because his father was a tough, hard man and I knew what the consequences would be if he ever found out. Eugene's risk-taking, or his weakness to have to share, was my reward. I belonged to something, although to what I didn't exactly know.

Two chieftains, with our bullets clasped tightly in our hands, we galloped down the street in a crazy run, past Toners, McCuskers and Canavans, with their fantail pigeons on the roof puffed up and coaxing the others to stop and land and roost in the early evening. As we passed Raffertys I could see the birds circling in their laps of the streets, twenty or thirty of them, their whoosh and draught, so low that they changed the air pressure overhead, the tumblers turning in mid-air. Groups of birds covered the sky – Clintons' birds, Canavans' birds, Crossans' birds – in different loops at different heights, flying and swirling over Rockville Street and the Falls Road, around and around and around, getting lower and lower until, in a large mass, all at once they descended on to their chosen roof.

We ran past Shields' house and McMahons and Chesneys and McAleavys and then Breslins and to Rockdale Street past McNieces, McMenemys, Meads, Dowdals, Devines and Finnegans, past Wards, and McKennas and into my back yard and the pigeon shed, where we sat on high bundles of Perri crisp boxes that crumpled into a cardboard chair, gift wrapping our skinny frames.

We opened our hands at the same time. Our bullets were both the same and we said nothing. But even as our bravado burned and our brazen tapping into the fault lines of our street glowed inside, we quietly wondered what we had done. We babbled about anything else – our 'orange-eye' bird and the swan's nest in the bog meadow, our promise to each other to build the shed higher and wider, the size of Clintons'.

We knew without saying that we had done so much that was wrong. Going into Eugene's parents' bedroom, sliding the wardrobe, removing the panel, opening the box of bullets, touching the steel and wood of the guns and taking our trophies. These things were more than forbidden – they were punishable.

We didn't see what we had done as an act of thievery, the taking of something that was not ours. It was more important. It was ownership of information. It was knowing something we shouldn't know. It was seeing things we shouldn't see. We sat on the surrendering boxes self-satisfied, older than our years.

That evening in bed, the crooked lamp on my wooden locker threw orange light across a plastic European Cup trophy that Celtic had won and across the giant face of Manchester United's smiling George Best, whose picture was tacked to my brother Peter's side of the bedroom wall.

I elbowed him in the back and I said, 'Look.' He swung a disinterested backwards punch at me. 'No,' I said. 'Look.' I stretched across the inches of space between our two single beds and put my upturned fist across his body, blocking the view of his *Hotspur* comic. Annoyed and bored with the stunt he pushed my hand away, so I stuck it closer to his face making him pull back. He finally looked.

Some years later, my friend Eugene would go to prison for IRA membership and in a few months time, my older brother Peter would go to Milltown Cemetery, shot dead from a passing car at fourteen years old on the footpath below our bedroom window on the Falls Road.

We can't have all the memories we wish for and sometimes make up a version of them in our heads and try to preserve them. And the times when we go to look for them, if we are lucky, they are still right there where we left them to be re-remembered as we wish to remember them.

In the tawny light of our bedroom I open my fist. The bullet falls from my palm on to Peter's comic, rolling on to his chest. The pressure of holding it all of that time has left a red impression across two of my fingers. He ignores my hands, picks up the bullet, turns on his back and holds it above him in the air.

'Fuck. Away. Off,' he says affectionately.

Johnny Watterson grew up on the Falls Road in Belfast before moving to Dublin as a teenager. He is now a staff sportswriter with the *Irish Times*.

How the Troubles shattered the 'quiet' of the North Coast
Coleraine, 1973

Hugh McGrattan

The North Coast area of the province, which is centred on the three towns forming what is often referred to as 'the Triangle', was generally accepted as being a 'quiet' area, little affected by the violence that daily blighted other districts throughout the Troubles. It is certainly true that, at least in the earlier years of the disturbances, life went on pretty much as usual. Soldiers of the regular army were seldom seen on the streets of the urban areas, security there being the responsibility of the locally recruited units of the Ulster Defence Regiment.

Local newspapers carried much more news forty-five years ago. Social media did not exist and the papers were the main source of information. Our two major titles were the *Chronicle* and the *Northern Constitution*, both long-established and well-respected broadsheets based in Coleraine. A large proportion of the news content was submitted copy, consisting of church and social organisation reports, political statements, sports reports, etc., all of which had to be checked and edited before publication. The work of the combined editorial staff of around a dozen reporters and photographers centred on traditional coverage of local councils and courts, as well as obituaries, features and coverage of the main sporting events, such as Irish League soccer and Gaelic Athletic Association fixtures. A well-supported page of Letters to the Editor was an important aspect of the papers' coverage and, as indicated, the responsibility of the editor or their deputy. Most of the supplied copy was published, for the ethos was of a community information service, publicising legitimate events and providing the local population with a comprehensive news service. With the new Northern Ireland Assembly elections imminent and reorganised district councils just starting work, our news columns were busy in the early summer of 1973.

Reports of terrorist atrocities, mainly in the more isolated rural areas and including bombings, shootings and murders, often appeared on our pages alongside the other news. Coleraine town, where our papers were based, and the neighbouring towns of Portrush and Portstewart, had not known the terror that had ravaged communities in other parts of the province. It was all to suddenly change.

On Tuesday, 12 June 1973, two IRA car bombs planted in the town exploded within minutes of each other. The first, at Railway Road, killed six people. Their ages ranged from sixty to seventy-six and most had been out for a day's quiet shopping, away from more bomb-prone areas. A total of thirty-four people were injured, some seriously, three losing limbs.

There had been the usual confusion over the exact location of the bombs, which were placed in two Ford Cortinas stolen that morning in Toomebridge. A ten-minute warning was phoned to the police at 2.34 p.m. but merely gave Stuart's and Society Street as the locations of two bombs. A judge later described the message as 'inadequate and misleading'. The first bomb went off at 2.50 p.m., almost opposite the head office of the Northern Newspaper Group. The second exploded ten minutes later in Stuart's, a long-established car salesroom beside the River Bann, wrecking the building and destroying a number of vehicles – but the bomb had been spotted in advance and the area cleared.

Several people, including myself, had lucky escapes. I should have been crossing Railway Road when the bomb went off but was detained by a cup of coffee at the new University of Ulster, a mile away, at the conclusion of a press briefing. Academic secretary John Hunter walked with me to the lift, then offered me a quick cuppa. It was only when we got to the cashpoint in the refectory that he realised, with embarrassment, that he had no money. Otherwise he wouldn't have asked me. I paid, not realising the depth of gratitude I owed him for his memory lapse. We were chatting ten minutes later when we heard the distant sound of the first bomb going off. I said a hasty goodbye and headed for the car park. Before I had got to my car, I heard another explosion. Now I could see the black smoke boiling up into the sky a mile away.

Cars had stopped at various points on my route back into town, with groups of people unsure of whether to continue. I was startled by several vehicles, some driving at speed, meeting me on Union Street, which was one-way. I turned into Railway Road, which was now a scene of chaos and carnage. People were rushing everywhere, helping the dying and the injured. The frontages of several buildings had been devastated. Spread out on the pavement, just below our reporters' room, were six bodies, covered by blankets. All around, people were still frantically searching the smoking cavities of what had been several shops. Bits of smashed vehicles littered the street. Later we were to learn that the roof of our office had been lifted several inches by the blast. A week later, part of a car was discovered behind a chimney.

I found our editorial department reduced to piles of overturned furniture and typewriters, with dust and papers everywhere. I retrieved a phone from the floor only to discover it was covered in blood. Our Limavady editor, Jim Donaghy, had been on a visit to head office and was facing the window when it exploded around him. He was now in Coleraine Hospital, where he was kept overnight. In true professional manner, Jim had got permission while there to talk to some of the survivors and to observe the magnificent efforts of the staff as they dealt with the injured.

At the time of the Coleraine bombs, the *Chronicle* and the *Constitution* were not long amalgamated under the banner of the Northern Newspaper Group. This had resulted in the considerable but inevitable plunge into new technology. Just three weeks previously, a new web offset printing machine had been installed. As a result, our papers were now able to carry extra pages of reports, and high-quality pictures with an impact that could not have been achieved in the past. Every one of our journalists was subsequently involved in the creation of what were then the most striking editions of the *Chronicle* and *Constitution* yet produced.

Several journalists from daily papers were also soon on scene and, in the twenty-four hours after the bombs, used our offices to prepare and submit copy and pictures. One bizarrely humorous incident remains in my memory from the night following the bombs. We were now finalising our own newspapers for weekly publication. Alongside the stories covering various aspects of the tragedy was a rapidly increasing file of customary reports from churches, political parties, councils, courts, sporting clubs and women's institutes. Our visiting colleagues were starting to get in the way and were told loudly but politely to get out. We had a paper to put to bed. It was a situation they understood and the world's press departed quickly and quietly.

Despite the horror and revulsion caused by the Coleraine bombs, attacks on our 'quiet' district were to continue. Long-established Dixon's of Church Street was destroyed by firebombs. Elsewhere, more lives would be cruelly lost. Portrush was to be the target of several unsuccessful attacks culminating in the devastating blitz on the holiday scene in August 1976, which saw a dozen businesses destroyed and much employment lost. But worse was to follow for the resort. On the evening of 11 April 1987, two part-time policemen, both well-known and respected local men with families, were gunned down on the main street by terrorists who fled in a stolen car. A happy spring evening thus became the worst outrage of the Troubles for Portrush. Mercifully, no one else on the crowded street was injured in this assault.

As the 1990s progressed and hopes grew of an end to thirty years of mindless death and destruction, one final but monstrous attack remains vivid in local memories. Destroyed on the night of Friday, 13 November 1992, were the newly refurbished premises of Moore's of Coleraine, the borough's largest store, along with adjoining shops and offices. An entire three-storey block was gutted, the cost of the damage being put at £10 million. An estimated hundred full-time jobs also disappeared that night. We filled the entire front page with a picture of the huge block of buildings ablaze. It was the kind of coverage we could never have envisaged back in the 1970s. I have a reproduction of that front page on my study wall. It was the last big assault on our community. The buildings have long been replaced, after years of work and huge cost, but that front-page vision of gutted walls and blazing background remains as a stark memorial to a terrible time that must never be permitted to happen again.

Hugh McGrattan has been a newspaper journalist, freelance writer and author in North Ulster for sixty years and is a former editor of the *Chronicle* in Coleraine.

The strike that set Northern Ireland apart
Northern Ireland, 1974

Don Anderson

'Did you know the Reverend Doctor is a secret drinker?' This was Gerry Fitt, MP for West Belfast, talking to me off camera in a small unattended BBC TV news studio in Westminster in the early 1970s. Gerry was a fund of anecdotes, many outrageously scurrilous, about political rivals. 'Gerry, we both know Ian Paisley is staunchly against the devil's buttermilk,' I replied with a grin. 'I have proof,' he said, moving over to a small drinks cabinet from which politicians could help themselves, and then sign for their noggins in a ledger. Opening the ledger, he showed me the handwritten line, 'Gin and orange – Rev. Ian Paisley.' He flicked to another date: 'Gin and orange – Rev. Ian Paisley.' Page after page he showed me, all with the same line, all in the same handwriting. In a previous idle moment Gerry had inserted these entries himself.

That was not a serious attempt at myth making, but early in my career I realised that Northern Ireland jealously guards its myths, through which journalists must navigate. I wrote a history of the 1974 Ulster Workers' Council (UWC) strike in the 1990s, based on material I had garnered from the main players at the time of the stoppage. The very name of that event is largely myth. The UWC barely existed and was used as a cover by the loyalist paramilitaries, who were in the driving seat from the beginning. But the mythical name stuck to this extraordinary event.

The early 1970s was a period of concentrated, vicious, murderous violence accompanied by intense fractious politics. Journalists got to know the leading players in Northern Ireland quite well. One such leading player was the aforementioned Gerry Fitt, but there were many others. Someone who rarely fraternised the same way was teetotaller and unionist Brian Faulkner, also a groundbreaking politician. By pioneering and leading power-sharing, he split monolithic unionism for good and thus ultimately ended his political career. Like Fitt, he was a consummate TV performer. I was trying to doorstep him as he left Stormont, positioning the camera crew at the west door and myself alone at the east door. Sod's law meant that he emerged to the camera crew but couldn't wait for me so he asked cameraman Dick Macmillan what he thought he might merit in the evening news. 'About a minute,' came Dick's brutally honest reply. Faulkner replied to a mythical question from a mythical reporter and rushed away. He had spoken for fifty-eight seconds. Later, back in the cutting room, I was impressed.

The 1974 UWC strike marked the collapse of the first power-sharing devolved government in Northern Ireland. The old majority-rule Stormont, which had lasted since partition, had been prorogued by London in 1972 amid persistent violence. The 1973 Sunningdale Agreement was an attempt to replace that institution with something entirely new – power-sharing with an Irish dimension – but the package outraged loyalists. Power-sharing lasted briefly from February to May 1974, headed by Chief Minister Faulkner with SDLP's Fitt as deputy. Had it survived it could have been a shortcut to the Belfast Agreement, saving thousands of lives, over a hundred thousand physical and mental injuries, and decades of misery.

The devastating effect of the stoppage was no myth. It lasted from 14 May to 28 May 1974. It began as a paramilitary, chiefly UDA, lock-out and siege of businesses but a pusillanimous response from government transformed the situation into a paralysing general strike within a week. The broad unionist community decided midway through the stoppage that government, whether Stormont or Westminster, was not governing and wasn't going to win. I once had slight difficulty in describing the huge impact, but not now. Now I say it was pandemic lockdown on steroids.

On the penultimate day of the stoppage, a dismal Faulkner, feeling betrayed by Whitehall, called a meeting of the civil service heads. The picture they painted of how things were in the most populated areas was horrific: electricity supply so low the grid was threatened, factories and offices shut, multiple roads blocked, no public transport, most filling stations closed, and hospitals having difficulties. Without enough power, animal feed mills and bakeries were halting, water and sewage-pumping stations were about to be overwhelmed, the army was unable to provide essential services, livestock on farms were dying, milk was being poured down drains because it could not be delivered.

The civil service heads warned that soon there would be the first resulting deaths among the very old, the very young and the very weak. And on that day the gravediggers said they were stopping. Finally, there were indications that there would be resignations among those senior civil servants because they could not carry on. Nightmare. The following morning Faulkner's political support among his own party collapsed and that was the end. The loyalist street parties were noisy and prolonged.

A heady victory, but it clouded a grave setback for loyalism towards the end of the stoppage, which was revealed in a broadcast address by Prime Minister Harold Wilson, a speech very strongly denouncing the loyalists. I remember feeling apprehensive when he called the UWC supporters spongers upon the British exchequer, asking, 'Who do these people think they are?' The loyalists believed their answer was the only answer, not fully realising that they had just demonstrated irretrievably that Northern Ireland could never be as British as Yorkshire. People in Britain had become aware of a bewilderingly wide spectrum of hostility, from loyalism through to republicanism (there had been no let-up in IRA operations). Harold Wilson reflected that accurately.

Just over a decade later, I watched as the Anglo-Irish Agreement for the first time gave the Dublin government an advisory role in the affairs of Northern Ireland, notwithstanding raucous unionist protests. Again and again after the UWC stoppage Westminster parties enacted measures unionism abhorred.

Harold Wilson was Labour, but his UWC question was also being asked among Conservatives. It was the Conservative and Unionist Party that had removed the old Stormont at a stroke. Over a quarter of a century later, in February 2020, Dominic Lawson – a senior, authoritative Conservative-leaning journalist – wrote in *The Sunday Times* an article entitled 'A united Ireland is the secret Tory dream'. In it he quoted Sir Patrick Mayhew, Northern Ireland Secretary of State in the mid-1990s, speaking to *Die Zeit*, the German newspaper, in 1993: 'People think we don't want to let Northern Ireland [leave] the United Kingdom. If I'm completely honest [we'd do it] with pleasure.' Upon such a bed of disinterest was laid the added complication of Brexit, which highlighted further that Northern Ireland was different to the point of Brexiteer exasperation. Mayhew knew it cost the UK more to support Northern Ireland than it did to be in the EU, a fact the exchequer was always aware of. Brexiteer leader Boris Johnson was recorded at a private dinner in June 2018 saying that it was 'just beyond belief that we're allowing the tail to wag the dog in this way ...' Northern Ireland was the tail. Yet unionism continued to believe that the union with the UK was unshakeable. The imposition of the Brexit Protocol ought to have laid that myth to rest.

But herding unionists into a corner was not what another giant in politics wanted. I saw John Hume in his home city shortly after the original Stormont had been prorogued in 1972. 'It's too soon,' he remarked to me. I didn't fully understand his meaning until some years later when I was sitting with him on a bench overlooking the sea in Donegal. We were putting the world to rights when he said, 'If the unionists ever got a taste of sovereignty, they'd never look back.'

He was exploring a political pathway that might give unsettled unionists what they desperately needed, which was protection for their cultural ethos, under threat from all sides. Decades later, unionists were briefly kingmakers in the Westminster parliament in the run up to Brexit, but it profited them little. The point Hume was making to me back then was if they threw in their lot with the rest of Ireland, they could stand to gain a devolved majority-rule Stormont, albeit perhaps for a smaller Northern Ireland. London is unlikely ever to grant anything like that again. But Dublin could.

Was the UWC stoppage worth it? Gerry Fitt told me the following: after a bitter Executive meeting about halfway through the stoppage, he picked up the nameplate at his ministerial seat, signed it, dated it, pocketed it. The SDLP had just walked out in despair because of an impasse over the projected Council of Ireland, part of the Sunningdale Agreement. So it was all over. However, a short time later that day, the party very reluctantly relented because they did not want to hand victory to the loyalists. 'It means,' said Gerry, 'that the stoppage actually prolonged power-sharing. It would have collapsed a week earlier over that Council of Ireland.' He wasn't joking this time.

Don Anderson began his career in the *News Letter*, then moved to the BBC as a TV reporter. He was Downtown Radio's first programme controller and subsequently deputy head of programmes and head of radio, BBC Northern Ireland. He is author of *14 May Days*, a history of the UWC Strike.

The phenomenon that was the Peace People
Belfast, 1975

Maggie Taggart

It is 1975. The Derry band, The Undertones, is just getting its act together and the wonderful playwright Stewart Parker has staged *Spokesong*, his rollicking musical drama about bicycles. Good news for the stage, but it was also an horrific time for tit-for-tat terrorist killings.

On one April night in Belfast, two Catholics were killed in McLaughlin's Bar in the New Lodge and five Protestants were killed in the Mountainview Tavern on the Shankill Road. I do not actually think I realised the terrible events I would have to report on as I celebrated getting my first staff job as a trainee at Downtown Radio. It was Northern Ireland's first commercial radio station, based in the Kiltonga Industrial Estate in Newtownards, next to Pritchitts milk-powder plant. Downtown did not begin broadcasting until the following year, March 1976. As a greenhorn, I spent the intervening months being trained in the skills of recording interviews, editing reel-to-reel tapes while out on the road and sending material back to base without the wonderful modern aids of digital technology, 5G phones and Wi-Fi.

In these days of relative peace, it is hard to believe the litany of violent incidents we woke up to in those days: bomb alerts, explosions, shootings and deaths. It was my job to drive to the sometimes distant locations where these terrible things had happened, find people to interview and report back in time for the hourly Downtown Radio News bulletins. I often wonder now if the people who kindly let me into their homes close to the incidents to use their landline phones, realised that the only way to get material back was to covertly unscrew their handsets, attach wire and metal cables known as 'croc clips' and phone the recordings into the studio. There had already been almost seventeen hundred deaths and countless injuries in the Troubles by the time Downtown went on the air, so I think I was somewhat numbed to the daily news of more bombings and shootings. But all these years later, I still hesitate to walk past a lone parked car – like many citizens of Northern Ireland, I am sure – just in case it hides a bomb that is about to detonate.

Adults were the usual casualties so when, on 10 August 1976, a getaway car rammed into a family out for an afternoon walk on Belfast's Finaghy Road North, it provoked outrage and sympathy from across the community. Anne Maguire was with her four young children – the incident left two of the children dead, one fatally injured and Anne with very severe injuries. Andrew was six weeks old, John was two and a half, and Joanne eight years old. The car was driven by an IRA man, Danny Lennon, who was being chased by an army patrol following a sniper attack in West Belfast. He had been shot and fatally injured by soldiers and his car went out of control, crashing into the family, causing carnage that shocked the world. Photographs of a mangled child's bike, a pram and the twisted railing served to emphasise the horror of the incident.

The deaths became the catalyst for the creation of an organisation that became known as the Peace People. One of the founders had a very strong personal reason for starting the movement calling for an end to conflict and violence: Máiread Corrigan's sister, Anne, was the children's mother. Betty Williams witnessed the crash and was inspired to take protest action. She joined forces with Máiread Corrigan and, later, with the journalist Ciaran McKeown. They organised a series of rallies and marches and the movement caught the zeitgeist of the time. Initially, they had immense support from people disgusted by the previous decade of killing, maiming and hate.

I met both women many times. I covered the first mass rally on Saturday, 21 August, eleven days after the killings. It was a huge gathering, mostly of women, held in the Ormeau Park in South Belfast, near my home. Plans were made for a second one a week later that would take place on the Shankill Road, Belfast's loyalist stronghold. It went ahead on 28 August, even though some community leaders on both sides warned it might provoke confrontation. In the event, it was a success, with crowds from nationalist and middle-of-the-road areas venturing across the city to join in. On the same day, a rally in Dublin attracted a huge crowd, estimated at fifty thousand.

The mood was a mixture of sadness, camaraderie, and exhilaration. It seemed that those present were galvanised by the idea that instead of sitting at home tutting at the latest atrocity on the TV, they could take dramatic action that would send a powerful message to the men and women of violence, forcing them to embrace peace. They were heady times, as rally after rally brought hopeful crowds out into the open to pray, sing and cry.

I was interested in the story because of my job as a news reporter, but our family also kept a close eye on the movement's progress because Máiread Corrigan worked as the confidential secretary to my late first cousin, John Lavery, the managing director of Guinness in Northern Ireland. He did not speak much of her, but we knew he supported her. The knowledge that she worked so closely with him somehow gave me a closer affinity with the Peace People. Later, I became a next-door neighbour of Ciaran McKeown's. As this mild-mannered man smoked his pipe in the back entry, we chatted through my garden fence and it was hard to credit the criticism he faced at the time. He was described as the Svengali figure behind the organisation.

As those rallies continued across Ireland north and south, it was a revelation to me to experience the atmosphere. There was quiet triumph that a group of hitherto silent people could defy critics and make their strong wish for an end to violence heard by those who were masterminding violent action.

In October 1977, Máiread and Betty were awarded the 1976 Nobel Prize for Peace. A strange quirk – the Nobel committee had not deemed the actual 1976 nominations worthy of the prize. The citation reads: 'For the courageous efforts in founding a movement to put an end to the violent conflict in Northern Ireland.' The prize money then was eighty thousand pounds sterling, and dissension in the ranks really kicked off when it came to deciding how to spend that money. Reporters were keen to know where the money would go, and I dare say critics were looking for a chink in the Peace People armour. It was a controversial issue and turned out to be a blow to public confidence in the organisation. Máiread Corrigan wanted to devote 'her' half to continuing the work of the Peace People, which was supported by charitable donations. Betty Williams declared she wanted to keep the other half to spend on different types of peace activism, a decision that was said to have shocked the rest of the group. I think it is fair to say that Betty's choice caused rifts that led to resentment, resignations and rancour. In the end, an uneasy compromise was reached, but it was the beginning of the end for those invigorating crowds I watched hugging, laughing and discovering neighbours of a different religious denomination. Within two years, the high-profile public witness of thousands of people had fizzled out.

It seems petty squabbles and internal disagreements were eating away at the joyful celebration of cross-community unity. Maybe it was a transient phenomenon that would never have lasted. For news reporters like me, once the public demonstration of euphoria had faded away, there was no longer a headline in the story.

In January 1980, Anne Maguire, the mother of the three children whose deaths were the catalyst for the Peace People, took her own life. Prior to her death, she and her husband, Jackie, emigrated and had two more children, but she never recovered mentally from that trauma. Máiread Corrigan later married Jackie, her sister's widower. The Peace People movement continues, but in a different form. Its remit is now much wider than appealing to local paramilitary organisations to 'reject the use of the bomb and the bullet'.

In a surreal postscript, my last meeting with Betty Williams, who had immigrated to the United States and then returned to live in Galway, was in the lobby of Belfast City Hall. I had gone with a BBC television camera crew in January 2020 to film the opening of a book of condolence for the late SDLP politician Seamus Mallon. Councillors and members of the public queued to sign the book but there, too, was seventy-five-year-old Betty Williams with an unexpected companion: the *Basic Instinct* Hollywood film star Sharon Stone. So forty years later, Betty hit the headlines again, photographed with her famous friend. Betty and Ciaran died six months apart, both at the age of seventy-six, while Máiread continues her international peace activism.

I have attended many protest marches over my years as a journalist, but I will never forget the groundswell of hope from people weary of violence in the summer of 1976.

Maggie Taggart has worked as a reporter in Northern Ireland for over forty years. She began as a trainee on Downtown Radio and most of her career has been with BBC Northern Ireland, BBC1 TV and BBC Radio 4. For twenty years she worked as BBC NI's Education and Arts correspondent.

The priceless Penny Marvel
Belfast, 1976

Don McAleer

I stood on Belfast's Royal Avenue one Wednesday evening in September 1976, watching smoke still wafting from the damaged side of the famous Belfast Telegraph building, and wondered if I still had a job.

I worked there as a reporter and at 4.15 that afternoon the IRA had driven a 100lb van bomb down the loading bay and into the heart of the building. It blew up minutes later, wrecking three of the four printing presses a couple of floors above and starting a big fire.

Wednesday was my day off that week so I learned of the attack on the 5 p.m. news. I immediately made my way there and, as I surveyed the scene with colleagues, my foremost thoughts were selfishly for myself. I was planning to get married and was arranging a mortgage for our first house. What now?

I felt angry but at the same time helpless to do anything about what had happened. Joe Patton, a printing worker, was seriously ill in hospital and died some days later. Other colleagues were injured. Part of the building was trashed but the editorial floor and some other parts of the large premises were usable.

The hundreds of staff on the paper must be eternally grateful to the fire service who, at risk to their personnel, went into the damaged building and quickly brought the blaze under control before it could spread and devastate the entire premises. It was ironic that the nineteenth-century building that had survived the wartime Blitz had again been in jeopardy.

As the dust settled, senior management surveyed the damage by torchlight. A further daylight inspection at dawn confirmed the decision to publish a paper. In many ways, the media is a big family and offers of help flooded in from all over, including from rival newspapers and printing firms north and south of the border. So the plan – to print a limited edition of the *Tele* using the one surviving press and the presses of the *County Down Spectator* – swung into action. Type was also set at a number of locations where hot metal was still used, including the *Irish News* and the printing works of the *Northern Whig*.

When word went out, via newsflashes on radio and TV, for journalists to report for work, it was a huge relief as many had feared they were jobless. We were still very much in business – defiance was the best answer to the terrorists. All staff, including many who were off duty or on holiday, reported in ahead of time.

I recall there was thick dust everywhere and a strong smell of smoke in the editorial department, but we eagerly got down to work. The news editor, the wonderful Norman Jenkinson, was at the news desk, doling out tasks to his enthusiastic team with the instruction to keep copy tight as space was very limited in the scaled-down edition.

Miraculously, the *Tele* came out that afternoon and was snapped up in newsagents and from the newsboys right across the city. It was priced at a token one penny – the Penny Marvel – but as a gesture it was priceless. It was a great joy as we made our way up Royal Avenue to hear the cries of '*Tele*, *Tele*' from the newsboys selling the paper – a familiar and welcome part of Belfast's evenings in those days. Eight of the distinctive BT delivery vans were destroyed in the explosion, but the remaining thirty ferried their bundles to newsagents across much of the province.

Enthusiasm was palpable in each member of staff and it seemed to grow in the weeks and months ahead as the presses were replaced, the building repaired and the *Tele* took its proud place on the news-stands.

As the spotlight moved elsewhere, staff could see the back story and the impact of the attack on the lives of those closest to us. There was no talk of counselling, which nowadays seems to be sprinkled around like confetti. It was a case of heads down and get on with it. And then there was the realisation that we were far from alone. Attacks happened every day and many, many people were affected in different ways – death and injury, as well as loss of jobs, property and the freedom to lead a normal life.

I had worked on the *Tyrone Constitution* in Omagh from 1965 to 1973 and then had joined the *Tele*. I saw the very worst of the Troubles at close quarters – murder, bloodshed, destruction on a huge scale. The incidents came in hundreds and thousands and, as journalists, we became somewhat inured to atrocities, distinguished one from the other to a large extent by their scale and callousness. They became a variation on a theme, but when one literally came to our own door it was so different.

Those who drove the Ford Transit van into a crowded newspaper building and then produced guns and opened fire on workers were mindless criminals. But it was the sinister minds at the top of the pyramid who were the real menace. It is an irony that amazes me. Those who sent the *Tele* bombers were the same people who composed statements supporting or justifying similar atrocities on a daily basis. When these statements dropped on the news desk, the very journalists who had been targeted were then expected to deal with the issue impartially, and they did. Whether that was a fair call was a matter above my pay grade, as they say.

The Troubles were a long and painful journey for nearly everyone in Northern Ireland and there were few whose lives were not impacted by the daily outrages. Many were not as fortunate as we were in the *Belfast Telegraph* – their places of work were wiped out and so were their jobs. Thousands died; many more were injured and carried the scars for the rest of their lives.

I was to see events from a totally different perspective when, in October 1977, I changed my career and moved to the Government Information Service where, among other things, I became a 'government spokesman'.

In the eyes of some, I was poacher turned gamekeeper, but I never saw it that way. And, in any event, gamekeepers have an important and honourable role. I was there to use my journalistic skills to convey government information to the media and the wider public. But the Troubles impacted heavily in the public sector too and I sometimes found myself drafting statements for ministers and departments condemning killings, attacks on business and the daily assaults that the population had to endure at the hands of paramilitaries of all ilks.

In addition to churning out press releases about routine government business and activities, it was often my task to explain to senior civil servants why it was necessary to react to certain claims and assertions by those who sought to portray a department or its actions inaccurately. But it was not all mundane statements, and tedious claims and counterclaims. In my thirty-four years as an information officer in the civil service, I saw many notable occasions from a very different angle and at close quarters. My job took me from 10 Downing Street and Buckingham Palace to Capitol Hill and the White House. I saw visits to Northern Ireland by royalty and presidents, the Anglo-Irish Agreement and the Good Friday Agreement. I saw the inside of government from the direct rule side and from the devolved aspect. It was all very interesting and important – an Ulster version of *War and Peace*. The peace is not perfect but better than the alternative.

As I now enjoy retirement, I can look back on an interesting career and reflect on the importance of journalism in holding government and other aspects of society to account. And on the need for government to be open and honest and to explain what it is doing or seeking to do. It is another matter as to whether either is being achieved. That's an argument for another time and perhaps another article.

Don McAleer was a reporter on the *Belfast Telegraph* and the *Tyrone Constitution* before joining the Government Information Service at Stormont, where he worked for more than thirty years.

Nairac – a collision of myths in a dark field
Dromintee, County Armagh, 1977

Roisin McAuley

I was a journalist for BBC Northern Ireland's current affairs series *Spotlight* when Captain Robert Nairac was reported missing on the morning of Sunday, 15 May 1977. The previous night he had driven out of Bessbrook barracks, South Armagh, in a civilian car, alone, wearing a donkey jacket and jeans. The car had been found eight miles away, in the car park of the Three Steps Inn, Dromintee, just over a mile from the border. A widespread search for him had begun.

The IRA put out a statement saying they had shot him. They said he had been well known to the IRA and had been a target for some time. He had admitted being a member of the SAS.

Some weeks later, as I recall, Dublin-based *Hibernia* magazine - it ceased publication in 1980 – carried a lengthy story about Nairac. He was a Catholic who had been educated at Ampleforth, the boarding school in Yorkshire run by the Benedictines, where the founder of the SAS, David Stirling, had been educated. The IRA had known Nairac was operating in South Armagh. He'd been a regular visitor to a pub in Crossmaglen. His movements had been followed by the IRA. He'd been tracked and targeted. It was a compelling and plausible story. The editor of *Spotlight* was intrigued by the Catholic ex-public schoolboy and British Army officer in the lion's den of Catholic, nationalist South Armagh. I was dispatched to find out more.

A contact put me in touch with 'a friend' in South Armagh. Over tea and scones in her house she told me 'they [the IRA] had no idea who he was'. The article in *Hibernia* was the IRA's attempt at damage limitation. She put me in touch with someone who might know the real story.

I remember the slap of the windscreen wipers as I sat in my car, parked on an unapproved border road, waiting to speak to the man who told me Nairac was 'the spy who didn't come in from the cold. He kept his donkey jacket on, even though it was a warm night.' The heavy coat had aroused the suspicion of an IRA member in the pub, the brother of my informant, as I later discovered. He asked three men, none of them in the IRA, to help him accost the man in the donkey jacket with the Belfast accent, whom he thought could be a loyalist setting up a target. The four of them followed Nairac out of the pub and tackled him in the car park. In the struggle, Nairac's Browning 9mm pistol fell out of his coat.

Panic ensued. The four had been drinking all evening. Nairac was sober. They bundled him into a car and drove him across the border and into a field at Flurrybridge in Ravensdale Forest, just off the main Belfast–Dublin road, where three members of the IRA, hurriedly summoned, joined them in a black farce of interrogation. They were convinced Nairac was a UDA spy from the Shankill. He had a convincing Belfast accent. He maintained, to the end, that he was a Catholic from Ardoyne. At one point, he wrested his own gun back and shot one of his attackers in the foot. They beat him over the head with a fence post. Finally, one of the IRA men summoned to the field, Liam Townson, shot Nairac in the head.

Townson and the men enlisted from the pub then left the scene. Three IRA members stayed to dispose of the body. They met up the following morning. They listened to a radio news bulletin and heard about the missing army officer. Until that moment, they thought they had killed a loyalist from Belfast. Realisation dawned. They went on the run.

After a four-day search, An Garda Síochána found traces of hair and blood, but did not find Nairac's body. It has never been found. My own guess is the men who disposed of the body did so in a hurry. There was no moon that night, they did not mark the spot. They fled to the United States.

For the *Spotlight* film, I went to England to interview Nairac's parents, his teachers and his friends. I got the impression of a romantic, a dreamer, a T.E. Lawrence figure. The shelves in his bedroom were lined with Bulldog Drummond stories, books by Edgar Wallace and other novels of derring-do about English gentlemen defeating foreign spies. He had kept a falcon at Ampleforth. He had a colourful view of history. He wrote essays that were more fantasy than fact, featuring knights in armour and daring rescues.

He had wanted to give up boxing at Ampleforth but was persuaded by his housemaster to continue. He went on to become not just a boxing blue at Oxford, but a boxer who would continue past the point when he had taken too much punishment and the fight should have been stopped. At Oxford, he enlisted in the Grenadier Guards and wore the uniform when sitting his exams. He liked acting. He was a great mimic. He remained close to his housemaster, on one occasion driving through the night from Oxford to Ampleforth to speak to him. A report in the Ampleforth archive praised his 'extraordinarily attractive personality with almost boundless enthusiasm, generosity and good humour', but added, 'his very qualities leave him with a certain naivety and lack of balance of judgement'.

His grieving parents had little idea of Ireland or its history. I got the impression they saw it as somewhere foreign, where Robert had been doing his duty. They spoke of his love of the English countryside, his dogs, his ferrets, his falcon and all wild things. His mother asked me to tell her about the place where he died. I described the field, the woods nearby, the small stone bridge over a stream. 'He could tame anything,' his mother said, showing me a photograph of her son in his Grenadier Guards uniform, talking to a group of boys in Ardoyne. Perhaps he thought he could tame Ireland. Who knows?

I see the Nairac story as a collision of myths in a dark field. The English romantic hero riding to the rescue, doing right, solving wrongs. The valiant Irish hero, wrapped in the green flag, fighting for freedom. It intrigues me still, as it has intrigued others, such as the late playwright and screenwriter Hugh Whitemore, who thought he might write a play about him, and Alistair Kerr, former soldier and diplomat, and author of *Betrayal: The Murder of Robert Nairac*. He is convinced that Nairac was gay. He also refutes the unproven allegations that Nairac colluded with loyalist death squads in the 'murder triangle' in counties Armagh and Tyrone. And over the years, I have been contacted by others who are drawn to the story of the maverick soldier and the mystery of his missing remains.

At a friend's birthday party in England about ten years ago, I found myself sitting beside a former officer in the Grenadier Guards. I asked him about Robert Nairac. He had known him. 'He was allowed too much leeway,' he said. 'We all liked him.' Neither statement surprised me.

Novelist and broadcast journalist Róisín McAuley reported for the BBC *Spotlight* programme during some of the worst years of the Troubles.

Remembering Lesley Gordon
South Derry, 1978 and 2021

Deric Henderson

The children of Culnady Primary School bowed their heads in prayer today and thanked God for the 'serenity and lovingness' that he had bestowed on little Lesley Gordon. Seconds later, her name was struck off the register. Her desk in the third row was empty. Her English and Maths jotters, a nature diary and an unfinished painting of an international airliner were still lying on her desk. On the back wall was another of her paintings, a multi-coloured monster. It was taken down and put away with her books in a drawer.

The children were asked by their principal Mrs Margaret Carson to say a prayer for Lesley and her brother Richard. Mrs Carson said, 'Lesley was an angelic child and probably the most popular in the school. She was bright and a girl of great potential. She was a delightful child, and I doubt if this school will ever forget her.'

These are the opening paragraphs of a report I filed for the *Belfast Telegraph*, and occasionally, on the anniversary of Lesley's death, I recall that winter's morning – being invited inside and listening to the grieving teachers; the silence; taking in the looks on the faces of her bewildered classmates. Still, after all these years, that story has never left me and I wondered what this innocent child victim of the Troubles had been like. Who was she?

On 8 February 1978, Lesley was killed when a booby-trap bomb detonated under her father's Ford Escort car just as they were leaving their home in Maghera to drive the three miles across the countryside to school. It was Ash Wednesday. She was sitting in the front seat, her brother Richard in the back, leaving enough space for the two friends they had arranged to collect on the way.

Willie Gordon was an education welfare officer. He was also a part-time member of the Ulster Defence Regiment, and as part of his daily routine of security precautions, he checked for devices underneath the car. That morning he knelt down to look, but didn't see the piece of fishing line wrapped around the air valve of the front driver's-side tyre and the valve cap. His wife, Georgie, stood at the door, cradling their third and youngest child, Lyndsey, still in her pyjamas, to wave them goodbye.

She then turned to go back into the living room to catch a glimpse from the front window as the car reversed away from the tiny lay-by at the side of the house at Grove Terrace. Willie stopped, changed into first gear, and just as he pressed on the accelerator, the explosion happened. Two more lives were claimed. Victims 1828 and 1829 of the Northern Ireland Troubles.

Lesley was just eleven years old. Her father was forty-one and Richard, who miraculously survived, was eight. Even though Maghera Primary School wasn't far from where they lived, the Gordons had decided to send their children to Culnady in the Upperlands area of south Derry – one of the many schools in that region where Willie, as part of his duties, examined and recorded the attendance records. With fewer than sixty pupils, there were fears it might have to close because of low numbers, so the Gordon children were sent there to help secure the school's future.

One of the first people who rushed out to see the damage and witness the hysteria was the next-door neighbour, Bella Turkington. The night before, she had been in Georgie's kitchen, where Willie had prepared small glasses of hot whiskey for the two women. According to friends, he never really talked about his duties with the UDR, and if he had any worries about his safety then he never shared them with the family. He had once served as a part-time RUC officer, and the first his wife knew of his change to a UDR uniform was when he dropped off three kitbags in the hallway.

He and Lesley died instantly. 'They were just sitting there, as if they had fallen asleep,' recalled one woman who was among the first on the scene that morning. 'But when you looked down ... the injuries were terrible. It was horrible.'

Georgie's father, John Watt, a First World War veteran who had survived the Somme, tried to get through to see for himself, but neighbours held him back.

Richard was pulled from the wreckage with a piece of shrapnel lodged in one of his legs. While his mother was taken away to be sedated and relatives looked after Lyndsey, he was taken in an ambulance to the Royal Victoria Hospital in Belfast where he was treated for head injuries. He needed skin grafts as well, and it was almost Easter before he was allowed home, having lost the sight in his left eye.

His mother visited him every day. She was driven in a car provided by the UDR to sit at his bedside. Once, a gun battle raged outside between the IRA on the Falls Road and soldiers on the rooftop. Richard was unaware that his father and sister had been killed, and on the day of the funeral, staff were asked to switch off the television because he might see news coverage of mourners gathering in the grounds of Maghera Presbyterian Church. The request was refused.

Later, he tearfully asked his mother their whereabouts. He suspected the worst but wasn't quite sure. 'They're not coming back, are they?' And she replied, 'No, they're not.' A friend said, 'It was heartbreaking for Richard; such a young lad who had been through so much, and you can imagine how Georgie felt. She found it very, very difficult. I remember calling at the house a few days after the funeral to see how she was coping. She came to the door looking dreadful and I'll never forget seeing the wee girl [Lyndsey] crying and clinging to her mother's skirt, and not understanding what was going on. She invited me in. It was just them in the house. No Willie. No Lesley, and Richard in the hospital. What could you say to her?'

Her husband kept a tidy garden which extended to the side of the house. He grew vegetables, and much of his free time was spent with his brothers-in-law, Jackie and Noel Watt, fishing for salmon and trout in the Moyola and Arivey rivers. He sold most of what he caught to local butchers and fishmongers, but always saved a salmon in the freezer for dinner on Boxing Day.

Stanley Leacock, a close friend, fished with him as well, and was on UDR duties when he witnessed the mushroom of black smoke drifting over Maghera seconds after the bomb went off. Four years later, he lost his right eye after being wounded in an IRA ambush when gunmen opened fire on his Renault car as he left the Mid-Ulster Hospital in Magherafelt with his wife Mildred and brother Harry.

He never forgot his pal from their days together in the 5th Battalion. A fortnight after the tragedy he wrote a ballad that he dedicated to Willie and the quiet and reserved little girl who, he remembers, was beginning to come out of her shell. Part of one verse reads:

Well, I lost a dear friend and comrade in nineteen seventy-eight;
And I hope and trust he and his child are happy inside God's gate.

Stanley said, 'I remember sitting with Willie at the funeral of an RUC man [Samuel Armour, killed by an IRA bomb just before Christmas, 1976] at Maghera Presbyterian Church and how impressed he was that so many Catholics were present. Little did we know then that he would be the next terrorist victim buried in that graveyard.'

Lesley was a bright girl and good at her schoolwork; probably good enough to pass her eleven-plus exam and qualify for a place at Rainey Endowed School in Magherafelt, eight miles away. Culnady Primary School closed in 2019.

Lesley was named after an aunt. She was quiet, sometimes outgoing without being cheeky, and when the weather was good she played with her friends – a girl called Arlene Richardson who lived a few doors away was the closest – before being called in for dinner. Her parents once bought her a tape recorder, and in the upstairs bedroom she shared with her sister – they had bunk beds – she sometimes danced to Showaddywaddy, her favourite pop group. Once her homework was out of the way, she watched children's television every Saturday morning.

She adored her grandparents, Georgie's mum and dad, especially her granny, and would often stay overnight with them at their home in Tamney Crescent at the far end of the town. She once told her mother she loved it so much there that she didn't want to come home.

Days out with her parents were always to Portrush. The beach first, ice cream, maybe something to eat, and then off to the amusement arcade to spend whatever money she had saved to play the slot machines and ride the dodgem cars. Barry's in the town centre was always the final stop-off before the family headed for home.

She belonged to the local Brownie pack that met once a week in a hall beside the Presbyterian church where, just days after her eleventh birthday, she read one of the lessons at the Christmas carol service. Her father was as proud as punch. Not long afterwards, he met a lady in the corridor of Ampertaine Primary School, Upperlands, during one of his inspection visits and she complimented him on how well Lesley had spoken. The woman said, 'His face just lit up. You could see what that meant to him. It meant an awful lot.'

There are framed school photographs on Georgie's living room wall of Richard and Lyndsey, on either side of one of Lesley which was taken not that long before she died. Georgie keeps a brass plaque presented to the family by the UDR in her bedroom, and Willie's and Lesley's names are among sixty remembered on memorial quilts, Patchwork of Innocents, dedicated to victims of the Troubles.

On the morning of the attack, Lesley pulled on her coat, gathered up her schoolbag and turned to her mother. Georgie reached down, held her close and gave her daughter a hug to confirm her love and affection, as Lesley whispered into her ear.

These were the last words her young daughter ever spoke: 'Have a nice day, Mummy.'

That was Lesley Gordon.

My breakneck journey to report Mountbatten's murder
Mullaghmore, County Sligo, 1979

Mike Parry

It was the bank holiday of 27 August 1979, and at the age of twenty-four I was running the news desk of the *Birmingham Evening Mail*. A ticker-tape (Press Association) newsflash came through: 'Explosion off the west coast of Ireland linked to boat of Lord Mountbatten.' Minutes later, the BBC reported that Earl Mountbatten had been killed along with other members of his family. The Provisional IRA had claimed responsibility.

I rang the chief news editor, Ian Mean, at his home. He said we had to get over there right now. We didn't have any reporters left in the office and he said, 'Okay, well, you'll have to go.' I got out to Birmingham Airport and amazingly there was a flight to Ireland. A couple of hours later I was in Dublin where I learned the full horror of the bombing carnage.

In addition to the earl being blown up, the explosion had killed a fifteen-year-old youngster, Paul Maxwell, who had been acting as boat boy, and the earl's grandson, fourteen-year-old Nicholas Knatchbull. Four other family members were badly injured, including Doreen Knatchbull, the Dowager Lady Brabourne, who died in hospital the next day. The Knatchbull family were Anglo-Irish aristocrats and connected to the Mountbattens by marriage. The other three, including Timothy, who was Nicholas's twin brother, survived.

Then I had to get to Mullaghmore, over on the west coast. I needed a hire car. But while I'd been in the sky, the national newspapers had booked every available one. I saw an envelope sticking out of a pigeonhole behind the Avis desk with the name Parry written on it – my surname. Somebody in Birmingham must have been on the ball, I thought. I told the lady behind the counter that it was my car booking. She grabbed the envelope and said, 'It's for Brenda Parry from the *Guardian*.' I feigned a ridiculous quasi-Irish accent and said, 'Brendan ... it's Brendan Parry.' 'Oh, okay,' she said, and handed me the keys.

I roared out of the hire car compound in a red Ford Escort and headed west across Ireland. In 1979, the cross-country roads in Ireland were sometimes no more than country lanes. It was disorientating. I had to plough on in pitch blackness and stop at every road sign to look for directions to the next village on the map. After four hours I finally saw a sign for Sligo – main town to Mullaghmore. I got to the seaside resort at 2 a.m. I got a treasured room in a local hotel. No point in going to bed – I had to be filing by 7 a.m. – so I just set out to find anybody and everybody, to discover what they'd seen, heard or knew. In the hotel, on the streets and down to the harbour.

A load of wreckage from Mountbatten's boat, *Shadow V*, was still piled up on the beach. I did a descriptive piece on the debris of the carnage. It was removed just after dawn. At 4 a.m. fishermen started arriving to set off on their little boats. One of them told me he believed the bomb could have been concealed in a lobster pot and that it might have exploded as the pot was pulled up from the sea. As dawn broke, I saw a number of people searching the hill behind the harbour. I trekked up there and a member of the Irish police, the Garda, told me quite openly that they believed the killers watched the boat go out from this hill and used a TV remote control to detonate a bomb they had placed on the boat the previous night.

One report after another came in and a huge manhunt was underway across both the Republic of Ireland and Northern Ireland – the border was just a few miles up the road. But as I was doing this story, there was another dreadful story unfolding at Warrenpoint, County Down, 115 miles away and just north of the border on the other side of the country. Two roadside bombs had exploded and killed eighteen members of the Parachute Regiment. No wonder the day became known as Bloody Monday.

On day one, I filed five different leads for five different editions of the paper. Everywhere I went I was picking up a new line – the police, the harbourmaster, the hospital, the rescuers, Classiebawn Castle where Mountbatten holidayed, the total shock in the local community. On day two, the pace was just as frantic. All sorts of forensic experts had arrived from all over the world. Because I was working for an evening newspaper I was free of the pressure to file by 3.30 in the afternoon so I drove north to Enniskillen to see if I could find the family of the boat boy, Paul Maxwell. One of the dreads of my whole reporting life has been knocking on the door of a family who have lost somebody, and when it's a child or a teenager it's even worse. The family weren't home but I talked to neighbours and filed a piece about this lovely young rugby-playing lad, so thrilled to be boat boy to Lord Mountbatten.

Returning to Mullaghmore, I joined all the other dozens of reporters in the bar. One of the guys there was Michael Sharkey from the *Evening Press* in Dublin. He told me his brother was a pop star called Feargal, who I'd never heard of but who, a few years later, hit the top of the charts in the UK and gave me an exclusive interview because I knew his brother.

Just before midnight, a barman called me over to the phone in the bar. It was Birmingham and they told me, amazingly, that they'd had a tip-off that two men were going to be charged with the murder of Lord Mountbatten in a Dublin court the following day. I had to get over there and I wasn't to tell anybody else. I got my gear together, slipped out of the back door of the hotel, slid into my trusty Escort and embarked on the reverse nightmare journey back to Dublin. All I can remember is how terribly pitch black it was and that the roads were once again deserted. I had an impending sense of doom, like I was entering a vortex from which I might never emerge. Again, I had to navigate from one village sign to another. My sense of trepidation heightened considerably when I suddenly noticed that I was almost out of petrol. This was a disaster. I was going to be stranded in the middle of Ireland all night when I should have been making my way to the Dublin court where two men were going to be charged with Mountbatten's murder. I was a drowning man and I needed a miracle. And then one happened.

I entered a hamlet – going no more than 20mph to try and preserve my petrol – and came across a village store with a petrol pump in front of it. Hallelujah. I would take the petrol and return and pay for it later: I couldn't pay for it then because I didn't have any punts. But the pump was locked. Even though it was 4 a.m., I had no alternative but to bash on the shop door to try to get the owners out to unlock the pump. I hammered away for a good ten minutes, causing other villagers to call out of their windows to tell me to go away … but I couldn't raise the occupants.

Utter despair set in. Maybe the owners didn't live on the premises. I sat down forlornly on a box of cabbages and figured that I'd just have to wait until somebody showed up in the morning. But would that be early enough to allow me to get to Dublin in time for the court hearing? I couldn't risk going on in the car in case I got stranded on a remote country lane. And then I heard a noise from behind the door. It was being unlocked. It opened and a woman in a nightdress with a cigarette in her mouth came out. She didn't say a word to me. She unlocked the pump and filled the tank up. All the time the cigarette remained in her mouth. I stood six feet away, fearing a blast.

When the tank was full she put the pump back in its cradle and held out her hand. I gave her what English money I had in my pocket. She didn't even look at it – she just walked off back inside, and closed and locked the door behind her. She hadn't spoken a word to me.

With a sense of enormous relief I resumed my journey. By 11 a.m. that morning I'd made it to the press gallery at the Dublin court to see Thomas McMahon and Francis McGirl charged with Mountbatten's murder. I filed before midday for all the main editions. The suspects had been stopped at a routine police roadblock two hours before the bomb even exploded, forty miles from Mullaghmore, following their overnight murderous mission. The Garda suspected their vehicle was stolen and, whilst questioning them, thought they were both very nervous and acting suspiciously about something. When questioned at the local police station McGirl blurted out, 'I never put no bomb on no boat.'

Thomas McMahon was subsequently convicted of the murder of Mountbatten and the three other victims and sentenced to life imprisonment. He was released under the terms of the Good Friday Agreement in 1998. Francis McGirl was acquitted on all charges. He died in 1995 on the family farm when then the tractor he was driving appeared to have rolled over on top of him.

Mike Parry is a broadcaster in radio and TV following twenty years of newspaper journalism in Fleet Street.

Football's night of shame
Dundalk, 1979

Jim Gracey

Sport, it has been often said in the Troubles aftermath, was the aspect of society that provided a semblance of normality in the midst of mayhem. True, our sportsmen, sportswomen and teams gave us much to cheer about and lifted our hearts at times when there was little to celebrate. Sport did indeed keep going in the midst of adversity. But, looking back as an on-the-spot reporter, the notion of sport as an oasis of peace and harmony is just a tad revisionist.

My job on the sports desk of the *Belfast Telegraph* did indeed seem normal compared to the work of my news-desk colleagues, who recorded more deadly scores as the body count mounted. But every now and then tensions on the streets spilled on to the terraces and sport migrated to the front pages for all the wrong reasons.

My own personal baptism of fire arrived just two months into my *Tele* career, ignited by that bloody August Bank Holiday Monday of 1979. Twenty-three people had died: four in the attack on Lord Mountbatten's fishing boat off the Sligo coast; eighteen soldiers in a double blast at Narrow Water, near Warrenpoint, all at the hands of the Provos; and, largely forgotten, a curious English visitor, drawn to the water's edge on the southern side of Carlingford Lough by the first blast at Narrow Water, who was shot dead by a panicking trooper who mistook him for one of the bombers. In the midst of the madness unleashed that sunny day, with community tensions stretched like piano wire and emotions off the scale, someone in the upper echelons of European football – and likewise the security services on both sides of the border – thought it a good idea to send Linfield to Dundalk, which is a few miles across the border in the Republic of Ireland, two days later for a European Cup tie. Talk about quenching flames with petrol.

Context is everything for those born in the ensuing decades. Today, a Dundalk–Linfield game would not raise an eyebrow, let alone the state of high alert that accompanied the fixture in 1979. Back then, Linfield was an exclusively Protestant team and club, drawing its support from staunch loyalist areas. The first Catholic players did not arrive until the 1990s. Today, the team is fully inclusive. Dundalk at that time would have been a safe haven for on-the-run republicans and their sympathisers. A combustible mix at the worst of times. The events of that Bank Holiday Monday made the violence that would erupt inside and outside Oriel Park two nights later an absolute certainty – the blood was up – and still it was allowed to go ahead.

Knowing what was going to happen, we journeyed like moths to a flame: our boss Malcolm Brodie in the driving seat of his Honda Accord automatic; colleagues Bill Ireland, Gordon Hanna and me, his passengers. Three great newspaper men and sports writers, sadly no longer with us, and me, too young and foolish to be apprehensive and for whom the trip seemed like a great adventure. The reports they filed that night were never going to be about football.

The normally bustling Dundalk we arrived in that afternoon was a ghost town, with the owners of pubs and shops hastily pulling down their shutters as word reached them of a pub wrecked by a busload of Linfield supporters in nearby Ravensdale. There wasn't a Blueman in sight when we got there, but an advance party had clearly arrived as a Union Jack was fluttering from the Maid of Erin statue in Market Square. It was the calm before the storm.

A blind man on a galloping horse could have seen the violence coming. Three thousand Linfield fans in a fleet of sixty buses descended on the border town where the local hoods were waiting, ready to defend their title. Gardaí, some not even in riot gear, were hopelessly unprepared, and outnumbered. Undisciplined stewards – bizarrely clad in white coats and resembling cricket umpires – attempted to drive back the rampaging Linfield hordes using wooden cudgels but were overrun. Worse still, the section housing the away fans was strewn with rubble that ought to have been cleared, completely negating the point of the police searches at the turnstiles. And a thin line of barbed wire was all that separated the goading Dundalk fans and police line from the snarling Linfield mob, who chewed it up and spat it out as they launched their attacks.

An estimated 150 to 200 of the 3,000-plus Linfield supporters were involved in the violence, but, fuelled by drink and anger, they generated the sound and fury of ten times their number. However regular fans later asserted that many of these 'supporters' had never been to a Linfield match before.

Unbelievably, at the outset, gardaí clodded stones back at them! The police baton-charged again and again but were driven back under the unreserved stand before calling in reinforcements. The trouble continued, despite appeals over the PA system by Dundalk and Linfield officials, and by Bluemen in the stands who were not involved in the violence and who tried to remonstrate with the mob. An uneasy peace settled, particularly after Warren Feeney scored the opening Linfield goal – though immediately after it, full back Terry Hayes was felled by a stone thrown from the Dundalk end. But more trouble was to develop. A tricolour was set alight at the Linfield end and, in response, the Dundalk crowd ripped up and burned a Union Jack.

Coming up to half-time, the violence worsened, with more stone-throwing and more baton charges. However, at this stage, the gardaí appeared to be settling for a policy of trying to reason with the fans – at that stage they made no arrests and allowed the Linfield supporters not involved in the trouble to keep things under control.

That plan soon broke down, however, and all hell was let loose during half-time, with vicious fighting, and Linfield fans up on the roof of the stand trying to remove the tricolour that was flying at full mast. Injured gardaí, many with blood streaming down their faces, were helped out of the ground and some stewards were also among the casualties. So, too, were a number of Linfield fans who had been arrested. We saw one dragged by police through the tearoom with blood gushing from a head wound.

Dundalk officials continued to make appeals for order over the loudspeaker: 'You are doing your club no good. Please stop firing missiles,' they pleaded, to no avail. Later, when the teams took the field again, some of the Linfield players, led by their player-manager Roy Coyle, walked straight to the Linfield section involved in the violence and pleaded for order. Legendary captain Peter Rafferty and Feeney, scorer of Linfield's goal, also appealed. Rafferty said afterwards, 'There was one boy, and the smell of drink from his breath nearly made me drunk. Quite honestly, I've never seen any of those people at Windsor Park before.'

They settled, but not for long. One fan climbed up on to the roof of the ground, and again tried to pull down the tricolour. He was tackled by a steward, who pelted the youth with stones and then retreated. And that was more or less the prelude for a big baton charge from gardaí. About three hundred of them rushed forwards, stepped over the barbed wire, which had been practically pulled asunder, and drove the Linfield fans back. More stones rained down on them, but they pushed on, driving the rioters back into the vast section of Linfield fans not involved, and who had earlier howled their disapproval of it all.

At one stage, stewards rushed across the pitch while the game was continuing, but renowned referee Pat Partridge hardly noticed it. Meanwhile, behind the Linfield goal, the supporters were being driven back further and further into one corner.

The casualty and arrest list by this time had increased significantly. Order of Malta members had set up an impromptu First Aid room under the main stand before the ambulances arrived. Then the trouble spilled outside into Carrick Road. Three houses, a supermarket and a filling station were attacked and had windows smashed as the Linfield fans made their way back to the buses taking them home, parked up by the Harp brewery. The buses, too, were attacked, with more windows broken. Several had been smashed on the way to Dundalk as well, injuring some Linfield supporters.

Meanwhile, in the Dundalk boardroom after the game, Linfield secretary Derek Brookes condemned the violence and, in particular, the troublemakers clad in blue. Their conduct, he said, had disgraced the club. 'Unfortunately,' said Mr Brookes, 'they ignored our appeals for order, and Roy Coyle did his best as well. Fortunately, the hooligans were greatly outnumbered by genuine fans, and the game itself was played in a magnificent spirit. There was hardly a serious foul.' Dundalk chairman Oliver Quinn said he was 'sad and disappointed'. Referee Partridge said he wanted to make no comment, and neither would the UEFA observer at the match, Leo Callaghan from Wales. 'It's all here in my notes,' he said. 'But I don't want to say anything. I'll be making my report.'

That report resulted in Linfield being held almost entirely accountable, being forced to pay Dundalk's costs to travel to the Netherlands as well as an additional £5,000 for damage sustained to Oriel Park. Dundalk were fined £870 for providing insufficient security at the match. In an ironic postscript, Dundalk went on to defeat Maltese minnows Hibernians in the next round before drawing Celtic. The events of that night forty-two years ago in Dundalk showed Belfast would not have been ready for a match like that had it been Linfield who progressed.

When order was finally restored as the Blue hordes left a shattered town, the 'score' was: 52 gardaí hurt; 50 civilians injured, including 3 Linfield fans and a girl who remained in hospital the next day; and 25 arrests made – mostly Linfield supporters, who appeared in court the next day and were fined.

And while the match itself yielded a £10,500 'gate', the Dundalk club revealed that the cost of staging the match, and paying for the damage would wipe out their profit. Linfield paid a high price, too, and not just reputational. UEFA chiefs quickly decided the club should carry the can for their supporters' actions and ordered the return leg to be played in Haarlem, Holland. Amid it all, a football match broke out, a credit to every player on the pitch and, fittingly, it ended in a 1–1 draw, Dundalk progressing with a 2–0 win, where Linfield's goal scorer at Oriel Park, Warren Feeney, missed a penalty.

That riot in 1979 was by far the worst I have witnessed in a football ground in forty-two years chronicling the game here, and there have been many: the battle on the pitch at the end of the 1983 Linfield–Glentoran Irish Cup final at Windsor; the 1985 final between the same clubs at which burning rafters rained down from inside the roof of the unreserved stand at The Oval; Linfield–Donegal Celtic in 1990; Cliftonville–Celtic in the week of the internment anniversary in 1984, when fans fought running battles with police who fired plastic bullets inside the ground, and when a service revolver was snatched and later used to murder an off-duty UDR soldier; and the murder of reserve police officer David Purse, who was on duty at a Crusaders match at Seaview in 1980. And so it went on through the 1980s and 1990s, the almost routine football disorder a microcosm of a violent and divided society.

The fact that Dundalk has played without incident at Windsor in recent years shows how far most of us have come in the long, drawn-out decades of peace- and confidence-building since. And that has to be the biggest blessed relief of all.

Jim Gracey was group sports editor of *Belfast Telegraph/Sunday Life*, and spent over forty years reporting on local, national and international sport, including five football World Cups. He retired in 2021 and serves as vice-chair of the Mary Peters Trust sport charity.

The gangster and the peacemaker who lived streets apart
Belfast, 1979

Gary Honeyford

The Troubles compelled choices. Some chose to inflict pain, others to spread the balm of compassion. Saidie Patterson and Jim Craig both hailed from Belfast's Shankill district. They walked the same streets but followed very different paths.

In the autumn of 1979 I was an uneasy novice being ushered into a dingy backstreet club off the Shankill Road with four other journalists by a bulky guy with a chubby face. Tommy 'Tucker' Lyttle was a UDA commander, media go-between and lover of greyhound racing.

In front of us was a neatly assembled 'terror tableau': Ulster and UDA flags framed a group of men in balaclavas and combat fatigues. Sundry weapons lay on the table at which three of them sat. The mask in the centre read a statement warning of impending 'action' against the IRA. Shortly after this event, two of the masks – James Pratt Craig and Arthur James Bettice – were arrested and charged. My colleagues and I were called as witnesses, a deeply uncomfortable experience for anyone.

Belfast Crown Court was a dismal place, drab and depressing. I remember little of Bettice but a lot about Craig. He was short and broad. Powerfully built. His spud-like face radiated menace, from the squashed features to the cold eyes, all propped up on the thickest of thick necks. His eyes never left me as I was asked to verify the *News Letter* report I had written. Bettice was freed while Craig was sent for trial. That made Craig suspicious and led to Bettice being killed by his own organisation, which claimed he was an informer. All fairly standard fare in the ebb and flow of the Northern Ireland tragedy.

Over the years, Jim Craig's name came up again and again. He was a Mafia-type figure linked to many murders, including those of fellow loyalists. I kept hearing about his racketeering, especially his extortion of money from building sites and businesses. As I knew, Craig could be very menacing. I was told of money destined for the UDA ending up in his back pocket, funding lavish holidays.

The police struggled to convict him because his victims were too frightened to testify.

In the end, his own organisation murdered him in an East Belfast bar in October 1988, accusing him of treason no less. He had colluded in the death of one loyalist leader too many. Shankill Road paramilitaries were fond of claiming that their only crime was loyalty, but the running joke in Belfast was that their only loyalty was to crime. Jim Craig personified that, although he was far from being the only one.

Craig distorted the Protestant faith which defined the Shankill area, using it to fuel division for his own ends.

Saidie Patterson simply lived that faith, drawing on it as a source of strength to help others. I knew little of her when I knocked on the door of 32 Woodvale Street one June day in 1980. It was a typical Belfast two-up two-down terrace, an unimposing home for a remarkable woman.

Saidie grew up in the grinding poverty of Belfast's linen mills but was not crushed by her circumstances. Her early life was dominated by the fight against the disparities of an industrial revolution that had brought great wealth to the few and great injustice to the many. She became a prominent trade unionist, holding court with Labour Party icons like Bevin and Gaitskell.

Then the Troubles brought the seemingly inescapable injustice of violence. Belfast's political and cultural fault line ran close to where Saidie lived, along the streets she walked and into the neighbouring Falls Road. Men and women on either side were joining terror groups, hiding guns in their attics … in waste bins … in the local parks.

Brasher, louder and angrier voices than Saidie's were prevailing. But through all the rage and sadness she never stopped calmly uttering her conviction that it was better to bury the hatchet than the dead. When the Maguire family tragedy sparked the formation of the Peace People, Saidie helped organise the seemingly impossible – a peace march along the fervently loyalist Shankill. Fifty thousand took part. They came from the Shankill and Falls and every corner of the island. Nuns and priests walked with Protestant ministers. It was a hugely symbolic emotional outpouring.

But peace was a dangerous pursuit in a Northern Ireland riven by visceral hatred. During another march, this time on the Falls Road, Saidie was attacked and badly beaten by a mob. She put her survival down to the courage of a group of Catholic women who came to her aid.

She was in hospital for months with an injured spine, but the episode merely stiffened her sense of purpose: 'I wear a steel support as a result, and I'm on crutches too – but there's nothing wrong with my tongue.'

It was a persuasive tongue for all its mild manner. I sat in the neat living room of her modest home enthralled by her turn of phrase, her experiences and her calm. Her faith was unshakable. Despite what she had encountered in the 'satanic' mills of her youth and the dark deeds of her native city, she truly believed that people were essentially good. Cynicism never touched Saidie. She wrote, encouraging me to 'keep up the good work. The pen is mightier than the sword.'

The contrast between those who helped and those who harmed has always intrigued me. During the pandemic lockdown in 2020, I listened to a Truth and Reconciliation Platform interview with former UDA man James Greer and one-time IRA member Anne Walker. Both were lured into violence but eventually turned away from it. I imagine their stories are typical of hundreds more as yet untold. They used a phrase that resonated with me: 'We lived by the news.' It seems obvious but we all did. Our days were book-ended, morning and evening, by the latest trauma and we journalists brought it into the homes of our neighbours. That is a weighty responsibility, but the media, like everyone else then, just got on with it. I always believed that however much people wanted to turn away, that reality had to be faced.

Decades on, fragments cling like leeches: a priest muttering to me, 'too much blood for any one day' after the Ormeau Road bookies attack; a note on the bloodstained floor of the Mountain Lodge Pentecostal Hall – 'Jesus Saves' in the hesitant hand of a child; the hatred in so many eyes; the tears, the incessant tears, in so many more.

Few have been left untroubled by the Troubles, but despair, violence and hatred did not prevail. I put that down in large part to those like Saidie Patterson; those whom the media described as 'ordinary people', but who were, in the circumstances, extraordinary.

Gary Honeyford was the Sky News Ireland correspondent. He also worked for the *Portadown News*, *News Letter*, *Sunday News*, RTÉ and was Reuters Television Ireland bureau chief.

Jumping on the bonnets of upturned cars
Dublin, 1981

Liam Collins

I was hungover that Saturday morning after a hard night in the 'office' pub, the Bachelor Inn, down a laneway known as Piss Alley near our offices in Middle Abbey Street, Dublin. After a perfunctory 7 a.m. hello to Paddy Murray, news editor of the *Evening Herald*, that morning, I put the head down to begin my shift, which was known as 'Daytown' and involved phoning every Garda station in the country.

Around 10.30 a.m., Murray stopped at my desk. 'There's a H-block demo starting in O'Connell Street at 2 p.m.,' he said. 'It'll get to the British Embassy around 4 p.m., right up against the deadline for the last edition, so I want you to do a bit of creative writing. I want two holding stories: one a riot, one a peaceful demonstration. Make the riot a good one, because if it kicks off, that will be the splash; if it's peaceful, it's a few paragraphs on page three.'

The H-block protests had been going on since the previous October and there had been a warm-up march to the embassy about two weeks previously. The group news editor, Ray Doyle, had rented an apartment with a bird's-eye view of the junction that would be the flashpoint if trouble started. Two reporters with an open telephone line had sat watching from a balcony. Nothing had happened.

This Saturday, 18 July 1981, no such comforts were available. Tensions were already high but the temperature seemed to soar that hot afternoon as the march passed through central Dublin. The chanting grew louder, the thump of makeshift drums seemed deeper and the sound of the whistles carried by many of the marchers seemed to prophesy impending violence. A window was shattered by a few stones to rhythmic chants of 'Gardaí … RUC'.

I bolted into a telephone box on Merrion Square and called the office. Murray answered. 'It's going to be a riot,' I told him. 'The trouble is already starting.'

'Should we run the riot story?' he asked.

'Yes,' I said.

At the junction before the embassy there were flimsy barricades and a thick blue line of gardaí across Merrion Road, barring the way. As more marchers funnelled into this dead end, the throngs arriving pushed those in front right up against the police barriers. Chief Superintendent John 'Robbo' Robinson exhorted his ill-equipped men to stand firm.

The junction of Merrion Road/Simmonscourt Road and Sandymount Avenue is the main artery into what is now known as D4, Dublin's most affluent neighbourhood. On one side are the six-foot railings of the Royal Dublin Society; on the other, a row of three- and four-storey red-brick houses, with balconies on the upper floors and garden walls topped with railings.

At around 3.45 p.m. the missiles began to fly from further back. Then, using the railings for leverage, groups of men, well trained in the art of the riot, had the walls and pillars fronting the houses broken apart in minutes. The loose bricks, bottles, stones and other missiles began to rain on the Garda lines. Iron gutters were ripped from the house fronts and used, along with the banners, as spears to try to force the Garda frontline to retreat.

Within minutes the junction turned into a battleground. In the first flush of violence, as the debris rained down, smacking and cracking on the police riot shields, one missile broke Chief Superintendent Robinson's leg. As injured gardaí were helped away from the line, new recruits appeared. Cars were dragged out of driveways, turned over and set alight. The roar of the crowd, the hammering of the missiles, the pungent smell of black smoke, the flash of petrol bombs exploding and the wail of sirens rent the hot afternoon air.

My concern was to get to a phone, confirm the riot story to the news desk and add some gory details. I climbed over a wall between two houses and made my way through the back gardens on to Sandymount Avenue. I knocked on a door and asked to use the phone, but was turned away by a man with a glass of wine in his hand. 'Can't you see I'm hosting a drinks reception?' he told me imperiously as he closed the door.

A couple of doors down an old lady, who didn't seem bothered by how wild-eyed with panic I had become, let me in and I phoned the office. Little did I know the riot story I had written earlier that morning was already running with the banner headline, 'Fierce Clashes at Embassy'. For the next twenty minutes I went backwards and forwards between the devastation on Merrion Road and the phone, relaying new developments and updating the story. It must have been after 4.20 p.m. when I ventured back for a last look.

I climbed the wall and dropped back on to the Merrion Road side without thinking. Then I suddenly realised the sound and fury was gone, replaced by an eerie silence broken only by the thump of batons on flesh and bone. A line of truncheon-wielding gardaí had passed my position and were engaged in hand-to-hand combat further up the road.

It was particularly vicious around No. 47, an unoccupied house that had been taken over by rioters, who hurled a gas cylinder and other missiles from the top floor windows. People were being dragged from gardens and even trees, which they had climbed for refuge, and beaten mercilessly. Some of the gardaí had lost their batons in the melee and were now using abandoned placards to attack anybody they could find.

The retribution was atrocious and self-preservation became my only concern. I crossed the road and kept my back to the railings of the Royal Dublin Society, behind which a line of Garda reinforcements was corralled. Suddenly an arm snaked out, went around my neck and pinned me against the railing. I thought I was done for when a voice said forcefully, 'Don't move and don't say a fucking word.' When gardaí came towards me with crazed eyes and batons drawn, the same voice shouted, 'Keeping going, lads – he's one of our own.'

Terrified, I stood stock still until eventually the waves of gardaí passed and the arm around my neck loosened. I turned, and as I came face to face with my protector, I had a flashback to events just four weeks earlier, when we were in the throes of a general election.

During the campaign I had travelled the country with Garret FitzGerald, the leader of Fine Gael, on his campaign bus, along with Frank McDonald from the *Irish Times* and Stephen O'Byrnes from the *Irish Press*. During the last week it was decided that FitzGerald would pay a visit to St Vincent's Hospital in Dublin, then take a helicopter to Dungloe, County Donegal, to rejoin the bus tour. We were waiting with a small knot of Fine Gael supporters as the chopper touched down in the Donegal village. As FitzGerald alighted, we were suddenly swamped by flag-waving H-block protesters. It was when the situation turned ugly that I noticed the Fine Gael leader's two armed bodyguards were missing. A couple of local gardaí finally shoved us into the sanctuary of the hotel and the danger passed. I asked FitzGerald what had happened to his protection unit and he looked at me blankly, realising for the first time that his minders were missing. I was already visualising the headline: 'FitzGerald Abandoned to the H-block Mob'.

Later, as the bus wound its way south and we were writing our copy for the following morning's papers, FitzGerald came down and sat with us. He explained that he had rushed out of the hospital and told the pilot to take off, leaving his armed protection detail sitting in a nearby car. 'I can't stop you doing a story, but if you do, the two detectives will at best be back in uniform tomorrow and at worst lose their jobs,' he said. When he left, the three of us considered the fallout from the story on the two men's lives and discussed whether or not to 'publish and be damned'. We decided an easy headline wasn't worth anyone losing their job. But later that night, after a few pints, I let the two detectives know what a close call it had been.

Now, as the riot receded in Ballsbridge, I turned and looked into the hard, cold eyes of one of those detectives, whose career I felt I had saved, and who had now saved me. 'One good turn deserves another,' he said curtly, then turned and was gone.

In the Bachelor later that evening, Murray slapped down a copy of the *Herald* and the edition of our rival evening paper, which carried a sentence that has stayed with me ever since: 'Rioters were jumping on the bonnets of upturned cars.' That was about the only thing that hadn't happened that hot violent day in 1981.

Liam Collins worked as a reporter and news editor with the *Sunday Independent* in Dublin.

The one thing we learn from history is that we don't learn from history
Derry, 1984

Eugene Campbell

It's a popular myth in the television world that looking through the eyepiece (or viewfinder, as it's known in the trade) of a TV camera somehow distances you from what you are seeing, but for me that was never the case. The camera becomes an extension of your body and you get to know every working and switch until muscle memory takes over and operating it becomes an automated sequence. A cameraman comes to know the camera in much the same way as a soldier knows his rifle.

But before you press the button to record, you have to look and assess. This might sound stupidly simple, and sometimes it is, but you have to understand what you're seeing – sometimes simple, often not. In my early years as a cameraman for UTV, I was based in Derry 99 per cent of the time. I worked alone on an almost daily diet of murders, bombings and riots. Very rarely would I film a 'normal' news story. Life was completely upside down but that was our normality. I was seven and living in Downpatrick when the Troubles started, so I neither knew nor remembered any other way.

Life was a diet of these tragedies. Mangled bodies and mangled wrecks; hatred in deeds and hatred in the eyes of people, young and old, who, despite having so much in common with their neighbours, would stretch every sinew to search out their minute differences in the name of flags, heritage and God. You could go mad (and many did) trying to peel back the onion-like layers of how we came to be where we were, who did what to whom, who started what, when and why.

I quickly became blasé about the utter futility and despair of it all, and found sanity in black humour and in the bottom of a bottle. A day's work was taped-off country roads where life was taken by bomb or bullet, or narrow tidy streets in grey cold light that could hide danger in every shadow, often followed by a fast drive to the office to make news deadlines. Evenings were usually drunken affairs, trying to wash away the memories of the day.

Our normality was abnormal. The words put to our pictures in TV reports had quickly lost any impact, unable to explain the extremes of the evil we'd filmed: murdered unborn children, lives stolen before their first breath; or a completely innocent schoolboy, kidnapped by grown men, tortured in the most sick and depraved way, before being murdered and having his young body burnt. (The people responsible still walk free.) Even worse things happened but still now, decades after, their evil is too much to revisit.

And yet we were only the spectators – observing, recording, remembering, parcelling up Irish history in its cycles of repetition.

I'd learnt to deal with all of this except for one thing: funerals. Through my lens, I've looked into the eyes of gunmen, or men in dog collars whose hateful words poisoned the naive, or the carpetbaggers in posh, polished suits, who always had answers, but I could not keep the gaze of a child standing by a graveside, burying their father or mother, whose life had been stolen. I couldn't look into their eyes because through their tears they were asking, 'Why?' and neither I nor anybody else could give them an honest answer.

The old saying is especially poignant here: 'The one thing that we learn from history is that we don't learn from history.' Heartbreakingly true.

Eugene Campbell was an award-winning senior cameraman with ITN for twenty-three years and a decorated war correspondent. He's now freelance, living in London.

The killing of Sean Downes
Belfast, 1984

Paul Johnson

It's the photograph that is lodged in my memory, never to be erased, no matter how many years go by. It's in black and white. A bit grainy. In the foreground, the heads of a dozen or so people, crouching but looking upwards. At the top of the picture are three armoured, police Land Rovers with grilles across their windscreens. It's the middle of the picture that is the focal point. A police officer, a burly figure padded out with a flak jacket, helmet on, visor up, stands side on, right arm nearest us, right index finger on the trigger of his two-foot-long gun, the stock wedged into his shoulder. The left arm is extended to a grip at the end of the barrel. There's another policeman in the centre. But the figure you are drawn to is on the right, a young man, early twenties, black tousled hair and a moustache, about two metres away from the end of the gun. In his right hand, he seemed to be carrying a stick, the diameter of a garden bamboo pole. He's leaning forward, as if stopping suddenly, left hand going to his chest, to his heart.

It's Sunday, 12 August 1984: the moment Sean Downes was killed on the Falls Road, a freeze-frame death in front of journalists and TV crews from around the world.

It was a sunny Sunday. But there wasn't any jollity in the air that day. There was a provocation to the government and the security forces. And the likelihood was that the provocation would mean confrontation. The two-mile march – including women, children and families, many young – to the rally site was flanked by police and army vehicles all the way. Along the route the occasional missile was flung at the police. Every side street was sealed off. Helicopters hovered low overhead.

Many of the crowd sat in the road to listen to speeches from a raised podium set up outside Sinn Féin headquarters. Gerry Adams was there. But this time the security forces were not interested in him. It was the man to his left, clutching the microphone, that they wanted: Martin Galvin, the thirty-four-year-old director of Noraid – the US-based group that raised funds for the Irish republicans – whose day job was, improbably, working as a lawyer in

New York City's Sanitation Department, and who was the subject of an order banning him from the UK.

It was the moment Galvin picked up the microphone and moved to address the gathering and the TV cameras that the police moved. Dozens of them charged into the crowd to try and carve a way through to their target. A photographer nearby was batoned as he waved his press card aloft. The shouting and screaming was instant, and then there were the cracks of plastic bullets being fired. Behind me, a man, blood pouring from a head wound, was being dragged into a front garden – a couple of youths smashed the door of a house to get him inside. Another journalist and I saw a low-slung pram abandoned in the middle of the chaos. We barged our way through and manoeuvred it to the side of a low wall, out of the way. Relieved, we looked inside. It was empty. Another man was unconscious to our left, with people trying to drag him away. Just a few metres away, there was a glimpse of the young man with the stick, running towards police and then a crack.

A plastic bullet is a solid, PVC cylinder, 10cm long and 3.8cm in diameter. It has an operational range of between 33 and 66 metres. At 45 metres its impact is in the severe damage category – meaning skull fractures, ruptures of kidney or heart and haemorrhages. The rules said it should not be fired from less than a 20 metre range and should be aimed below the waist. The rules didn't mean much that day.

Galvin escaped through the houses and back gardens of the Falls Road. His object was provocation and publicity. On those terms, it was a grim success.

One person was dead, four seriously injured and twenty people hurt. The remarkable photograph by Alan Lewis of the *Daily Mail* was published the next day, so it was all the more puzzling that, at a hastily called press conference, the RUC chief constable, the pugnacious Sir John Hermon, didn't seem to have seen it or heard about it. If he had, he surely wouldn't have claimed – during what became an ill-tempered session – that his officers had fired into the air, not at any targets in the crowd; that the reporting was hyperbolic; and that force was only used because a riot had broken out. That angry, reflex version didn't hold for long in the face of the evidence. But it was quickly replaced by another, this time from another senior RUC officer, who explained that the bullet had ricocheted off a wall and then hit Sean Downes.

Media bias is not a new theme. Coverage was slanted, said Ian Paisley. And the BBC was particularly to blame. Unionists won recall of the Northern Ireland Assembly in order to vent anger at the reporting. In London, some took an opposing view: Shirley Williams, of the Social Democratic Party, called it Belfast's Peterloo. David Steel, leader of the Liberal party, called it a police riot.

Eight months later, in April 1985, Constable Nigel Hegarty, twenty-seven, appeared at a Belfast court charged with unlawful killing. It emerged that in a statement made on the day, he said he had fired from a distance of 20 to 25 yards (18–23 metres). At his trial, it emerged that Sean Downes had been convicted, as a sixteen-year-old, of membership of the junior IRA and possession of a weapon. Mr Justice Hutton said he believed Hegarty when he said he believed his life and those of his colleagues were in danger. He took into account 'the stress of the moment and the obvious determination of the deceased'. Hegarty was acquitted.

Sean Downes' funeral took place three days after he was killed, an estimated five thousand people joining the cortège to the vast Milltown cemetery. In the crowd were Adams, Martin McGuinness and Danny Morrison. It was only when the shiny nameplate on the side of the coffin was visible that it became clear that the victim's name was not Sean but John, and that was how he was known to his family.

Postscript

John Downes left a widow, Brenda, aged twenty. She had been at the rally but had gone home, with their eighteen-month-old daughter Claire, when trouble broke out. She tried to get the court's decision overturned and believed her solicitor was making progress. At one point Brenda went to Australia but 'you can't run away' and she returned to Belfast, immersing herself in the Irish-Palestine support campaign, women's causes and Relatives for Justice.

That solicitor was Pat Finucane. He was shot dead by the UDA, with security force collusion, in 1989. The reverberations of the killing last to today: in March 2021, the Council of Europe said it would open a review after the British government refused to order a public inquiry.

Nigel Hegarty returned to service in the RUC.

Mr Justice Hutton became Lord Hutton. At one point, his name, address and car registration appeared on an IRA list discovered by the RUC. He moved his family to Scotland. Years later, in 2004, he chaired the inquiry into the circumstances surrounding the death of Iraqi weapons expert David Kelly. Hutton absolved Prime Minister Tony Blair, reserving his criticism for the BBC.

Sir John Hermon retired as chief constable in 1989. In 1997 he published his autobiography entitled *Holding the Line*.

Martin Galvin tried to repeat his appearance of that 1984 day in 1989 but was arrested and deported to the US. He went on to oppose the peace process and Sinn Féin's role in it.

The day after John Downes' funeral, I went to Donaghadee, a small seaside town, bedecked in red, white and blue bunting and Union Flags, for another funeral. Sergeant Billy McDonald, aged twenty-nine, was the two hundredth member of the RUC to die at the hands of terrorists since the beginning of the Troubles. He was attending a lecture as part of his criminology studies at Ulster University when a bomb planted in a wall cavity was detonated. He had hung on to life for nine months, recovering consciousness only once, dying just hours after John Downes was shot dead. Inside the church, the congregation sang 'The Lord's My Shepherd' as another congregation had done the day before when saying goodbye to John Downes.

Paul Johnson was Ireland correspondent of the *Guardian* from 1984 to 1986. He was deputy editor of the *Guardian* for twenty-five years before retiring in 2020.

Covering paramilitary funerals
Belfast, 1984

Michael Fisher

My first marking in August 1984 – as a member of RTÉ's 'Northern staff' led by Jim Dougal – was to cover the funeral in West Belfast of Sean Downes, who had been killed by a plastic bullet fired by an RUC officer. Thus began twenty-six years of reporting the Northern Ireland conflict that encompassed many tragic deaths on all sides. Although the Sinn Féin leadership was present, Downes's was not a republican funeral. The security forces kept their distance and Mr Downes was buried in his grandfather's grave. In the analogue era, there were no mobile phones for reporters so my audio for the RTÉ radio news at 1.00 p.m. was fed to Dublin via a telephone in the church sacristy.

In March 1987 I witnessed an IRA 'show of strength' when two masked gunmen emerged through the crowd in the confined space outside the Long Tower church in Derry at the funeral of Gerard Logue. They opened fire over the tricolour-draped coffin with the security forces observing from a distance. This led to Bishop Edward Daly of Derry ordering a ban on paramilitary trappings, including flags, at funerals.

By the time it came to senior IRA member Larry Marley's funeral in April 1987, I was better versed in what to expect: watching for who was present and who was absent; the disposition of the security forces; the comments by the bishop or clergy; the reactions of the local community. Marley had been one of the masterminds behind the escape of republican prisoners from the high-security Maze prison in September 1983, so I had assumed there would be a strong security presence, with the RUC attempting to prevent any 'show of strength'. I did not think it would take three days of behind-the-scenes discussions before the stand-off with security forces was resolved and the funeral allowed to take place. Such funerals, like the one for hunger striker Bobby Sands in 1981, have proved an essential part of the republican tradition. Gerry Adams said the Marley funeral was the largest 'display of republican support since the hunger strikes'.

My report on the Marley funeral was factual, and deliberately low-key, although I left a gap for the actuality not subject to a ban to convey the scuffles between the police and the crowd. There were strict reporting rules – known as the Section 31 guidelines – for RTÉ journalists in those days of the Troubles. These prevented the national broadcaster from interviewing anyone who was a member of a paramilitary group and, additionally in the case of republicans, anyone from their political wing, Sinn Féin. In describing the Provisionals, we were careful to refer to an IRA member and never used any self-styled military title.

Larry Marley's killing by the Ulster Volunteer Force was said to be a retaliation for the IRA having shot dead John Bingham, a leading UVF member, in North Belfast. As an RTÉ reporter, that funeral had required a different and more sensitive approach. One local camera crew got sufficiently close to the house where a private service was held. When the coffin was brought out, it was draped in a UVF flag. Ballysillan Crescent, where Mr Bingham lived, was a cul-de-sac, so crowds had gathered at the top of the road. I joined them, attempting to blend in, without the notebook, pen, microphone or tape recorder that might have identified me as a journalist. Members of the Orange Order provided a guard of honour around the coffin; Protestant Unionist councillor George Seawright was one of the pall-bearers. That weekend, the Dublin-based *Sunday Tribune* newspaper carried a large colour photograph of the Bingham funeral on its front page. It showed the size of the cortège emerging from Ballysillan, with delivery lorries carrying dozens of wreaths. Somewhere in the photograph you can spot me!

A few months before my retirement from RTÉ News, I covered the funeral of a loyalist in Belfast. Bobby Moffett was a former member of the Red Hand Commando group, linked to the UVF. He had been shot dead by the UVF on 28 May 2010 while standing at a street corner on the Shankill Road, following a personal dispute. Some locals claimed the UVF had warned them not to attend the funeral. Family, friends and neighbours gathered at the house of his elderly mother, Susan Moffett. Someone took a deckchair from the house so that she could sit down while the remains were being carried out. No one attempted to prevent the small group of media from watching. The atmosphere that sunny morning was very peaceful, calm and dignified, unlike the tense atmosphere at some paramilitary-related incidents I had covered. By the time the mourners left the housing estate and turned on to the Shankill Road, several hundred people had joined the cortège. Hundreds more lined the route, sending out a clear message to those responsible for the killing.

While it was possible for me not to be recognised as a reporter at a funeral in Belfast, there were two controversial republican funerals in County Monaghan at which my work as a television news reporter, combined with family connections, meant I was immediately recognised.

Séamus McElwain, from Knockatallon beside the border with County Fermanagh, was a leading IRA member who had escaped from the Maze in 1983, so he was given a republican send-off. This funeral, in April 1986, required a cautious approach from me as an RTÉ journalist: I knew there were those in the crowd who would be quick to allege censorship if a full report did not appear. A UTV colleague and I arranged that the UTV cameraman would stay close to the farmhouse of the McElwain family – where six men fired shots over the coffin. The cortège then made the slow journey along country roads decked with black flags to the church, followed by hundreds of mourners.

I based myself three miles away, beside St Mary's chapel in Urbleshanny, where there was a large Garda presence. The Requiem Mass was celebrated by parish priest Canon Bernard Maguire. Before he sprinkled the coffin with holy water, the paramilitary trappings were removed. The remains were allowed into the chapel, and the 'guard of honour' wearing combat jackets and masks proceeded alongside. Prominent among the mourners were Sinn Féin's Gerry Adams and Martin McGuinness. Scores of blue-helmeted gardaí lined the outside wall of the cemetery, but there were no incidents as Mr McGuinness gave the graveside oration, paying tribute to McElwain as an IRA 'volunteer and freedom fighter'.

Jim Lynagh from Monaghan town was one of eight IRA members killed by undercover British soldiers during a gun and bomb attack on Loughgall RUC station in County Armagh in May 1987, during which a civilian also died. The same East Tyrone IRA unit had blown up a nearby police station the previous year, using a 200lb bomb carried in the bucket of a JCB digger, which was also their tactic for Loughgall.

When Lynagh's body was released from the mortuary, his remains were taken home via the main border crossing at Aughnacloy. A few hundred republican sympathisers, including Sinn Féin representatives, gathered at Moybridge to meet the hearse. The cortège then moved through the nearby village of Emyvale, close to where I now live, where the IRA chose to pay a final tribute to Lynagh, one of the most active paramilitaries in the border region. As the highly experienced RTÉ news cameraman John Coghlan recorded the scenes, three armed and masked men wearing combat jackets emerged and fired rifles into the air in a show of defiance. They then ran into a nearby pub and escaped.

There had been a discreet Garda presence on the edges of the funeral procession. A Garda car had been parked at the side of the pub to monitor the crowd. In the confusion, as the IRA 'guard of honour' made their escape, the crowd overturned a Garda vehicle – with one detective inside – into a stream. Another detective fired warning shots into the air from his Uzi sub-machine gun as his colleague extricated himself from the car.

We then had to return to Belfast as quickly as possible to get the camera footage on to the main evening news. These were the days before twenty-four-hour news gathering and live satellite links. The dramatic pictures were also sent to the BBC in London under a sharing arrangement. The next day we returned to Monaghan for the funeral itself. The Mass was held in the cathedral and afterwards Lynagh was buried at Latlurcan Cemetery, where Gerry Adams addressed mourners. Again, Section 31 restrictions meant that RTÉ could not broadcast his words.

A similar experience with fast-moving events came at the funeral in 1992 of the three IRA members killed in Gibraltar. As explosions went off close to where Gerry Adams and Martin McGuinness were standing, I borrowed a mobile phone from a colleague and got through to RTÉ's flagship *News at One* radio programme to describe the frenzied scene at Milltown Cemetery, as loyalist paramilitary Michael Stone ran away firing shots while pursued by some of the huge crowd. It was the only time in my career I was afraid for my own safety and that of my colleagues.

My late aunt, who welcomed me to Belfast when I first arrived in 1984, reminded me I was privileged to be reporting on people and events that would be part of history. When I look back and remember those times, and especially those funerals, I know that she was right.

Michael Fisher is a reporter with the *Northern Standard* in Monaghan. He previously worked with BBC News in London, BBC Radio Birmingham and, for over thirty years, with RTÉ News, mostly in Belfast covering the Troubles for radio and television.

The Mafia, the IRA, Johnny Depp and me
Cork and beyond, 1984

Ivan Little

It started with an ITN weekend-reporting shift in London. And it ended with my appearance in a Hollywood movie starring Johnny Depp. In the intervening twenty-five years, the intriguing story of the IRA's *Marita Ann* gunrunning ship took me to Boston on the trail of American mobster and Provo supporter Whitey Bulger, where I met the FBI and the family of one of Bulger's murder victims as well as undercover cops and lawyers. I also ended up face to face with the IRA leader who led the Irish side of the gunrunning operation and the former Provisional who tipped off the authorities about the *Marita Ann*.

It was on my birthday in September 1984 that I flew from Belfast to London to work for a couple of days with ITN. But no sooner was I in the door than I was out again, flying back to Ireland with an ITN crew, this time on a private jet that was waiting at Heathrow. The brief was to get pictures of a fishing boat called the *Marita Ann* that had been captured by the Irish navy, who had fired tracer bullets before boarding the ship 120 miles off the Kerry coast. We duly spotted the *Marita Ann* at sea, and award-winning cameraman Sebastian Rich filmed it from the air before we headed off to Cork to edit a report for ITN (after downing a few glasses of champagne to celebrate my birthday).

Later that evening we were at Cobh harbour to record the IRA gunrunners – including well-known Kerry republican Martin Ferris – being frogmarched in handcuffs off the ship. The others who were held were Irishmen Michael Browne, Gavin Mortimer and John McCarthy, and John Crawley, a US citizen and former US marine. The next morning we were given access to the terrifying armoury of weaponry being unloaded from the *Marita Ann*. It included 160 guns, dozens of rockets and grenades and over seventy thousand bullets – total value: $1 million.

Next stop was Dublin for the appearance at the Special Criminal Court of the men who had been arrested. I'd been due back in Belfast the following morning for my day job with UTV but ITN asked me to go with their crew to shoot footage of the arms haul being driven to Garda headquarters from

County Cork. On our way south we saw a convoy of security forces lorries heading north on the opposite side of a dual carriageway but by the time we were able to turn around we couldn't see any sign of it. We later discovered that, in an only-in-Ireland moment, the drivers had stopped off for a cup of tea at the Irish Army's Curragh base – which explained why we'd lost them. When the lorries finally arrived at the Garda Síochána's headquarters at Phoenix Park in Dublin, we were waiting to film what I imagined was the final part of the *Marita Ann* jigsaw for me.

But how wrong I was. Sixteen years later, in 2000, UTV sent me to Boston to make a documentary about the discovery in a shallow grave of the body of murdered Irish-American John McIntyre, who had skippered the *Valhalla*, the trawler that had taken the arms from Massachusetts and rendezvoused with the *Marita Ann* for a handover in the Atlantic. It transpired that Whitey Bulger, an infamously fanatical and vicious gangster who sang Irish rebel songs in the IRA bars of Boston, had financed the shipment and, like the Provos in Ireland, was furious when the *Marita Ann* was intercepted. He wanted to unmask the tout.

Bulger, the ruthless leader of Boston's Winter Hill Gang quickly convinced himself that McIntyre was the informer, and his suspicions were reinforced after the British and Irish authorities falsely briefed journalists in Ireland that the information had come from America. The fake steer was to protect the real source of the tip-off – IRA leader and British intelligence agent Sean O'Callaghan. McIntyre paid with his life, with Bulger – who had ordered his execution – helping his men to do his vile dirty work after their victim had been lured to a house in Boston. Bulger and his henchmen at first tried to strangle McIntyre with rope but they couldn't finish him off and he begged for a bullet in the head. McIntyre was then shot and Bulger's gang pulled out his teeth in a bid to make any positive identification of his body almost impossible. But it was established he was indeed John McIntyre.

In 2000, in a neat house in Quincy, just outside Boston, I met McIntyre's mother, Emily, and brother Chris. Over tea and fruitcake they cursed Bulger, who had been on the run for years with his partner Catherine Greig. At another meeting during the same trip, the director of the FBI in Boston, Barry Mawn, told me he had no doubt about the mobster's involvement in the McIntyre slaying. He showed me an FBI chart on the wall that revealed Bulger was second only to Osama Bin Laden on their 'most wanted' list.

The next part of my *Marita Ann* voyage took me to England to interview double agent Sean O'Callaghan for my documentary. In a swish hotel in London, O'Callaghan readily admitted that he gave his handlers in British intelligence chapter and verse about the *Marita Ann*, which had been due to bring its deadly cargo into County Kerry, where IRA men were waiting in cars to transport the guns to arms dumps. The British told the Irish authorities and the operation to seize it swung into gear. O'Callaghan said he had been with Martin Ferris right up until the moment he boarded the trawler in Fenit, County Kerry. He added that McIntyre had nothing to do with the leaking of the information. Over dinner, I told O'Callaghan that McIntyre's family despised the source of the *Marita Ann* tip-off just as much as they hated Bulger. He wasn't surprised, and he wasn't particularly remorseful.

A few years later, a bizarre twist of fate found me talking about O'Callaghan with Martin Ferris. Wearing my other hat as an actor, I'd been touring Ireland with a Martin Lynch play, *The History of the Troubles (accordin' to my da)*, which was a black comedy about the impact of the Troubles on one man, played by me, and supported by a series of characters created by Conor Grimes and Alan McKee, who were also involved in the writing of the piece.

We were staging the play in Tralee's Siamsa Tíre theatre for nearly a week, and one night after the show an Australian lady called Maire and her friends joined us in the bar to discuss the production. Maire invited us to come for drinks after the play the next night at the bar outside Tralee that she ran with her husband, Martin. We never turned our backs on a party and, within minutes of receiving a warm welcome from the locals in the pub, I found myself sitting next to Maire's husband and instantly recognised him as Martin Ferris, who by that stage had become a Sinn Féin TD in Dublin.

I told him I had 'met' him once before and went on to explain that in the other half of my double-life I was a journalist who had reported on his 'departure' from the *Marita Ann* twenty-six years earlier. We talked at length about everything under the political sun but if I was expecting an inside track on the *Marita Ann* or O'Callaghan, I was sorely disappointed.

In 2011, Whitey Bulger and Catherine Greig were arrested in Santa Monica, and Bulger was later given a series of life sentences for eleven murders, including the McIntyre killing.

But a different type of sentence was waiting for Bulger. In 2018, the eighty-nine-year-old Mob boss was found dead in his cell in a West Virginia jail after some of his many enemies finally caught up with him and beat him to a pulp. In a gruesome echo of the McIntyre murder, Bulger was left unrecognisable by his assailants.

Three years earlier, a Hollywood film about Bulger called *Black Mass* had been released. The monster was superbly played by Johnny Depp, who managed to portray his evil savagery with ease. In one scene, in which the practicalities of the gunrunning plot were discussed, Bulger is seen meeting Belfast IRA leader Joe Cahill in a private room in a Boston bar called Triple O's. The two conspirators break off their negotiations to watch a news report on the television about violent clashes between the security forces and republicans in Derry after an IRA funeral.

By a bizarre coincidence, the reporter's voice they hear in the ITN report is mine.

Jimmy Graham: a man I never met but cannot forget
Derrylin, County Fermanagh, 1985

Gareth Gordon

There was a time when no week seemed to pass without a visit to Fermanagh. Not the idyllic land of lakes and mountains, but the one stained by bloodshed and killing.

At first, what met me in Derrylin on 1 February 1985 seemed familiar. Much too familiar. It's a matter of regret that I can't remember the names of all those whose murders brought me to Fermanagh. But I'll never forget the name of Jimmy Graham, and this is why.

Jimmy Graham was a member of the Ulster Defence Regiment. He was also a bus driver, and on this Friday morning that job brought him to a primary school in Derrylin, on the border with Cavan, to bring children for swimming lessons in Enniskillen. The Provisional IRA knew he was coming and, as he waited for the children to arrive, they shot him dead. He didn't stand a chance.

And so it was that other journalists and I stood at the white tape until a policeman came to escort us to the school so we could speak to the principal about the horror at the school gate. Quotes gathered, I walked back down the path towards the bus. Its door was open. I stepped inside ... and froze. I don't know why I assumed the body was gone. But it wasn't. And I saw more than I ever wanted to see.

There are worse things than standing behind white tape shielded from the truth. This was what waited on the other side, and I never want to see it again. I looked around to see if anyone had noticed: this was a crime scene I had blundered into. Turned out the police scenes of crime officer had been delayed. So the victim remained on his bus, lying on his back in the aisle between the seats. He had managed to get out of the driver's seat but not much further. I stepped back off the bus, shocked to the core.

Back in the Belfast newsroom of my paper, the *News Letter*, someone thought I should write up the experience for the next day's front page. I told them 'no' with more force than I'd intended. And I never did write it until now – and only with the Graham family's permission.

There's another reason why the murder of Jimmy Graham stood out, even by the bloody standards of Northern Ireland: this was far from the first time a member of the Graham family had been singled out.

Ronnie Graham was the first to be murdered. He was ambushed in June 1981 while delivering groceries for a local shop. Five months later, his brother Cecil Graham died, two days after he had been shot as he visited his wife's family home to see his five-week-old son. His wife and his baby had been temporarily staying with her parents because the baby was born prematurely and required constant care. Both brothers, like Jimmy, were members of the UDR. Now all three were dead.

It doesn't stop there. Their sister Hilary – also a member of the UDR – had been knocked down by a car that crashed through a vehicle checkpoint in November 1979. She suffered internal injuries and died more than two years later.

Four siblings gone, three murdered in separate attacks – the only incidence of this happening during Northern Ireland's long Troubles.

In heartbreaking interviews with the South East Fermanagh Foundation victims' group, Jimmy Graham's wife, Lily, and daughter, Sharon, revealed that the IRA had tried to murder Jimmy several times. Once, in 1980, the children watched as their father returned fire at men who ran off through the fields near the family home. A fortnight before the final fatal attack, he received a letter telling him to 'clear the country'. Sharon said that was something that 'he would never do'. In the early hours of the Sunday morning after he was murdered, when his remains had been brought home, they said 'two carloads of boys' had driven past, 'shouting and cheering and blowing the horn'.

Jimmy's murder meant money was scarce and Sharon had to leave school at fifteen to pay the bills. Lily Graham said she still missed her husband desperately: 'especially birthdays ... even the Twelfth of July when he'd be getting ready to go out, sash on him. Christmas? There's no Christmas any more – there's no nothing any more.'

In his book *Bad Blood: A Walk Along the Irish Border*, Colm Tóibín recalls meeting two men in south Fermanagh who told him some people in the area believed an abnormally large number of Catholic young people had been killed in car accidents as 'revenge' for what happened to the Grahams:

'What do you mean, revenge?' They weren't sure whether to tell me or not, they looked at each other. No, they didn't mean that these young people had been killed deliberately, but the older people said it was because of the Grahams. Had I heard of the Grahams? I had, I said. They were the three brothers who were killed one by one by the IRA, the last while he was waiting to drive a bus full of Catholic children to swim in Enniskillen. Yes, one of them said, the older people maintained that the accidents were a sort of revenge for what was done to the Grahams. God, you know, did I understand? It was God. It seemed like a large number of young people from the same area, I said, to be killed in accidents. They nodded grimly. I said I didn't think it was God. No, they agreed, they didn't either. It was just something which was said.

I read, and reread, the passage again and again and my mind went back to that bleak Friday morning in 1985 and the yellow school bus riddled with bullets outside a school, and I thought of a man I never met but cannot ever forget.

Gareth Gordon is a political correspondent with BBC Northern Ireland. He previously worked for the organisation as a radio reporter and for the *News Letter* and *Coleraine Chronicle*.

An Englishman in New Lodge
Belfast, 1986

Simon Cole

So, there I was having a pint in Robinsons. It was 1986; my first trip to Belfast as an ITN reporter. I was enjoying a Guinness and agreeing it tasted better in Ireland when I was approached by a small man, who'd obviously had a drink.

'Are youse army?' he whispered.

I said, 'No, why?'

'You're dressed like an army officer, so I'd be careful if I was you.'

I examined myself: blazer, blue shirt with fake regimental tie, fawn chinos and shiny brown shoes. I got it immediately, having come from a military family. It was my first taste of how everything in Northern Ireland at that time was on a hairspring. It was a hugely exciting experience for a reporter because the UK effectively had a civil war on its doorstep. Crews from all over the world came to cover the conflict, and Belfast's hotel bars were a great place to congregate, compare notes and drink too much.

It didn't take me long to learn the ropes. Back in those days, ITN didn't have a permanent Ireland correspondent, so teams were sent in for a month at a time. With the workload and the drinking, it was about as long as a body could stand. Most of the crews had done many tours of duty and were kind enough to look after me. They were brilliant. We had big teams – reporter, camera, sound, lights, fixer and picture editor. The latter was invariably left in the restaurant to pick up the tab when the rest of us got a shout about a bomb or a killing.

I was shown around the city as a sightseer. I saw the fortified police stations; the murals; the pavements painted red, white and blue; the magnificent City Hall; the Harland & Wolff cranes; Milltown Cemetery. But a city is not about the fabric, it is the people. And how I enjoyed the people of Northern Ireland.

Like any city in a virtual state of war, there was a culture of *carpe diem* because no one knew where the next bomb or bullet would strike. The resilience and humour of the people was wonderful to experience. And I was always staggered by bereaved families wanting to go on camera and pay tribute to victims of the Troubles. They were wiped out emotionally but still came, red-eyed, to the door to talk about the loss of their loved one. It was hard to stay neutral in those moments.

But we had to stay neutral. Whatever sympathies we might have harboured for one side or the other had to be kept hidden. I remember once in a report talking about an incident 'in the Ardoyne'. I got hate mail sent to UTV because of my lack of local knowledge: it should have been 'in the Ardoyne area of Belfast'. After that, I bought a stack of books and immersed myself in the history of the conflict, as well as talking to as many learned locals as I could. Again the ITN crews imparted their knowledge and, after a couple of tours, I considered I had the feel of the place and was getting the politics right.

In those days, ITN had a cubbyhole office in the UTV building – Havelock House on the Ormeau Road. We worked hand in hand with the UTV teams – they had local knowledge, we turned out at all hours of the day and night. We shared pictures, information and drinks – we were all on button three on the television. The ITN office was famous for having a large hole in the wall – it was circled with a scrawl saying 'Terry Lloyd was here'. Terry was one of ITN's top reporters as well as being one of the nicest men I've ever met. His grandfather, Michael, was a policeman in Dublin who was shot dead in the 1920s. From his Ireland reporting, Terry progressed to covering world hotspots. Sadly he was killed in the invasion of Iraq in 2003.

To return to the hole: Terry, like any television reporter, was very proud of his work and it is always hugely disheartening when your report is dropped from the bulletin. The legend goes that Terry and his crew had worked their rocks off to produce a cracking report and it was dropped from *News at Ten*. Terry, having had a drink, took out his frustration on the UTV wall and punched a hole in it. I guess he didn't feel much pain – the wall was a stud and his hand was probably anaesthetised!

At this point, I'd like to pay tribute to Terry and his work in Northern Ireland. He had worked his way up to correspondent level with ITN from a news agency in the Midlands and along the way had acquired the knack of being able to talk to anyone. He was clubbable, humorous and totally professional. We all still miss him.

Like most of us covering Northern Ireland, Terry enjoyed the downtime. We often stayed at the Europa but usually preferred the Wellington Park because of its bacchanalian Friday nights. We ate well in restaurants like La Belle Epoque. I remember one particular night when the ITN crew was at a table (I can't remember the venue for reasons that will become obvious) and a group of Irish lads were at the next one. All of us were taking a drink. The Irish contingent started singing, so we had to match them and it turned into a competition. It ended when one of our crew (I'll spare his blushes by not naming him) disappeared and returned with a washing-up bowl in his hands, singing a hit song. As we all joined in and sang lustily, he used the bowl to drum the rhythm of the song on our heads in turn. It was great fun until I turned round at the wrong moment and received the bowl smack on the nose. Serviettes filled with ice were hastily assembled as my poor nose poured blood. But we didn't stop drinking!

The corollary to this was that the next morning I had a huge mark on the top of my nose. We got sent to a controversial shooting in Aughnacloy and I told our fixer to do the report and the piece to camera as I looked so bad. All well and good until I received a massive bollocking from my boss for not appearing in the piece.

Another memory from that time is my long Driza-Bone raincoat. I'd been lucky enough to holiday in Australia in 1989 and bought this long black coat. It was very stylish and, buttoned up, it covered me from neck to toe – very useful for those foul, wet days on the road in Northern Ireland – and it was coveted by Gerry Adams. We were covering a march in Derry in the most appalling weather and walking backwards to get the shot. A drenched Adams was at the front with Martin McGuinness, and he asked me if he could borrow my coat. In the tradition of staying neutral I politely refused. On another occasion, in equally inclement weather, we were covering an IRA funeral in Milltown Cemetery. As was our practice, we stayed a discreet distance away from the grave and stood at the exit. So there was I in my long, black coat. As the mourners passed us, many said, 'Thank you, Father.' The crew and I lived on that tale for a week.

There are many memories from my time in Northern Ireland. I've chosen not to dwell on the big news events – and there were many – but instead to give a snapshot of life on the road. It was fun, tiring, emotional and often immensely sad. And we should never forget that more than 3,500 people lost their lives in those terrible times.

There is one cameo I will always remember. There was a crew changeover and we were all in the Europa when the fresh lighting man arrived with three massive suitcases. We all expressed our shock that he'd brought so much stuff. He confessed that two of the suitcases contained his curtains from home and he was going to put them through the hotel's dry-cleaning service – on expenses of course!

Simon Cole was an ITN reporter in the 1980s, later becoming an executive at Sky News.

All around was chaos
Killeen, County Armagh, 1987

Rod Nawn

As the weak spring sunshine threatened to break through in Newtownards, the prospect of a pleasant journey with long-time friends for a busy weekend in Dublin was a welcome if familiar break to routine for Ireland rugby union international Nigel Carr. It was just before 7.30 a.m. on the last Saturday in April 1987 that he prepared for the short trip from home to Belfast's Stranmillis area to rendezvous with teammates David Irwin and Philip 'Chipper' Rainey.

At that time there was a new layer of excitement for these elite sportsmen. The inaugural Rugby World Cup would take place in Australia and New Zealand in May and June, and the training sessions that Saturday and Sunday were critical in the final preparations for the tournament, the still-amateur sport's first global venture. Ten Ulster players had earned their seats on the plane to Wellington for Ireland's opening match against Wales, and this weekend, coach Mick 'Doyler' Doyle – who combined life as a veterinary surgeon with his rugby duties – would put the finishing touches to the squad's preparations.

The previous night, Carr had packed his overnight bag and training kit, had checked and double-checked everything. On Saturday, he dressed quickly, slipped on a pair of trainers for the 120-odd mile journey to the Dublin training camp and bade farewell to June, his wife of just a few months.

'There is something of a *Sliding Doors* thing in our collective memory of that morning,' he told me. 'I have a distinct impression still of how, on the way into the city, all the traffic lights were on green. I had an uneventful, swift trip to meet Davy and Philip. But Davy still insists we didn't get on our way to Dublin on time; that I arrived later than planned because I'd been confronted with red lights at every junction! Just banter. But on time, early or late, our day might have unfolded differently.'

Carr's kitbag was added to the pile already in Irwin's car boot and, just after 8 a.m., the trio was on its way, briefly along the M1 motorway, then on a route that would include Newry, Dundalk, and Drogheda before arriving with Doyler. The three young men – who were all born within a year of each other and who had been fellow students and players at Queen's University –

gossiped and laughed about the sort of inconsequential matters that litter everyday conversations.

Irwin turned on the radio. Madonna's number one, 'La Isla Bonita', offered a familiar soundtrack; Carr's eclectic musical tastes were sated by Labi Siffre, Mel & Kim, Fine Young Cannibals and Starship. 'It was a fun trip – rugby, girls and music were the usual topics of conversation,' said Carr.

Rainey, yet to play for Ireland despite his form as Ulster's full back, was making himself as comfortable as possible in the back seat. He could entertain the hope that he could at last win that first cap if Hugo MacNeill's grip on the green jersey loosened. McNeill had visited Rainey's Ballymena club the previous evening and was cadging a lift to Dublin with another Ulster teammate and Ireland fixture, Trevor Ringland, and team manager, Syd Millar. They were on the same journey, maybe in front, possibly behind.

Northern Ireland was still a very unpredictable place in 1987: the political situation disheartening; the continuing, lethal madness of violence an everyday companion. The distress and suffering, the crisis in government, were never far from the thoughts of serious, intelligent people. Carr was established as a forensic scientist and had more than a passing professional acquaintance with the consequences of violence, while, as a doctor, Irwin dealt daily with frailties and the darker shades of life. Rainey had graduated in engineering and was embarking on a career in business.

This weekend their mission was built on optimism – literally playing their part in sport, an important passion and distraction for so many. As a player, Irwin had an enviable record, making his international debut in 1980 as a twenty-one-year-old three-quarter. Two years on, he was a Test-playing British and Irish Lion in New Zealand. Carr had long been hailed as the brightest wing forward talent in the northern hemisphere. He was capped first at twenty-five, promptly becoming part of Ireland's 1985 Five Nations and Triple Crown-winning side. 'I'd felt for a while that if I got my chance, I would take it,' he says. Soon he'd be voted on to a World XV for his rugby intelligence and all-round excellence. Within a year he'd be a fully-fledged British and Irish Lion, playing in Cardiff against the Rest of the World XV in a one-off Test at home.

The traffic grew worse as Irwin drove past Newry towards the border with the Republic. Everyone in the car knew the routine well – usually the most striking indications that one jurisdiction had ended and another had begun were the gawdy neon advertisements offering the chance to change sterling currency into punts. There would be occasional, random checks of vehicles by the RUC and army, but there was little noticeable security presence that morning, no physical border.

For about a mile between Northern Ireland and the Republic, cars and lorries travelled unimpeded by officialdom; two countries merging easily, one into the other on that short, unpatrolled strip of road at Killeen. It was a crossing used weekly by tens of thousands, but in Ireland's turbulent modern history it had, on a few dreadful occasions, been an area vulnerable to well-prepared IRA attacks.

From a distance, Irwin noticed an aged Ford Cortina apparently abandoned at the side of the Belfast-bound lane. Just as he began to think about why it was there, there was a sudden flash of fierce light and a resounding crash. Irwin's passengers have few memories of the moment in time that would leave an enduring, nightmarish imprint on their lives.

Dazed but amazingly alert, Irwin knew it had been a bomb. He looked across to Carr on his left, clearly more than just stunned, his face twisted in pain, then checked on Rainey. He lay motionless. Irwin feared the worst. Irwin somehow extricated himself from the tangled metal that had moments ago been his car. He dragged Rainey away from the vehicle, the acrid smell of 500lb of explosive mixing horribly with the stench of petrol fumes and smoke. Carr remembers the noise of the car bomb vaguely and that the main impact on David's car seemed to be on the passenger side. 'My feet were trapped – it could have been so different. Davy was brilliant. He struggled to free my legs; pulled and twisted my uncooperative body to release it,' Carr says. 'He had to rip my feet out of my trainers before hauling me away.'

Irwin was at first astounded, shocked and angry. There was no rush to the scene of carnage by the security and emergency services that were just hundreds of yards apart on that border. The real threat of a further ambush dictated caution. 'It was surreal: cars, lorries, vans passed at speed,' he recalls. 'We needed help: my pals were severely injured. I could see two crumpled shadows in a car on the opposite side of the road. They couldn't have survived.'

All around was chaos. Only gradually did assistance arrive. The couple in the tangled wreckage was now the focus of frenzied attention from stunned gardaí and RUC officers. An ambulance arrived eventually. Carr was carried on board and, as it swept away towards hospital, he recalls that there were rushed, quiet whispers about 'deaths'. He thought instantly of Chipper.

Rainey, too, was taken to hospital as the rescue operation gathered pace, while Irwin remained at the scene, offering help where he could. He looked again across the road, debris everywhere: his instinct was sadly right, no one in the car on the opposite side of the road had survived. The occupants, Lord Justice Maurice Gibson and his wife Lady Cecily, had died instantly. The couple had returned by ferry from a holiday in England just that morning and had been escorted from Dublin port to the Louth–Armagh border by two gardaí officers. Just half a mile away, an RUC team was waiting to accompany them home to Belfast. It was one of the IRA's deadliest and most high-profile assassinations. The outrage was palpable as the news spread. The rugby trio had been travelling south and were directly alongside the Gibsons' northbound Ford Escort when the abandoned Cortina released its lethal payload.

Amazingly, Rainey recovered and, with Irwin, he was well enough to travel to New Zealand in mid-May. Carr had fractured ribs, abdominal bleeding and chipped bones in his leg and arm, while soft tissue damage exacerbated a recurring knee problem that had blighted his sporting career in previous years.

'I was in hospital for a week or so, and I remember some of my first visitors were colleagues from the Forensic Science Service who would been involved in examining the scene at Killeen. I still targeted going to the World Cup, but I soon faced the reality of my injuries. The squad invited me to the pre-tour dinner, but I already felt like an imposter. What could I contribute from the other side of the world?' Carr recalls without bitterness. 'I was determined to get back to the game. I trained hard that summer and autumn and, within a year, I played for Ulster again and somehow managed to get recalled to the Ireland set-up too.

'I was determined that the injuries, and that bomb, would not define me, but I could never reach the standards I'd always set myself. My top-flight career was effectively ended that Saturday morning, 25 April 1987. I have no axe to grind. Perhaps I might have made a Lions tour, won more Irish caps, but what I did for my club, Ulster and Ireland was special.

'David, Philip and I have still never really discussed that morning's events together. We know what we know, and the dreadful price the Gibson family paid. We have a close friendship that was shaped by more positive days. I do know that for all he did for me at Killeen I've never properly thanked Davy, who was absolutely brilliant in the aftermath. But I think he knows.'

Rod Nawn is a former weekly newspaper group editor and a news and sports producer for Ulster Television and BBC Northern Ireland. He is now a freelance broadcast producer and writer.

Seared into my mind forever
Enniskillen, 1987

Jim Flanagan

A telephone call to my home in Glengormley on the morning of Sunday, 8 November 1987 set in motion a chain of events that would remain seared into my mind forever. The man on the telephone was esteemed *Belfast Telegraph* news editor Norman Jenkinson and, on this occasion, he had no time for small talk. A bomb had gone off near the cenotaph prior to the Remembrance Day service in Enniskillen. There were many casualties – men, women and children – and I was to get there as soon as possible.

At that precise moment, little did I know I was about to witness the aftermath of one of the most heinous IRA atrocities of the Northern Ireland Troubles – a crime against humanity that sends shivers down my spine to this day.

In the preceding years, as a senior reporter on the *Telegraph*, I had covered many tragedies. Some people have a misconception that because journalists were dealing with death and destruction on a daily basis, we were somehow immune to the sorrow and devastation around us. I can only speak for myself but can say that, for me, nothing was further from the truth. As a young boy and teenager growing up in North Belfast in the 1960s and 1970s, I had personal experience of the mayhem spiralling out of control across the city – and I detested all of it. Lives destroyed, families heartbroken and cherished childhood friendships torn apart. Trying to make sense of it all was one of the main reasons I embarked on my chosen career.

It was with a feeling of trepidation that I arrived in Enniskillen that Remembrance Sunday, not knowing quite what to expect. By the time I had driven to the town the rescue operation was well underway. Many people had been killed and seriously injured, and security forces and civilians were using their bare hands to sift through rubble in the frantic search for survivors. Just minutes before the main Remembrance parade had been due to start, the 40lb bomb had exploded, causing a wall to collapse and trapping most of the dead in the debris.

As news of the massacre spread, families arrived on the scene, desperately seeking information about their loved ones. Among the people who were there, there was a determination to help the victims, mixed with feelings of shock, anger and injustice at what had happened. I headed to the Erne Hospital, to where many of the most seriously injured had been taken. Doctors and nurses, many of whom knew the victims personally, fought valiantly to treat the growing number of casualties. Local Ulster Unionist MP Ken Maginnis stood with relatives at the main entrance, doing his level best to keep them informed about a very fluid, ever-changing and distressing situation.

At one stage I saw a helicopter land on the hospital lawn, and a severely injured man was wheeled out on a stretcher and airlifted to hospital in Belfast. I subsequently found out he was well-known Enniskillen High School headmaster, Ronnie Hill, who was to spend the remaining thirteen years of his life in a coma, being cared for by his devoted wife, Noreen, and his family.

As the day wore on, the full scale of the carnage was becoming apparent and by teatime, when Secretary of State Tom King arrived in the town, the names of those murdered as they gathered in their Sunday best for the solemn Remembrance service had become known. The eleven people killed included three married couples, a retired policeman and a student nurse, Marie Wilson, who died some hours after the bombing. Her father Gordon, who was also injured in the blast, created worldwide headlines when, within hours of the massacre, he gave an interview saying he bore the bombers 'no ill will'.

Within forty-eight hours of the bombing, the funerals got underway and the town of Enniskillen came to a standstill as the nation mourned. Many of those in attendance had been caught up in the bomb and still bore the scars of the attack. Some, clearly distressed, were in wheelchairs but were determined to pay their respects.

Such was the scale of the atrocity that, although I was there to do my job, at times I felt like a bit of a nuisance, intruding on private grief, and I made sure I did not stray anywhere I was not wanted. Over the next two weeks I spent a lot of time in the town and, despite their deep personal grief, I was treated with the utmost respect by heartbroken relatives of the victims. Such is human nature that some wished to express their views while others preferred to keep their thoughts to themselves.

Ten days after the bombing, the Prince and Princess of Wales paid a morale-boosting visit to the injured in the Erne Hospital. Prince Charles, of course, had personal experience of the grief caused by the Troubles as his beloved mentor, Lord Mountbatten, had been murdered by the IRA near Sligo in 1979, one of the first stories I had ever worked on as a young reporter. He was extremely moved by the testimony he heard at the hospital, as was Princess Diana, who, in a moment of poignancy, cradled a baby who was born a few hours after the explosion in her arms.

I had somehow hoped that the gravity of the Enniskillen bomb would highlight the futility of violence and mark a turning point in our troubled history. Looking back I see how gullible I was to think things would change. I was a twenty-seven-year-old reporter relatively recently married with a one-year-old son and it was the only time I seriously considered upping sticks and getting out of Northern Ireland. I'm not ashamed to say that leaving crossed my mind but it was just a passing thought in the midst of a very dark period in our history.

There were to be more dark days, of course, but now things appear to be moving in the right direction. While people still have their differing views, they appear to be willing to pursue political objectives through peaceful means. A twenty-first century breakthrough, you might say!

I would like to end on a positive note. I have undertaken my own personal journey and now live with a heart implant, thanks to the skills of doctors at the Freeman Hospital in Newcastle-Upon-Tyne – a second chance that was so cruelly denied to so many of my fellow citizens in our beautiful country. I'm a grandfather now and I can only see better days ahead for my children and grandchildren. We owe it to their generation to never repeat the mistakes of the past.

Jim Flanagan was deputy editor of the *Belfast Telegraph* and editor of the *Sunday Life* and the *Ballymena Guardian*.

How Gordon Wilson moved me, and the country, to tears
Enniskillen, 1987

Mike Gaston

'I know that voice! You're Mike Gaston.' Welcome words in the immediate aftermath of one of the biggest tragedies of the Troubles. I turned round and was met by a diffident smile and warm handshake from Mick Breslin, editor of the *Fermanagh Herald*. The setting was the entrance area of the Erne Hospital, which was awash with fearful relatives hoping for news of a loved one and anxious journalists desperately seeking story lines.

Mick's was the first helping hand I got in the awful, awe-inspiring week that followed the Enniskillen Remembrance Day bomb. It was to be by no means the last. Indeed one of most powerful memories I've carried through the half-lifetime since then is of the almost endless compassion of the folk of Fermanagh.

Mick was quick to make the offer I most needed to hear at the time: 'How can I help you?' Although we'd never met before that moment, he'd realised that I was more than a little lost, and struggling to make sense of the senseless. We compared notes on what we'd heard so far, the distillation of unconfirmed reports and strong suspicions. He suggested a few names of people I might talk to.

Just as I thanked him and made to leave, he said, 'Here's someone I should introduce you to. His father and sister were both caught in the bomb. They're being treated here in the hospital now. He might give you an interview.'

With that, he introduced me to a visibly pale and shaken young man called Peter, who was waiting to hear about his sister. She was in intensive care. Peter declined my invitation for an interview at that stage. Instead he gave me his telephone number and a promise that his father would talk to me that night. I was to hear, just a little later, the sad news that his sister had died.

And the toll continued to rise. When I'd arrived in Enniskillen less than two hours after the explosion, six people were known to have died. The final death tally was to be twice that number. Sixty-three were injured, thirteen of them children, and the lives of many more would never be the same.

There were all too many heartbreaking stories to follow. The first, for me, was hearing young minister the Reverend David Cupples tell his packed church that they'd lost six of their older members. David had only begun to lead the congregation at Enniskillen Presbyterian Church two months earlier. It was his first post as minister in charge. His voice cracked with barely suppressed tears as he said, 'We have lost Billy and Nessie Mullan, Kit and Jessie Johnston, Ted Armstrong and Johnny Megaw ...' After a long pause, in which he bravely recovered his equilibrium, he went on to thank those folk for the love with which they had welcomed him into their church, the wisdom they had shared with him, and the fellowship that he and the rest of the congregation would miss from here on.

After the service, I went back to the BBC studio in Enniskillen, which overlooks a bend in the River Erne. I rang Peter Wilson as agreed and he invited me to the family home. He said the house would be hard enough to find. Luckily, I was offered a lift by BBC colleague Charlie Warmington. He'd attended the same church as the Wilson family for almost twenty years.

We were met at the door and ushered into the crowded sitting room like welcome visitors rather than prying reporters. In an armchair by the fire sat Gordon Wilson, face flushed, arm in a sling, listening attentively as a neighbour talked to him.

The conversation amongst the mourners present was hushed, awed, warm and supportive. Some spoke of the special bond between Gordon and his youngest daughter, Marie – 'she was his wee pet, you know' – not realising for the moment that Peter and Julie-Anne, Marie's siblings, were sharing their own grief in the same room. Others spoke of the preparations Marie had been making for her upcoming twenty-first birthday party. She'd just come home that weekend from her student nurse post at the Royal Victoria Hospital in Belfast.

There was a knock on the door. It was the undertaker. Gordon had to make funeral arrangements. Tea was offered. Gordon came back. I asked if we could talk. The room cleared as if by the wave of a wand. While I'd been clinging to my tea, I'd realised how close to the surface my own emotions were. One of my daughters was seriously ill and my mum had terminal cancer. I was wending my own way towards that valley.

As Gordon sat back down beside me, I softly shared my condolences then asked him to say in his own words what had happened that morning. What took place next was beyond breathtaking. In his soft, lyrical, Leitrim accent, Gordon wove a spell that went on to capture the hearts of half of the English-speaking world. He told of his love for his youngest daughter, Marie; the joy of finding her hand under the rubble that crushed them both. About his terror when she stopped answering his questions. Of his heartbreak when she said for the last time, 'Daddy, I love you very much.' He spoke of his pride in her profession. Of the love in her being. About the conviction that they would meet again and his determination to bear no ill will against the bombers. 'Dirty sort of talk won't bring her back,' he said.

I sat mesmerised by his words. Absolutely no urge to interrupt or to imprint an ego-driven question on to what I knew then was a once-in-a-lifetime interview.

Aware of how much those emotionally charged few minutes had cost Gordon, I thanked him profusely. He in turn shook my hand as I left the room. Charlie was waiting for me and, wracked by barely suppressed sobs, I made it to his car.

My lifelong friend Wilson Harte was the intake producer for the next day's *Good Morning Ulster*. After I played the interview down the line to the studio in Belfast, he rang back completely stunned. He said that in all his years of covering the worst atrocities of the Troubles he'd never heard anything like Gordon's words. He'd also never seen a room full of seasoned broadcasters with tears in their eyes and on their cheeks.

The interview went right round the world that night. I later heard that it reduced the Queen and the prime minister to tears when they heard it on the *Today* programme. Historian Jonathan Bardon said, 'No words in more than twenty-five years of violence in Northern Ireland have had such a powerful, emotional impact.' International peacebuilder William Ury, in his book *The Third Side*, said, 'One person's act of forgiveness can sometimes move an entire nation,' and quoted the Gordon Wilson interview as the example. It's widely believed that the bombing was a turning point in the Troubles. It undermined support for the IRA and Sinn Féin. Gordon Wilson's words are also believed to have dramatically reduced loyalist tit-for-tat retaliation.

A levelling quote came from BBC Northern Ireland news editor, John Conway. He said that what made the interview work was giving Gordon the space to speak without interruption. Put more bluntly, I'd managed to keep my mouth shut and let Gordon's words speak to us all.

Thereby hangs another part of the tale. Gordon Wilson reached many people with his words of love and forgiveness. We heard what we wanted to hear and kept on asking for more. A few days later, I met some of his friends in the town. I asked them how he was. 'Exhausted,' they replied. I suggested they tell him to take time out. For himself and his family. To say to him that he didn't have to agree to every request to speak. He'd already done far more than he needed to.

I stayed in touch with Gordon, Joan and Peter. I was privileged to be invited to an award ceremony by the Methodist church worldwide that honoured Gordon's contribution to peacebuilding. I was also present at three family funerals. The first was when they laid Marie to rest in November 1987. In December 1994, I attended the funeral of her brother, Peter, who died in a tragic car accident. Gordon died the following summer, and I went to his funeral also.

Many years later Joan Wilson, who had endured so much pain from family tragedy, summed it up in a newspaper interview. 'Some people say that time heals, but it doesn't. It only teaches you how to cope better.'

Mike Gaston was a reporter with BBC Radio Ulster and Associated Press Radio in the 1980s. He was nominated as Sony Reporter of the Year following the Enniskillen Bombing.

The army killing of GAA player Aidan McAnespie
Aughnacloy, County Tyrone, 1988

Declan Bogue

21 February 2021 – we're sitting at our desk on a crisp winter morning. The air outside might sting your lungs. There's a stillness in everything all around.

Thirty-three years ago to this day, conditions were identical as Aidan McAnespie made his way past the Aughnacloy border checkpoint on the Monaghan Road to continue to the Aghaloo O'Neills football pitch. His day stretched out with possibility, but first there was a spicy local derby against Killeeshil to fill the morning.

And then a bullet from the border checkpoint a hundred yards behind him cut him down.

For years leading up to this moment he had been the victim of constant harassment by soldiers who would hold him for hours at a time at the checkpoint. Because he worked in a poultry plant and checked on cattle across the border, this became a regular experience for Aidan, so much so that his family knew that when he didn't return home, he was being detained again. One relative later reported a solider as having said that they had a bullet there with Aidan's name on it.

On this Sunday morning, a bullet fired from a machine gun went into his back and, as he lay on the ground, cars swerved past to make their way on through the checkpoint, oblivious to the carnage, deaf to the whistle of the bullet.

An eighteen-year-old soldier had fired it. Into a twenty-three-year-old lad.

In an RTÉ radio documentary aired in 2018, neighbours recounted how there were cheers coming from the barracks at the time of the shooting. And how the road was later closed and gunshots went off, the implication being that some fresh ricochets were being gouged into the tar. The bullet that killed Aidan was one of three discharged.

Charges were brought against Grenadier Guard David Jonathan Holden for manslaughter but were later dropped. An RUC investigation concluded that the killing was accidental. One of the claims was that Holden's hands were wet and the gun slipped. That version of events was later weighed against the fact that it takes nine pounds of pressure to pull the trigger on such apparatus.

A 2008 Historical Enquiries Team found that the soldier's explanation was the 'least likely version' of what had happened, adding the chances of this happening were 'so remote as to be virtually disregarded'. In June 2018, the North's Public Prosecution Service announced they would be charging Holden with gross negligence and manslaughter.

Nowadays, a squat monument sits where McAnespie fell.

The club had seen it all before. In November 1973, one of the key club officers, Francie McCaughey, was entering his milking parlour when a bomb went off. He died eleven days later. The Ulster Freedom Fighters claimed responsibility. Three suspects were arrested. One said the motive might have been because McCaughey had recently purchased land behind the local RUC station for use by Aghaloo O'Neills. He claimed the land was 'in a loyalist area'.

Eighteen months later, McCaughey's brother-in-law Owen Boyle was at home in his kitchen when he was shot through the window. He died within a fortnight. The Protestant Action Force claimed responsibility.

Both murders are understood to have been the grisly work of the Glenanne Gang, an informal group of loyalists that included soldiers from the Ulster Defence Regiment, police officers from the Royal Ulster Constabulary and members of the mid-Ulster brigade of the Ulster Volunteer Force.

Aghaloo O'Neill's had only been established for eighteen years and had three members murdered.

At this remove, decades on from the establishment of the Belfast Agreement, such killings seem of another world. But then so much of that period is thankfully alien. Any revisiting of that time snaps you like an unexpected blow.

In *Lost Lives*, the book that details all the deaths relating to the Troubles, thirty-six victims who were part of the GAA are listed. There is no argument that they were all were murdered because of their involvement with the GAA. But a good number of them certainly were.

Why did that happen? There are no definitive reasons. There is only context. And context is subject to the prejudices of anyone.

In the North, the GAA is a symbol of nationalism. The Irish tricolour flies at games. 'Amhrán na bhFiann' is played before significant games. Such trappings are embedded. While the membership is a much broader church and includes plenty from all faiths and none, with various political beliefs, those associations were enough for those intent on slaughter.

Political leadership was then as it is now: unyielding and unapologetic. Sammy Wilson of the DUP once made mention of the GAA being 'the IRA at play' – a comment that was grossly offensive, spectacularly ignorant and that wilfully endangered the lives of the membership.

In pragmatic terms, for those intent on doing damage, GAA members were 'handy marks'. What could have been easier for paramilitaries than targeting a man who was alone, locking up the gates of a clubhouse on a dark night in a rural part of Ulster? This happened to Bellaghy chairman Sean Brown, who was abducted and then shot dead in May 1997. The same gun was used seven months later to kill senior team manager Gerry Devlin at the gates of St Enda's GAA club in Glengormley.

Media reporting of incidents of vandalism and arson committed upon GAA premises frequently missed the point. A dreadful phrase – tit for tat – was used to excuse the likes of a deliberate fire that destroyed St Joseph's Ballycran on the Ards Peninsula in May 1993. Recent attacks on Orange Lodges would be included in the reports as if to provide justification. Throughout the Troubles, the perception of the GAA and its commitment to a united Ireland caused discomfort and fear to loyalists.

Under a heading of 'Basic Aim' in 'Chapter 1 – Aims and Ethos' of the official GAA guide, point 1.2 notes: 'The Association is a National organisation which has as its basic aim the strengthening of the National Identity in a 32 County Ireland through the preservation and promotion of Gaelic Games and pastimes.' For loyalist paramilitaries, that aspiration was reason enough for their savagery. That the vast majority of the players, coaches and volunteers who make up the GAA populace are blithely unaware of those words counted for nothing.

More visible pointers are left out there to dangle in the wind. When the GAA was being established in each county, the 'Association swept the country like a prairie fire', as the first secretary, Michael Cusack, put it.

There were huge levels of autonomy in each county and yet, the make-up of county boards and clubs became a power struggle between clergy and republican forces. The subject is given the space and time it deserves in historian Paul Rouse's magnificent account of the first All-Ireland hurling final, *The Hurlers*.

The clubs throughout Ireland are named after a mixture of saints, republican figures, local chieftains and ruling clans.

The GAA made it clear through president Pat Fanning what it felt about internment at two rallies held in Casement Park in the early 1970s. Those interned in prisons such as Long Kesh immediately set about playing Gaelic football tournaments with the blessing of prison authorities.

One of the greatest curiosities about the GAA, and certainly one that outsiders would be confounded by, is its unofficial caste system that discriminates against those from Ulster. The extent to which teams suffer prejudice is disputed, but it is a deeply held conviction in pockets of Ulster. Despite the airy pronouncements about Irish unity, northern GAA officials have grown accustomed to encountering discrimination, while northern teams have been verbally abused by their southern counterparts on the field of play.

In his autobiography, *The Outsider*, Fermanagh native Peter Quinn details his time in the early 1990s as GAA president. It brought spectacular advancement as he began the transformation of the Croke Park stadium and a general modernisation of the sporting body. However, he was fighting a rearguard action against what he felt was a hostile media who wished to paint him into a corner for his nationalism.

When it came to writing his account of those years, he spelled out how delicate that period was: 'One did not have to be involved in any form of political activity, never mind paramilitary activity, to be a target. Most of our members who were murdered in those years had no involvement in any kind of illegal activity; just being a member of the GAA was enough to have them killed,' he wrote. 'That is not to condone what was happening on the other side – it could not be condoned either, in any society. Murder is murder and must be condemned, whoever commits it or whatever the motivation. But the GAA was not murdering people. Nevertheless, its members were being murdered, simply for being members.'

Perhaps it is aspirational to feel that the passing of time will unravel all of these stories and the attitudes bound up within and allow some context in a post-conflict world. For now, it's still a matter of picking our way through the stepping stones, with the water coming up around our ankles.

Declan Bogue is a freelance award-winning writer and author who has written extensively on sport, with a special interest in historical events.

Twists and turns, patterns and connections
Belfast, 1988

Gavin Esler

Celtic art involves the endless repetition of patterns, interconnected spirals and knots. When I think of Northern Ireland during the Troubles, I have a similar sense of twists and turns, patterns and connections. The story which follows is true, but I am still unpicking the knots. It is about the first and only time I was hijacked, but it is also about much more.

It begins with a phone call I received at the BBC studios in Belfast from a caller who insisted that a 'senior commander' in a loyalist paramilitary group 'wanted a word with me'. I turned up to a dank, dusty hall in East Belfast and sat alone in a corner of a large room that smelled of stale sweat. After half an hour, the man who 'wanted a word' bounced across the shabby wooden floor, and it turned out he wanted many, many more words. He was a big man, heavily muscled, and he neither shook hands nor smiled. Instead of 'hello' he said one sentence: 'I am speaking to you as someone deeply involved in violence.' Then he sat down and we talked for two hours. This 'senior commander' clearly knew a lot about me – that I'm Scottish, from a Glasgow Protestant background, with family roots in County Antrim. He wanted to persuade me that, while the IRA were undoubtedly terrorists, he and his group were righteous because they were 'counter-terrorists'. He had read a lot of books on guerrilla warfare and argued that the police and British Army could never defeat the IRA, but his brand of 'counter-terrorism' could, by separating the IRA from its supporters in the Catholic community. These IRA supporters were not, he insisted, 'innocent civilians' but terrorist 'accomplices'. He was eloquent, passionate, and suggested I was utterly naive if I did not understand that his campaign to 'make IRA supporters pay' would eventually cut off the oxygen the IRA needed to exist. He was, of course, trying to justify sectarian assassinations and, as I discovered later, he was a charismatic recruiter of young loyalists to his cause. When he himself was murdered, his legacy was an organisation of ruthless killers whose violence outlived him. I witnessed it myself, first-hand, a few months after his death.

I had moved to London, working for the BBC's *Newsnight* programme, but

I returned often to Northern Ireland when the repetitive pattern of violence twisted into another series of knots. In March 1988, three unarmed IRA members were killed in Gibraltar by British Army special forces, the SAS. Their bodies were returned for burial in West Belfast's Milltown cemetery. I filmed the scene, a repeat of the pattern I had seen so many times before – a huge, disciplined and respectful crowd; IRA marshals; the assumption that perhaps the IRA would, in the choreography of death, fire shots over the coffins. I stood with one of the editors of this book, Deric Henderson, reflecting that we had stood side by side so many times before, at so many funerals before, wondering so many times before if the killings would ever end.

Then, suddenly, a loyalist gunman later identified as Michael Stone appeared, a man from East Belfast who would have known and undoubtedly have been influenced by the arguments from the 'senior commander' I had met. Stone ran into the funeral crowd, threw hand grenades and opened fire at mourners with a pistol. He killed three and wounded fifty others, making his escape by running downhill towards the M1 motorway, pursued by other mourners, and creating another series of twists in the spiral of violence. Catholic areas of West Belfast erupted. Cars and buses were hijacked and set alight. The cemetery was in chaos, but the wounded were eventually ferried to the Royal Victoria Hospital, not far away.

I had an existing arrangement to interview a priest who had worked for years trying to bring reconciliation to Northern Ireland, Father Alec Reid. He was based at the Clonard Monastery, also in West Belfast, and had maintained strong contacts within the IRA and the republican movement. Given the chaos, Father Reid was surprised to see us but recorded an interview, appealing for calm. My TV crew left while the producer and I had a cup of tea, said our goodbyes, and walked to our car. As we did, four men were watching us from the exit of the monastery car park.

'Provos,' I whispered to my producer, meaning Provisional IRA members. As we drove out, the men jumped across the exit and I had to stop the car. I rolled down the window to talk, but before I could speak, one of the men stretched inside and pulled the keys from the ignition. 'What the–'

'We're taking the car,' the man with the keys said calmly, 'in the name of the Irish Republican Army.'

'Don't be daft,' I responded (probably I swore). But I added, 'The IRA doesn't hijack reporters' cars.'

'This is not a reporter's car,' the leader of the group said. 'It's a hire car. You drive a dark blue Ford. This is a commercial vehicle, and we're taking it.'

A legalistic argument followed about definitions of 'commercial vehicle'.

I recall that the name of the Irish Republic first proclaimed in 1916 was invoked, and the Provisional IRA 'active service unit' (as they would have described themselves) finally opened the boot, took out my briefcase, handed it to me, and apologised for the inconvenience. They then drove away at speed, leaving the producer and me vacantly wondering what to do. But within a minute the hijacked car sped back just as rapidly as it had left, stopped in front of us, keys in the ignition, engine running, doors flying open. The four IRA men ran down the street of terraced houses opposite the monastery, in through unlocked front doors, through the houses into back gardens, over fences into other houses, until they were gone in seconds, just as a British Army foot patrol came running down the street giving chase, their rifles pointing in our direction. The Provos had almost run into an army roadblock.

'It's our hire car,' I yelled at the soldiers. 'Taken off us. Can we take it away?'

'No,' one of the soldiers yelled back. 'It's a crime scene. We need to leave it for the RUC.'

My father had often lectured me that there is no point in arguing with a man holding a gun, and after a loyalist assassin, an IRA squad and now an army patrol all within two hours, I could understand my father's wisdom. To skip the boring details, the hire car company got their car back; the producer and I filed our lead story for *Newsnight*; and the intricate Celtic artistry of violence in Northern Ireland took another twist a few days later when two British soldiers were murdered on the day of the funeral of one of those murdered by Michael Stone. In Northern Ireland, the past is never dead. It's not even past.

I went off to America for most of the next decade. I came back to Northern Ireland occasionally, including with Bill Clinton's envoy, Senator George Mitchell, and with Clinton himself. After the Good Friday Agreement I went back more often, speaking at book festivals, seeing friends, and drinking a few pints in the old haunts, now feeling safe. The shadow of the gun had mostly gone. And then more than twenty years after the events in Milltown cemetery, I was heading to a book festival event, picked up by a driver who said he recognised me from TV. His face seemed vaguely familiar. He told me he had been a republican 'political prisoner' at the Maze prison, and we chatted amicably about the Troubles and people we both knew. Then, as we stopped at traffic lights, he leaned over towards me and said, 'You know me, don't you?' 'I do,' I replied, without remembering who or how or why. He drove off.

I spoke at the festival about my latest book, and forgot all about the conversation, until I woke up very early one morning several months later. I was shaken by the revelation of something long buried. I did know that taxi driver. It was his hands that had grabbed the keys of my 'commercial vehicle'. It was his voice that had argued about the legality of hijacking me in the name of the Irish Republic of 1916. And it had all happened because the charismatic commander of a loyalist death squad had convinced young men that it was righteous to kill for God and Ulster.

Like the spirals and knots of a Celtic brooch, the Northern Ireland Troubles looped us all together over thirty years in our basic humanity, despite all the cruelty, terror and death. The 'terrible beauty' Yeats had seen in Easter 1916 contained deep within the knots and patterns a little twist of that most precious of all qualities: hope.

Gavin Esler is the author of five novels and four works of non-fiction, most recently *How Britain Ends*. He began his career as a writer and broadcaster with the *Belfast Telegraph* and BBC Northern Ireland.

For me, the story of the Troubles is told in silence
County Fermanagh, 1988

Fergal Keane

We kept our distance. The custom was to call the local clergy in advance: 'How does the family feel about cameras?' Sometimes they wanted us there to convey the grief and pain caused by murder. Other times the message was to stay away, or film from a distance. The republican paramilitaries saw funerals as events heavy with the symbolism of sacrifice, moments of political and media potential. The loyalist organisations were more likely to be hostile.

But Jillian Johnston's family were not political. They were country people, living in the lakelands of County Fermanagh, close to the border, in what I had always thought was one of the most beautiful parts of Ireland – a land of woods and water and well-tended fields where, in the words of W.B. Yeats, 'peace comes dropping slow'. It was a place in which to walk and fish or take a boat and laze away the afternoon.

Except that beneath the bucolic imagery other realities coiled. Here and across the borderlands men watched their neighbours and plotted murder. They might do the killing themselves or pass on details of movements – the comings and goings of a rural life – to gunmen from another county who would come to commit the act of killing. That line of Heaney's about 'each neighbourly murder' resonated ominously along the border.

In March 1988, Jillian Johnston was twenty-one years old and planning her wedding to Stanley Liggett, a local boy she had met at a dance in Kesh, a few miles from where she lived. On the night of 18 March, Jillian and Stanley had just pulled into the yard of her family home and were sitting eating chips in the car when IRA gunmen opened fire. Jillian was shot twenty-seven times. Stanley later told a journalist that the last thing he remembered before blacking out was hearing Jillian's mother say that Jillian was dead.

The couple met when they were teenagers and had been inseparable. They made plans to move to England, away from the shadow of the Troubles, once they married. Neighbours called her a girl who had a smile for everyone.

I reported on many murders in the four or so years I spent in Northern

Ireland, yet it is the imagery of Jillian Johnston's funeral that comes back most often when I think of those times. It struck me with an emotional force I have never been quite able to fully explain to myself.

I remember the bewilderment on the faces of family members, friends and neighbours. How could Jillian – the kind, loving, warm, always helpful Jillian – have been murdered? Jillian of all people. The IRA issued a statement saying she was shot by mistake. The target had been Jillian's brother who, they claimed, was a member of the Ulster Defence Regiment. This was a lie. The family had no connection to the security forces. Later the Sinn Féin leader, Gerry Adams, said her murder had been 'a mistake'.

How often we heard that word. Mistake. The wrong information. How it must have felt to hear such a word attached to the butchering of your child. The local community was left wondering who it was that pointed the killers in the direction of the Johnston yard.

The shooting came in the middle of the worst period of my own time in Northern Ireland. It had begun with the shooting of three unarmed IRA members by the SAS in Gibraltar on 6 March. Ten days later, the funeral of the three was attacked by a loyalist gunman, Michael Stone, resulting in three more deaths. Three days after that, at a funeral of one of Stone's victims, two army corporals were murdered by the IRA after driving into the procession by mistake. The atmosphere of that time was fevered. There was a sense that anything could happen. The fragile boundaries of what was permissible in the name of a cause had been shattered. The papers and the airwaves were dominated by the terrible images of Stone's apocalypse and the corporals lying stripped and broken on waste ground. What next, we wondered?

Away from the drama in Belfast, the murder of Jillian Johnston captured little media attention. A cherished child, a beloved fiancée, a girl who had been a source of goodness in her community was gone. But it mattered out here on the edge of the country. It would matter as long as one person who knew her was left alive.

The killing went on for another decade after Jillian's death. I was overseas when the Good Friday Agreement was signed in 1998, ten years and one month after her murder. I thought of her that day. I did not see her as one story I had covered among many, nor as a fellow islander murdered in the name of uniting Ireland, but as a good, decent human being lost to her family, her boyfriend, community and country.

Nobody was ever brought to justice for the murder of Jillian Johnston. It is likely nobody ever will be. In the years since I have often wondered about the gunmen. What did they see from their hiding places? In the rush of adrenaline and noise that accompanied the firing of their automatic rifles could they see the figures thrown about inside the car and, if so, did even one of them register a flicker of regret? Is there any haunting now as they edge towards old age and look back to that March night in the yard when Jillian Johnston's future was extinguished by their gunfire? Our island is still an island of secrets. The men who pulled the triggers will not speak. The past will be buried. The men who opened fire will rationalise. They will tell themselves that they were fighting a war and that in all wars there are innocent victims.

The churchyard was quiet on the day of Jillian's funeral. There was neighbourly solidarity. But these people of the lakeshore were not ones for public displays of emotion. Their grief was all the more shattering for its reticence.

For me the story of the Troubles is told in silence. Silence after silence. The silence of kitchens, sitting rooms, bedrooms where the bereaved stared into the distance thinking of the husband, father, son, brother, wife, sister, mother who would never come home. It is the only fact that never changes. The dead stay dead.

Fergal Keane is special correspondent with BBC News. He has covered conflict in many parts of the world.

The inquest on the Rock
Gibraltar, 1988

Paul Harris

The barman at the poolside terrace seemed a likeable sort of bloke. Not too chatty – but always keen to get updates from us on what was happening a few hundred yards down the road. There, at a coroner's court flanked by palm trees and armed guards, one of the most sensational stories of the fight against IRA activity abroad was unfolding day by day – the inquest into the SAS shooting of three IRA terrorists in Gibraltar. We think the barman arrived about a week after I had helped to set up the press room on the top floor of the Holiday Inn, in an area beside the pool, overlooking the town and the sea beyond. Perhaps we should have been glad that he did. He was quickly on the scene when some Belfast supporters of the dead found their way through hotel security and into the room. A *Sun* newspaper splash about the shooting of Mairéad Farrell, Danny McCann and Seán Savage, based on evidence from the inquest, carried the headline: 'Why the Dogs Had to Die'.

Angry and menacing, the intruders were looking for a *Sun* reporter – any *Sun* reporter – to throw off the roof. The barman quickly joined journalists to calm the men down, and escort them out of the hotel. He was there again when another crew came up to the terrace as reporters were preparing to leave after four weeks of covering the inquest.

'Lawful killing' had been the verdict. The Belfast boys disagreed. Chatting to the barman, they appeared to have guessed that he wasn't local.

'So you're from England?' one of them asked. 'Where are you living there?'

'Hereford,' the barman replied. And everything went a little quiet …

The inquest into the deaths was opened in September 1988, six months after the blood and bullets of the Troubles came to the Rock. Hundreds of thousands of words have been written about it since, and on the rights or wrongs of the SAS thwarting a suspected bombing mission by shooting all three dead in a fusillade of twenty-nine bullets.

The Press Association team's reporting of the hearing – filed by telex as running copy by me, Deric Henderson and Press Association (PA) crime reporter John Steele – was a crucial backbone to the coverage of the story in

UK newspapers. Likewise, the PA service was eagerly monitored in Whitehall, providing minute-by-minute information on how the highly controversial inquest was proceeding.

The court building had been specially adapted to accommodate strict security, and to ensure the anonymity of MI5 and SAS witnesses involved in 'Operation Flavius', the complex undercover plan that swung into action when intelligence suggested the IRA were planning an attack on the British military in Gibraltar. These witnesses gave evidence from behind a curtain on one side of the witness box, to render them visible only to the coroner, lawyers and jury. Alas, the proud court cleaners had buffed up the oak panelling on the other side of the witness box to such a brilliant sheen that it was possible to see the face of the first secret service witness reflected in the varnish. I included this detail in my first report of that day's evidence. The report was picked up immediately in London. When we came back after a break, the oak panelling had been covered up.

The press pack in Gibraltar included some of the best-known names in journalism, many of them long-time chroniclers of the conflict back home in Northern Ireland. Despite the seriousness of the subject, there were many light moments on the Rock, culminating – as tradition dictates – with an end-of-hearing party. Coincidentally, we found ourselves in the same restaurant that the leading barristers and solicitors involved in the case had chosen for their farewell dinner. After some good-natured banter we sang them the song we had composed about everything that had happened – a dozen or so irreverent verses, to the tune of 'My Old Man (Said Follow the Van)'.

Warming to his role in the performance, Ted Oliver, a veteran Northern Ireland reporter, clambered on to the barristers' table and pulled from his belt a replica 9mm Browning water-pistol. Then, singing the chorus, he pumped a volley of shots into the motionless, less-than-amused face of Treasury Counsel John Laws, the Oxford-educated barrister who represented the British government at the inquest.

I encountered Oliver and many others in the Gibraltar press pack during my twelve years with the PA, and twenty-six with the *Daily Mail*, when I was a frequent but merely transient visitor to the province. I am still indebted to the ones who helped a naive young reporter to navigate the political complexities and physical dangers in those early days.

Scenes I would subsequently witness, such as the 1987 Remembrance Day bombing at Enniskillen, always made me think that the Troubles, as they became known, was too pale a label for the reality. I would stay at hotels that any visiting reporter will instantly recall – principally the Europa in Belfast, proud holder of the most-bombed hotel in Europe accolade. Even in the early

1990s, some airline stewardesses told me they still claimed 'danger money' to stay overnight there (shortly before stepping nonchalantly into the city's burgeoning Golden Mile of pubs, bars and restaurants on the hotel's doorstep).

In Derry (that's Londonderry if you worked for the PA or the *Mail*) it was always the Everglades; elsewhere, a scattering of places recommended by the resident press corps whenever I headed out of town in a hurry. My annual holiday for several successive years was spent covering marches and mayhem at Drumcree. Not much sun, sand and sangria, but plenty of barbed wire, bile and petrol bombs. I often ended up having two bonfire nights: one at home with the kids; the other on 11 July, when the locals had a rather different interpretation of firework spectaculars.

Every time I returned to Belfast over a period of about fifteen or twenty years, the city seemed to have buildings missing here and there. A bomb would destroy them, the rubble would be cleared and flattened, and the authorities would turn it into a temporary car park. We used to joke that it was a sinister campaign by the Provisional NCP.

I became a familiar face (perhaps unwisely) on the trail of Johnny 'Mad Dog' Adair; was the target of regular verbal abuse and hectoring from the Reverend Dr Ian Paisley (who wasn't?); and had frequent encounters with Gerry Adams. Once, when introducing myself, I spontaneously stretched out a hand. He seized it tightly, turned towards Martin McGuinness, who was beside him, and declared, 'Get this! I'm shaking hands with the *Daily Mail*!'

But you didn't always have to travel to Northern Ireland to witness terrorism or its aftermath. It came to you. Sometimes, close to home. In 1983, an IRA bomb got within a few yards of killing one of my editors and his family as they were Christmas shopping at Harrods, in a blast that claimed six lives and left dozens injured or maimed.

Six years later, an RAF corporal and his six-month-old baby daughter were murdered while his wife was driving them near the British air base in Wildenrath, Germany. The baby died from a bullet to her skull. The family lived three streets away from my home in London. I still remember their tears as they told me how they had lost their beautiful little girl; then their anger at the IRA's cold expression of 'regret' in a statement issued afterwards.

Occasionally, however, the Troubles could allow inspiring stories to emanate from disaster, death and tragedy. I will never forget a surgeon at Belfast's Royal Victoria Hospital humbly explaining to me in intricate medical detail how he had saved a baby's life by operating 'in miniature' to rebuild her tiny body after it was shattered by IRA gunfire. Or the staunch courage of the campaigning McCartney sisters, who told me at their home in a Catholic enclave of East Belfast of the monstrous threats and intimidation they were enduring from IRA members after they broke a republican 'vow of silence' to expose the savage murder of their brother Robert, and the cynical, criminal cover-up that followed it.

The violent thread that ran through most of the stories emerging from Northern Ireland during that period was part of everyday life for those who covered the Troubles full time. A few months after I returned from Gibraltar, Deric Henderson stayed with me at my home in Harrow, north-west London, for some rest and relaxation. That day, some robbers raided a local post office. They had mounted a metal girder to a van and charged, rhinoceros-like, through a steel security door. The Flying Squad, undercover officers and teams of police marksmen were waiting for them. In the chase that ensued, one of the robbers was shot dead a few doors away from my house, another killed elsewhere, and a third wounded. More than thirty shots were fired at police, injuring one officer, in what a witness described as a Wild West gun battle.

Deric surveyed the scene with the calmness of someone who had spent half a lifetime reporting on murder, torture, bombings and unspeakable atrocities. 'Harrow,' he said. 'Very dangerous place.'

Paul Harris was chief reporter of the Press Association in the 1970s and 1980s and spent three decades at the *Daily Mail* before retiring as chief news feature writer in 2015.

Too close for comfort – standing by a 1000lb bomb
Derry, late 1980s

Vincent Kearney

'Don't move, don't move.' The words shouted by a British Army officer running towards us were barely audible due to the noise of the rotor blades of the helicopter in which he and a unit of soldiers had just arrived. I was with Willie Carson, a diminutive, charismatic and legendary freelance photographer from Derry, whose work appeared in newspapers, books and magazines across the world. We were standing beside what had been described as a large IRA bomb intended for a passing police or army vehicle. We had heard the helicopter arrive and circle overhead a couple of times before landing in a field a few hundred yards away. We had watched as soldiers disembarked and immediately started running towards us.

I asked Willie to take as many photos as possible before we were told to go back outside the police cordon where we belonged.

It all started with what at the time – the late 1980s – was a very routine call to say that a large IRA bomb had been found just outside Derry. I was later told the IRA had alerted a priest or politician – the device had failed to detonate as intended and they were concerned that civilians could trigger it. I was a cub reporter with the North West edition of the *Belfast Telegraph*, and Willie Carson was just the man you wanted to be with on a job like this. His local contacts and reputation ensured he could open doors that remained closed to most others.

When we arrived at the RUC cordon, it was on the downward slope of a hill, meaning we couldn't see what lay beyond. A police officer, who not surprisingly knew Willie, said a 'very large' bomb had been left behind the wall of a bungalow, probably fitted with a command wire. I asked if we could walk to the top of the hill to have a look at the scene, while Willie made the point that he needed to see the bomb to be able to photograph it.

Willie's pleas paid off and the officer lifted the white tape, telling us we could have a few minutes. Standing on the brow of the hill, we could see the bungalow a few hundred metres away, but we couldn't see the bomb, so decided to get closer.

When we arrived at the bungalow we could see two large plastic barrels, each up to slightly above my waist, that had been placed against the inside of the perimeter wall beside the road.

As Willie took photographs, I made a few notes about the scene, the appearance of the barrels and what looked to be a dark powdery substance. It was at this point that the helicopter arrived, and we could hear the officer leading the charge shouting.

Fearing the soldiers might just possibly think we were IRA members rather than curious members of the media, I slowly raised my hands into the air, notebook in one, pen in the other. Willie did the same, waving his camera.

The words being shouted were now much clearer, and more intense, as the army patrol ran at speed across the field that separated us: 'Don't fucking move. Don't fucking move.' We both stood perfectly still until the army unit stopped about a hundred metres away. 'What the fuck are you doing here?' asked the officer who had been shouting instructions at us. I explained that I was a reporter with the *Belfast Telegraph*, that Willie was a photographer, and that we were simply trying to do our jobs. I offered to show him ID. 'Why did you break the police cordon?' he replied, as the unit he led glared in our direction. Not wanting to drop the police officer in it, I said we had been there a while and had not seen a cordon. We were then told we could put our hands down, 'but stand still'.

'How did you get into the garden?' the officer then asked. 'Which way did you come?' Pointing to the brow of the hill where we had stood a short time before, I told him we had walked from there down through a field and then through the front gate.

'Did you touch anything?' he asked. I explained that we had walked around a little bit to take photographs and make notes but hadn't touched the barrels. His next words remain the most chilling I have ever heard in the course of my career: 'This bomb hasn't been defused yet.' Willie and I had looked at each other in shared shock.

'You got here before us. That's why there was a police cordon,' the officer said. 'Don't move. There could be pressure plates.'

At that point, two of the soldiers moved towards us, stopping a few metres from the gate. One of them dropped to his knees and began to move forward slowly on all fours, head down and looking closely at the ground in front of him. When he reached the gate he stood up and asked me to show him where we had walked, and I pointed out the parts of the garden we had been in. He then hunkered down and looked closely at the bases of the barrels that contained a large bomb we had just been told could still be live. The soldier then slowly went back out the gate and told us to follow in his footsteps.

'Right,' said the officer when we were back outside. 'You two, get out of here, now. Go back the way you came.' We didn't have to be told twice. While we had walked down from the hill, it was full speed ahead on the return journey. Given the differences in our height and stride I made it to the top well ahead of Willie, without once looking back to check his progress. Breathless when we reached the top, we briefly glanced back and agreed that we had just had a very lucky escape. Later, the police said a device containing around a thousand pounds of explosives had been defused.

To this day I don't know if there were pressure plates – perhaps the bomb had been planted to take out a police or army patrol but had a faulty firing mechanism, or the telephone warning was a trap to lure soldiers to the scene. I asked those questions, but they weren't answered.

I don't know if Willie Carson and I were actually in any real danger. I don't know if the army officer exaggerated the danger as a result of anger at our actions, and in an attempt to teach us a lesson. If it was the latter, it worked: one thing I do know about that afternoon is that what happened gave me a healthy respect for police cordons.

Vincent Kearney is northern editor for RTÉ news. He has also worked for *The Sunday Times* and *Belfast Telegraph*.

Kelly: the talk show that defied the Troubles
Belfast, 1989

Gerry Kelly

1989 wasn't the ideal year to launch a live television entertainment/chat show in Northern Ireland. P.J. O'Rourke, the celebrated American political satirist and journalist, had just published his book *Holidays in Hell: In which our intrepid reporter travels to the world's worst places ...* Belfast had a chapter all to itself. With write-ups like O'Rourke's, it's not surprising that Northern Ireland had become something of an entertainment wilderness. Very few international artists were including Belfast in their touring schedules and celebrities were giving the city a wide berth. There weren't many venues either – there was no Waterfront Hall, no SSE Arena and none of the fine centres that we have today in Derry, Lisburn, Enniskillen, Strabane, Newry and so on.

The challenge facing us was enormous. By definition, an entertainment/ chat show needs big showbiz names, music of all genres, local and topical stories of interest and competitions – a little light-hearted relief at the end of the week. But how could we ask personalities to come to Belfast when the city was regularly making headlines for all the wrong reasons and frequently being compared to Beirut, then engulfed by a ghastly civil war?

What we needed was a bold approach, a comprehensive charm offensive and a lot of good old-fashioned BS to attract the reluctant world of celebrity. One thing we had decided from the start was not to include any political or Troubles-related interviews. Local television was awash with political programmes at the time and so we felt the television audience, come Friday night, was ready for something less depressing – a ninety-minute escape from the daily agenda of bombs, bullets and mayhem.

It was an ambitious project for any local TV station, even without the added difficulty of combatting the world's perception of Northern Ireland. The first Kelly show aired on Friday, 15 September 1989 – the start of a steep upward learning curve – and continued for the next seventeen years and 570 shows. It was a tough first year behind the scenes for the team but gradually we began to make valuable contacts within the showbiz fraternity, both in the UK and in Ireland. Very quickly, we had amassed a large loyal television audience – a vindication of our belief that Northern Ireland was ready for a programme that showed a different side to life here.

But as much as we tried to avoid including debate about the Troubles, the realities of what was happening in Northern Ireland often impacted the programme. On Thursday, 5 December 1991, a huge 1,000lb car bomb exploded in Glengall Street in Belfast, causing millions of pounds worth of damage to the Europa Hotel and the Grand Opera House. The next night, I introduced the show live from the Europa Hotel, amidst all the resultant carnage, proving that the resilience of the people of Northern Ireland would never allow a paramilitary organisation to bomb Christmas out of Belfast.

During a commercial break, I returned to the studio to continue with the show. However, minutes later, a phone call was made to UTV claiming a bomb had been placed in the car park at the front of Havelock House. It was apparent that the group responsible for the car bomb had not been happy with how we had introduced the programme that night and decided to retaliate in the only way they knew. The police arrived and we were forced to close the live show down and evacuate the entire audience. No one could get to their cars and so the audience, the guests on the show and everyone who was working in UTV that night were ushered out a back door to a church hall on Donegall Pass, which had thankfully opened its doors for us.

By 2 a.m. the bomb was declared a hoax and we all were able to return.

Our guests that night – who included Bond girl Honor Blackman, Frank Windsor from Z Cars and Irish folk group The Fureys – were all remarkably unfazed. In fact, The Fureys treated us to an impromptu performance in the church hall, much to the delight of everyone there. As I drove home that night, I couldn't help but smile to myself. Yes, I was annoyed we'd had to close down the show but I knew we had rattled a few cages. I realised the Kelly show mattered.

Over the years, we had two other similar nights but things got a little more personal at the end of 1992, the year after the Europa bomb, when I received the first of three death threats. All of them utter nonsense of course, but a stark reminder of what life was like away from the rarefied bubble of making television programmes.

Bomb scares and death threats aside, there was one other event that both annoyed and infuriated me in equal measure. It would become apparent that – in Northern Ireland in the 1990s – even a chat show could not escape being categorised as either orange or green. John Taylor – now the Right Honourable the Lord Kilclooney and deputy leader of the Unionist Party from 1995–2001 – accused the Kelly show of having some kind of hidden agenda and implied that we used some form of religious or political bias when choosing our guests.

In an article in the *Belfast Telegraph*, he insinuated that we were running an increasingly nationalist agenda.

Our hard-working team of researchers spent their entire week chasing their tails, scouring newspapers and magazines, contacting agents and making numerous phone calls to get the best possible guests for the programme. To think it would matter to them, or to the programme, what religion or political views anyone had was utterly ludicrous. And yet Taylor's comments hurt at the time.

Years later, the mayor of Derry City Council presented me with the city's coat of arms. In one corner of the crest is a skeleton and when I asked what it signified, he jokingly replied, 'Oh, that's a Protestant waiting on a ticket for the Kelly show.' Humorous though his answer was, I still felt a pang of anger – not at him, obviously, but at the fact that a few thoughtless words written years previously still reverberated around the province.

As the years went on, the show began to build quite a strong brand reputation in the minds of international booking agencies, which meant that we were now automatically included in the promotional tours of their artists. Because the show aired late on a Friday night meant, of course, that anyone flying in could not return home that night. All our guests were put up in the Europa Hotel which, considering its dubious reputation as the most bombed hotel in the world, could have been viewed as a risky and even dangerous choice. It turned out to be quite the opposite for our guests, actually. Almost everyone asked to stay there. Perhaps it was a macho thing – good for the ego or street cred or something to boast about with their peers: they'd risked life and limb to stay at the Europa.

By the end of the 1990s, with the Good Friday Agreement in place, the attitude of booking agents towards Northern Ireland had changed dramatically. We were now able to book A-list guests like Garth Brooks, Kylie Minogue, Dolly Parton, Sir David Frost, Michael Parkinson and Sir David Attenborough, among a host of others.

In the 2000s, we thought the time was right to break with our long-standing ethos of being a politics-free zone and invite both Gerry Adams and the Reverend Ian Paisley on to the show. Following the recent election, their parties (Sinn Féin and the DUP respectively) had become the biggest in Northern Ireland. Our agenda was very clear. We wanted them to appear on separate weeks because we knew that if they appeared together, any discussion would only degenerate into the usual series of recriminations that we had all grown so sick of over the years.

The thrust of the interviews would not be about what had happened in the past but what plans each party had to lead us into a new Northern Ireland

and, considering their diametrically opposed views, how they could possibly ever work together. We were confident that both parties would welcome the opportunity for their leader to speak to a different type of television audience, a unique opportunity to get their message across to people who were not necessarily avid followers of current affairs.

Sinn Féin agreed, the DUP was more cautious.

We decided to go ahead with the Gerry Adams interview and hoped that Ian Paisley would follow suit the next week. In the commercial break before Gerry Adams' appearance, I informed the audience who my next guest was and said that if anyone felt uncomfortable, they could leave the studio for the next twenty minutes or so and return towards the end of the programme. No one left. Adams' answer to one of my questions during the wide-ranging interview would ultimately have far-reaching political significance. He said, 'The war is over.' So, there it was. For the first time he had actually said the words that unionists and journalists alike had been demanding from him for over a decade.

With such positivity, the stage was now set for Ian Paisley to take up our invitation to appear on the show the following Friday. Sadly, he declined. Such a disappointment. I genuinely regretted that decision and could never understand what the DUP thought they would lose by their leader's appearance. Still, who would have thought that within twenty-four months of that interview, a new Northern Ireland Assembly would be up and running, led jointly by two lifelong enemies, Martin McGuinness and Ian Paisley.

From the start of the Kelly show in 1989 until its end in 2005, life in Northern Ireland had been transformed. A difficult period to do a chat show? Maybe, but I wouldn't have missed it for the world.

Gerry Kelly is an award-winning radio and television broadcaster. From 1989 to 2005, he was the eponymous host of *Kelly*, the most successful and longest-running chat show in Northern Ireland.

The tiny white coffin that made me ashamed of my homeland
RAF Wildenrath, West Germany, 1989

Michael Macmillan

Of the long list of stories that I covered as a journalist working at home and abroad in the 1970s, 1980s and 1990s, I am regularly asked which one I remember most. I could answer the Gulf War, the Palestinian intifada, the fall of the Wall, the Romanian Revolution, Tiananmen Square, the miners' strike and many others. The answer, though, is closer to my roots.

On a bitterly cold day at the end of October 1989, more than two hundred RAF personnel and their families lined up in the hangar at RAF Wildenrath in West Germany. On two trollies lay coffins that were draped with Union Flags. The tiny white one carried the body of a six-month-old baby, the other contained the body of her father, an RAF serviceman. They had been shot dead by an IRA active service unit that had been marauding around the British bases of the Rhine, looking for easy targets. Why this RAF corporal and his little daughter fitted the bill, only their attackers knew.

Then a foreign correspondent for BBC TV News London, I stood with the mourners and stared at the ground as they sounded the last post. I was overwhelmed by a deep sense of shame for where I came from. What on earth could have justified such cruelty and brutality. To think that such an event might be a cause for celebration in some quarters was beyond comprehension. I was angry, upset and disgusted.

I had spent much of 1989 based in Washington DC for the BBC and, prior to that, five years as North of England correspondent for ITN. Before that, I was political editor at UTV. While, by 1989, reporting the Troubles was no longer a daily task, I had been to Germany before in that year, after an IRA booby-trap bomb attack in Hanover. Then the target was Lance Corporal Stephen Smith, his wife, Tina, and their four young children. The bomb was under their car. Corporal Smith died and his wife and children were badly injured. The IRA team responsible for this attack would, of course, strike again.

On 7 September, Heidi Hazell, a German national, aged twenty-six, was sitting in her car outside her home near Dortmund. A man wearing British

Army battle dress approached and began firing at her with an AK-47 high-velocity rifle. She was shot more than a dozen times. The gunman had thought that she was a sergeant in the British Army. They had got it wrong. It was Heidi's husband who was in the army and she was simply his German wife. Unapologetic, the IRA released this statement:

> As we intend to continue our campaign until the British Army withdraws from Ireland, the outcome of last night's attack reinforces a warning we gave on August 2 1988 for civilians to stay well clear of British military personnel. This warning applies to the use of vehicles personally belonging to British soldiers and all modes of military transport.

So, on 26 October 1989, another horrible sequence of events would unfold at a filling station near the RAF Wildenrath base. Corporal Maheshkumar Islania, his wife, Smita, and their baby daughter, Nivruti, had stopped in the car park to buy groceries at the station's shop. They would have paid no attention to the Ford camper van that had pulled up beside them. Their errand completed, the Islanias, with Smita at the wheel, prepared to drive off. Two IRA men jumped out of their van and opened fire with their high-velocity rifles. Witnesses said they kept firing through the rear window of the car. Their task completed, the gunmen jumped back into their vehicle and headed for the nearby Dutch border.

Maheshkumar was dead and so was the baby. Smita survived. She was seen cradling her baby at the roadside, refusing to release the child from her clutches. It was a devastating, heart-wrenching scene.

Standing in the hangar at Wildenrath on that day, my mind was back in Belfast, remembering the countless shootings, bombings and funerals I had covered, but noting the unique macabre aspect of this occasion. I had never before reported on the murder of a six-month-old child. But it was the added ingredient of my homeland, and how it had visited its hatred upon these poor unsuspecting victims, that made me feel in some way answerable to the sea of bewildered, tearful faces that had gathered to watch and pay their respects.

They carried Nivruti and her father to the RAF aircraft waiting on the tarmac to fly them to Brize Norton. No one could forget the image of the lone RAF officer holding the tiny white coffin in his arms. That picture would lead my report for the BBC Six O'Clock News and be used in the main headline sequence for the bulletin that evening. In those days the Six was the most watched TV news programme in the UK with a nightly audience of six million people.

I remember labouring over the script. This report could not just be a mere statement of facts. It had to present to our audience the monstrous nature of what had happened and the callous disregard that had been displayed for these most innocent of victims. I chose my words very carefully – I wanted each one to bite home and bite hard.

On an average day in national and international news I would have expected my report to have been close to the top of the bulletin, maybe the lead story, given the tragic content. Sadly, there was major competition for airtime. The chancellor, Nigel Lawson, had resigned and my report was consigned to the end of the news. Despite that, after the bulletin had aired, the BBC's foreign editor, John Mahoney, phoned me. He had emotion in his voice. He said there wasn't a dry eye in the newsroom. Maybe I had done my job.

Then, of course, there is the story of the man who German police suspect led these attacks, Dessie Grew. From Moy, County Tyrone, he was the eldest of a family of seven girls and four boys. Grew was top of the class at school, excelled at both O level and A level, and was a keen GAA player. His seeds of hatred were sewn when his family were burned out of their home in 1972 by loyalists. Six of the family were injured and it was an experience he would never forgive or forget. Grew was shot dead by the army in 1990, a year after the German attacks, as he was retrieving rifles from farm outbuildings near Loughgall. His brother Seamus had been shot dead by the RUC eight years previously in controversial circumstances that became part of the Stalker investigation into the alleged targeting and killing by police of IRA suspects.

At Dessie Grew's funeral, Gerry Adams gave the oration. He described him as a 'freedom fighter, a patriot and decent upstanding Irish citizen'. That deeply held belief, shared by so many people, symbolises the gaping wound that Northern Ireland has always wrestled with, fuddled with the concept of right and wrong, truth and lie. It is a place riddled with guilty consciences, unsolved crimes, buried bodies and bitter division.

They often talk of a hierarchy of victims. There probably should never be such a priority list but we all have one and, in formulating mine, I shudder to think of the nightmares of Smita Islania as she relives the moment that her husband and six-month-old baby were shot dead in front of her. For me, she is at the top of that list and of all of the terrible violence, wars and scenes of devastation I have witnessed during my journalistic career, this is the story that wounded me most.

Michael Macmillan was Middle East correspondent for BBC TV News and, prior to that, a correspondent for ITN's *News at Ten*. He started his broadcasting career at Downtown Radio and later became political editor of UTV.

We didn't emote because that would get in the way of the work
Belfast, 1992

Darragh MacIntyre

Sometimes it is the sound. The pain made concrete in wailing anguish.

I was working with a camera crew on the afternoon of 5 February 1992. We were filming in a Chinese food shop around the corner from Sean Graham bookmaker's shop on the Ormeau Road in South Belfast. While we went about our business, the camera lingering over the exotic spices, two gunmen were murdering people less than a hundred yards away. They had walked into the bookies and shot all around them. Mission accomplished, the gunmen sped away in a waiting car. Chance had decided who died and who lived. Five people murdered. The youngest, fifteen. Seven people injured.

We knew nothing of any of this. Then suddenly we were pulled back into Belfast's reality. Sirens pierced the scented calm. Loud and very close. Stepping outside, we found terror. The terror of women mostly. Mothers, sisters, daughters rushing from the red-brick terraced streets to get news of their loved ones. In my memory, the sirens fall silent. The images blur. But I still hear the sounds. Screams. The roars of pain. Human grief. Many years later, I would become friends with one of those impacted most that day. Billy McManus had rushed to the bookies knowing his father was probably inside when the attackers struck. Long after, when I was making a film about the shooting, I reviewed news footage from the day, and there was Billy, just outside the door, desperate to get to his dad inside. His father, Willie, aged fifty-four, was indeed among the dead. That day I did my job. Took notes. And tried to be useful to my more experienced colleagues from Ulster Television who were already on the scene.

I had worked on and off in Belfast for five years, so I knew the drill: get the pictures; get the interviews; try to establish the facts. In that order. Your job was to make sure that your team could tell the story as best as possible. There was one unspoken golden rule – don't let the story get to you. Even as you were swimming in a sea of others' pain, there was an onus on you to push on. Your role was to be detached, even dispassionate. It makes sense. How could you do

124

your job if you allowed yourself to be captured by the huge emotional charge of what you were witnessing?

In many respects, we were like emergency teams from the police or ambulance service. Later, often in pubs, you could talk through what you'd seen with other journalists. Those evenings, medicated by alcohol, were when most of us processed our experiences. If people cried, and I'm sure they did, they did so in private.

In the next years at the BBC I reported on more murders, though I was never the go-to news reporter, so I know other colleagues saw much worse and much more often. I am sure none have ever forgotten the horrors and terror that they stepped into – and then had to compartmentalise so they could do their job. The most enduring moment for me happened in the early afternoon of 4 November 1992.

The newsroom had got a tip-off about a shooting on the edge of Belfast city centre (an amateur radio ham earned a living listening to police communications). I was sent along with the crew. We were at the scene, in the network of streets just over the Ormeau Bridge, within fifteen minutes of the shooting, but a cordon was already in place. The murder victim lay on the street. Somebody had attempted to gift a smidgen of dignity to the man: his corpse had been covered, but his feet were visible, lifelessly splayed apart.

Locals pooled at the outer limits of the perimeter. Neighbours stood outside their front doors, some in hushed conversation. Everyone looked down the street to where the latest victim lay. That's what we were doing too. The cameraman focused first on the body, then dutifully collected 'cut-away' pictures of soldiers, the public and, of course, the street name.

I stood by the crew, scanning the scene for anything that might provide a relevant image for the story or, better, a potential interviewee. To anyone who didn't live through the Troubles, it might be difficult to comprehend but there was little unusual about this scene in Belfast at the time. Another day, another murder.

Out of the corner of my eye, I saw a woman, walking jauntily along on an adjoining street. I noticed her precisely because everything about her contrasted with what was going on around the corner, on the street where I was standing. A young woman. Late twenties, early thirties maybe. If there was ever a look that defined happiness – that was her that day. Head high, carrying her shopping, striding home.

Today's news lay in waiting for her.

At the white tape, two men glanced up in her direction. A sudden huddle before they turned towards her, lifting their hands out of their pockets and taking tentative steps towards her – then the moment Roseann Gilbride was told what was around the corner. I saw all this. I saw the moment someone's life was torn apart. Dreams of a lifetime of fun and joy, shattered.

The camera caught her an instant later as she turned down the street towards where her husband, and the father of their three children, lay dead. Some men tried to comfort her, but she pulled away, dropped her bag and ran to her Michael. Michael, aged thirty-six, had been visiting his parents for lunch. Roseann had planned to join them.

I processed this scene as a working journalist. Then, and now, our job was to bring the awful reality of violence to the public. You step back from the emotional pitch of what you have witnessed and do your level best to tell the story of that day's horror. But I never forgot that moment, when someone's world went from gorgeous light to the very darkest in a second.

Some years later, I was leaving journalism. I was heading to a new life in Donegal with my wife and two children. My last shift was at Drumcree in 1998. I finished in Portadown at 8 a.m., just as news was coming through of the killing of the three Quinn children in Ballymoney. The boys – Richard, aged ten; Mark, aged nine; and Jason, aged eight – died after their home was firebombed by the UVF, murdered even as the peace process was well underway.

One month on and we were travelling to our new life. We were driving in convoy – my wife in one car, me in another with our two girls, our dog and our suitcases – heading due west out along the M2 and then over the Glenshane Pass. My wife, Sharon Hall, was a journalist too. She'd covered the Troubles for even longer than I had and, like me, had a habit – all journalists had – of listening to every news bulletin.

We were going to run a pub within sight of Errigal mountain, and get a restaurant up and running, but the routine of listening to the latest news hadn't left either of us.

It was five o'clock, 15 August, and the news came on. The Omagh bomb. The first reports didn't reveal the true horrific scale of the loss of human life. But it was clear that many people had died and that many people had been injured.

We were just outside Dungiven when we pulled the cars over and parked up on the side of the road. Sharon and I got out and hurriedly considered reporting in for duty. Omagh, as the crow would fly, wasn't much more than thirty miles away. It took only a second or so to rationalise that it wasn't our role any more. Dozens of journalists were already on their way.

And then, suddenly, we both started to cry. And hold each other. We stood there sobbing for minutes, not a word between us, before we got back in to the cars and drove on with the bewildered children.

I wondered even then why this bomb, these killings, had affected both of us in such an emotional way. It had never happened before.

Later it would emerge that twenty-nine people and two unborn children had been killed in the bomb. Hundreds were injured. We didn't know those details then, but we did know that people had lost their lives, that something awful had visited Omagh, a town we both knew well.

Looking back, I think it was actually quite simple: our job had protected us from the full emotional context of the Troubles. We didn't emote because that would get in the way of the work. There was an invisible ring fence that protected us from having to deal with what we were seeing and meeting on a near daily basis.

This was the very first time we were outside of that ring fence, looking on like most citizens of this place, without any guardrail to lean on.

Darragh MacIntyre is a reporter with BBC *Panorama* and BBC *Spotlight*. He has worked as a journalist in Northern Ireland across three decades.

How a bomb ended my journalism career
Bangor, 1992

Colin Bateman

I never wanted to be a journalist. I wanted to write the Great American Novel. American because America was where all my influences came from – in books, movies (not 'filums') and TV. There was virtually nothing good about Northern Ireland – there were no writers from here (that I'd heard of); if there were ever movies about here, they were always rubbish and the accents were all over the place. Meanwhile, in the real world we were all busy killing each other. When the world wasn't shedding tears over us, they were laughing at our craziness – at Paisley ranting, at Hurricane Higgins rebelling, at Georgie Best drinking for Ulster. It was all quite embarrassing. So, no, I didn't want to write the Great Irish novel, nor the Great Northern Irish novel; not even the great Bangor novel, which is where I lived. No, I wanted to write the Great American Novel. But that's a hard thing to do when you're a spotty, incredibly shy, seventeen-year-old punk rocker starting out as a cub reporter on the *County Down Spectator*.

I really didn't want to be there. I only had the job because my dad, who knew I loved writing, fibbed – or let's face it, lied – about why he wanted me to pop into the *Spectator* office for a chat with its editor, the formidable Annie Roycroft. Annie was just about the first female newspaper editor in Ireland – the same age as the Queen, a Sunday-School-teaching spinster, the paper was her life – she was the *County Down Spectator* in human form. She was just going to have a chat with me about what life was like on a newspaper. It was a shock when she sat me down and told me to write three hundred words on why I wanted to be a journalist. I didn't, but being the obliging type, and too shy to say no, I wrote what might be the finest work of fiction I've ever written. I walked out with the offer of a job.

I started at the tail end of the 1970s. If I couldn't be a great novelist, then I could be a great journalist, like Woodward and Bernstein bringing down the president, or that reporter in *The Odessa File* hunting down old Nazis. There weren't a lot of Nazis to be found in Bangor; there wasn't a lot of anything. There was all kinds of madness going on up in Belfast, and there had been for ten years. But Bangor, even though it was only a dozen miles away, was different. We had what might be called a 'good' Troubles. A bomb every couple of years. An occasional terrorist murder. It would be considered a lot for a small town in, say, Surrey, but for Northern Ireland, it was nothing. Part of the reason for that was geographical – there was only really one main road in and out of the town, so if terrorists did decide to target us, there was always the worry about how they would get home in time for supper without having their escape route cut off. The town was considered safe enough that off-duty soldiers from Palace Barracks in Holywood were allowed to spend their downtime here, mainly in The Helmsman disco. They were young, fit and had money to spend, so they were popular with the local girls, and not so popular with the local boys. The fighting we had on our streets on a Friday night had more to do with testosterone than Troubles. Eventually it got so bad that the soldiers were banned from coming, and the boys got their girls back. Because Bangor was safe, it also meant that a lot of police lived here, which made it safer again. So we did okay out of the Troubles.

The *Spectator* dealt in council and courts, in burglaries and the Boys' Brigade and junior football. For many years, the most popular feature was 'Rat of the Week', in which some unidentified citizen was chastised for stealing a charity box, or driving off from a minor crash without reporting it, or pushing a boy off the sea wall into the sea. (It was my brother who was pushed. And back then, before the bloody marina, we still had a sea to fall into.) The feature eventually had to be discontinued when people began to compete to get into it.

I eventually became deputy editor of the paper, and I got quite settled in what was a relatively stress-free job. I got no nearer to writing the Great American Novel. It was always the dream, it was always next year, but it never happened. The deputy editor's main responsibility on a small paper is to stand in as editor when he (by now Annie had retired, and Paul Flowers was the editor) goes on holiday. I'd done it a few times and was quite relaxed about it.

Then came 22 October 1992. I was in charge of the paper that week. We worked, as normal, until late on Wednesday night. We'd finish off the front page the next morning, so it would be as up to date as possible when the paper started printing at lunchtime on Thursday.

I went home, went to bed – and then the windows were rattled by what felt like a sonic boom. It was a bomb, and a big one. I jumped up and into the car and raced into town. The IRA had detonated a 200lb bomb. They had basically destroyed our entire Main Street. There was smoke everywhere, shop alarms, police sirens – just pandemonium.

NOBODY wants to see their hometown destroyed. NOBODY wants anyone injured (four police officers were hurt). BUT, if a bomb is inevitable, if it HAS to happen, then as the deputy editor of the *County Down Spectator*, you really want it to happen on a Wednesday night. Any other night, it's old news, it has already been covered elsewhere, but a Wednesday night means your front page the next morning is going to be the one everyone wants to see. This was the biggest news story in Bangor – possibly EVER. And I was in charge of the paper. I was captain of the ship. It would be my ticket out of parochial little Bangor. Everyone in the media would see what I was capable of, and I would probably be an ITN foreign correspondent in Beirut by the end of the week.

Except I froze. I absolutely froze. I knew what I was supposed to be doing, but I just couldn't do it. I should be interviewing people, I should be marshalling our reporters and photographers, I should be leading from the front, but I was absolutely paralysed. Having observed the mayhem, I got into the car and drove home. I got back into bed and pulled the covers over my head. My hometown was in a state of chaos, and I was hiding. It was a sickening feeling, but there was also a sudden realisation that I had NEVER wanted to be a journalist. I wasn't equipped for it. When I was faced with my first real test as a journalist, I wanted nothing to do with it. I didn't want to be writing about real things, I wanted to be making things up.

I went into work the next morning expecting to be sacked on the spot. But the thing was – nobody had noticed. Everyone had done the job they were supposed to do – the reporters had reported, the photographers had taken their pictures. Now it was my job to help turn it all into a newspaper. It was a big broadsheet, but we dropped everything from the front page and ran with a giant picture of our Main Street with the headline 'DEVASTATED' superimposed over it. Then we had page after page of coverage, which I think rivalled anything one of the big nationals could have done.

Great team, great work, great paper – but something had changed in me. I wanted to write novels, and I'd been putting it off for too long. Very shortly after that, I began writing *Divorcing Jack*, which if not destined to be the Great American Novel, was at least to become one of the Greatest Bangor Novels ever written – or certainly in the top ten.

Colin Bateman is a bestselling novelist, screenwriter and playwright. He rose from cub reporter on the *County Down Spectator* to the dizzying heights of deputy editor on the *County Down Spectator*.

A war hero murdered by loyalist cowards
Belfast, 1992

Ciaran Barnes

John Lovett, an elderly neighbour of mine, was murdered alongside two other innocent men in the 1992 James Murray's betting shop massacre. A dozen more were injured. John Lovett was an RAF veteran who had fought in the Battle of Britain. After that, he was stationed in India and Burma, where he was captured by Japanese forces and held in a prisoner camp until the Second World War ended in 1945. His killer, Stevie McKeag, was a UDA gunman, who specialised in murdering Catholics in enclosed spaces. McKeag's other victims included Philomena Hanna, a twenty-six-year-old mother of two, who was shot in the pharmacy where she worked in April of the same year.

I was at home on a Saturday afternoon watching television when I heard the cracks of the assault rifle and hand-grenade that devastated the bookies. My ma thought it was a bin being kicked over in the entry at the rear of our home just off the Oldpark Road, but I guessed different. I ran out on to the road, and as I made my way down to the bend near the interface at Rosapenna Street, I could see smoke coming from the betting shop – the remnants of a hand-grenade thrown inside by the UDA minutes before.

By that stage, dozens of men and women were running on to the Oldpark Road – a common sight when bombs exploded and shootings occurred. Folk disregarded their own safety to check on their loved ones – something that was understandable back then. When I reached the bookies, a man stood outside waving his arms, telling the crowd to stay back. Smoke filtered from the doorway. Ambulances arrived a short time later. I was one of the first on the scene of the slaughter – a young teenage boy who instinctively knew that Belfast had to change.

This was a time before huge supermarkets like Tesco. Shopping was done in rows of tiny stores packed together. On the Oldpark Road you had a bookies, bakery, butcher, hairdresser, video rental shop, newsagent, chemist and grocer all joined together in a neat little terraced row. Anyone running down that road was naturally filled with dread, not knowing which one had been attacked.

The bodies of the dead and wounded were taken out by paramedics. It reminded me of football games – back then, injured players were transported off the field on hand-held wooden stretchers – the difference being the players weren't draped in white sheets with evident bloodstains.

In the days after the James Murray's massacre, there was a clamour to have the Oldpark Road fenced off. Crowds gathered at the no man's land between nationalist Rosapenna Street and unionist Manor Street demanding a barrier be installed between the communities. The parish priest from Sacred Heart, the church that is less than a hundred yards from James Murray's Bookmakers, was Father Don O'Rawe. Even as a young teen I had no time for organised religion, but his sermon to the crowd struck a lifelong chord. He talked about not allowing the hatred that polluted the hearts of the bookies killers to infect our own. It stays with me to this day.

Seven years after the James Murray's attack, I started my career as a journalist. The events of that day – and the desire to convey the attack's impact on a small, tight-knit and brilliant community – pushed me towards this industry. What I didn't envisage was how hard it is to write about the place where you come from and the people you know. Until this moment, I have never penned a single word about that conundrum, or the name John Lovett.

The war hero's impressive military record was mentioned at the time of his shameful murder and features in the *Lost Lives* book – the encyclopedia on the Troubles that should be required reading in every secondary-level school in Northern Ireland. John re-entered my thoughts in 2016 when a UDA mural appeared to Stevie McKeag in the Shankill estate. The mural features a poppy – a symbol wholly inappropriate as McKeag was the killer of a British military hero.

The same week the mural was painted I had a pint with former *North Belfast News* journalist Evan Short in the Frames pub in Belfast city centre. A talented reporter and old schoolfriend, he understood my reluctance to write about a killing spree of which I was a witness to the aftermath. Armed with information regarding John Lovett's war record and my memories of the bookies attack, he tracked down John's niece Maud Evans. She told Evan, 'You could have written a book about John. He was very good-natured, and he would have done anybody a good turn. He liked gambling and that's why he was at the bookies. He didn't drink and loved practical jokes.'

What struck me while reading Maud's words is that trying to avoid writing about the places you come from and people you know often becomes an impossibility. UDA leader Johnny Adair's C Company planned the James Murray's bookies massacre and is reported to have thrown a party afterwards to celebrate. Two other innocent civilians were murdered in the attack: Francis Burns, aged fifty-two, and Peter Orderly, aged forty-seven. Many more were injured in the mass shooting and bombing that took place inside a tiny space no bigger than an average living room.

I've interviewed Adair dozens of times over my twenty-year career as a journalist, but never quizzed him about the slaughter. I know him well enough to know he would deny involvement, but does that excuse the question not being asked? It's a matter with which I wrestle.

What I do know is that the UDA killers who butchered the innocents in James Murray's Bookmakers are in no way reflective of the majority of decent people who live in the Shankill estate. The men and women there are hard-working and generous, and I am proud to call several of them friends.

Among them, ironically, is Stevie McKeag's former partner. She is one of the most courageous people I know and someone who utterly rejects sectarianism and religious hatred. What both she and I, and thousands of others, understand is the impact of growing up beside an interface and the psychological toll it can take.

During the late 1980s and early 1990s, the bend on the Oldpark Road at Rosapenna Street, where the James Murray's Bookmakers killings occurred, was probably the most dangerous place in Northern Ireland. In separate attacks, some years apart, UDA members Billy Quee and Norman Truesdale were killed nearby by republicans, as was Protestant civilian Sam Rock. Catholic Dermot McGuinness was gunned down by loyalists at the off-licence next to James Murray's Bookmakers. Father-of-five Sean Rafferty was shot dead by the UDA at his home round the corner, and taxi driver Hugh Magee was murdered as he drove his cab on the Oldpark Road.

A friend once joked that anyone who lived through the Troubles in North Belfast suffers from post-traumatic stress disorder. When the laughing stopped, it dawned on me that he might be right. Nationalists and unionists of my generation – aged forty and over – still walk those streets with caution. Taking the long route to get to a safe destination is hard-wired into our brains and, despite being irrational, it's what we still do. The bend on the Oldpark Road where the James Murray's Bookmakers attack occurred is one of those dangerous places.

Twenty-seven years after the ceasefires, the area remains a modern-day no man's land; a place where you can still identify someone's religion depending on their direction of travel. I pass it in my car frequently, never on foot, and often think of the needless slaughter that occurred in the surrounding area. I also wonder whether the UDA members who lay poppy wreaths at memorials on Remembrance Sunday think of John Lovett. The Battle of Britain veteran who helped prevent a Nazi invasion of England and who survived a Japanese torture camp. A war hero murdered by cowards, and someone whose sacrifice is practically forgotten, while the exploits of his sectarian killer are exalted.

Ciaran Barnes is chief reporter with the *Sunday Life* newspaper and has reported extensively on the Troubles for over twenty years.

A chilling car journey with 'Mad Dog' Adair
Belfast, 1993

Maggie O'Kane

One Friday morning in October 1993, I arrived from London to do holiday cover for the *Guardian* correspondent in Belfast, and there was only one big story in town: the ongoing, mad loyalist killing spree that saw Protestant paramilitary death squads surpass even the IRA killings of 1993, murdering forty-eight Catholics that year.

Most of the victims were drinking in the wrong Catholic bars at the wrong time on a Saturday night. And the myth was that there was only one Mr Big – Johnny Adair.

That October weekend, despite surviving three assassination attempts by the IRA over the years, Adair wasn't so hard to find. He was then twenty-nine and had been picked up regularly since he was twenty-three to be questioned about murdering Catholics. When the RUC stopped him, cruising in the Catholic Falls Road – with a six-inch cardboard cut-out of a Celtic football player swinging gently from his back window as a decoy – he would wind down the window and say, 'That's so-and-so's house there, isn't it?' as he pointed to the house of a well-known Catholic or Sinn Féin councillor.

Adair knew his streets and their streets. At thirteen, he had watched a forty-five-year-old Protestant bus driver called Harry Bradshaw slowly dying at the wheel of his bus. Murdered by his own for strike-breaking during the loyalist workers' strike. He said, 'I still remember the driver, still seated at the wheel of the bus, and watching him turn grey in the daylight.'

During the first weekend of that same loyalist workers' strike in May 1974, I was twelve years old and hanging out of the side windows of our top-floor dormitory in the Protestant town of Ballynahinch, just outside Belfast. We were a bunch of excited girls and scared nuns watching loyalist workers marching up the hill to get us, but then they just marched back down again.

Back on the Shankill, Adair's teenage life continued. The Ulster Defence Regiment refused his teenage application to be a reservist, so he became a loyalist paramilitary.

I grew up in Dublin and eventually became a war correspondent for the

Guardian. By the time I got back to Belfast in October 1993, aged thirty-one, I had covered the fall of the Berlin Wall and Eastern Europe (for RTÉ), the Gulf Wars, Bosnia, East Timor and Afghanistan.

Being back in Belfast, looking for Adair, was supposed to be just another job. But that brief weekend October trip to Belfast was different – deeply personal and disturbing. And, looking back on it, driven by something or someone who still felt she had a lot of prove to somebody.

Two things helped me find Adair – the first, ironically, was my own father's brief stint in the RUC, which had ended badly for the young, handsome twenty-one-year-old Catholic, Peter O'Kane. His four older brothers – Seamus, Joe, Paddy and Sean – gave him a hard time for joining the enemy, so he took up a driving job with Coca Cola.

One of my dad's old former comrades in the RUC was Detective Chief Inspector Jimmy Nesbitt, who had led the investigation into the Shankill Butchers – UVF killers who, for seven years, had abducted Catholics in their black taxis and, after torturing them, cut their throats with a butcher's knife. Nesbitt had been in charge of the Shankill Butchers investigations and was now tasked with sorting out the current spate of loyalist killings.

'Ah, "Mad Dog" Adair?' Nesbitt said. Yes, he would meet me that Friday afternoon. 'And how's Peter doing down in Dublin?' Nesbitt was nearing retirement. He was brave, intelligent and matter-of-fact. He didn't tell me much, except that the police called Adair 'Mad Dog' and that the loyalists were operationally very tight and possibly moving into explosives.

My second break that led to Adair also came from my father. He had played football for the mainly Protestant-supported Belfast team Crusaders and he had won two Northern Ireland amateur caps. Joe English, a leading loyalist, was a big Crusaders fan. I found him in the Crusaders bar after a match that Saturday evening. 'Big Peter the goalie!' said Joe English in disbelief when I presented myself to him in the pub, trying to sound as posh and English as possible.

Joe English took me drinking to the Cloughfern Arms, up in Rathcoole on the outskirts of North Belfast, in the company of the young men of Ulster's Young Militants, one with a tattoo that read 'KAI' – 'That's "Kill All Irishmen",' he explained to the girl from the English *Guardian* newspaper. As the night wore on, I explained to Joe that the *Guardian* was interested in speaking to the UFF inner council. Joe said he would help – he wanted the *Guardian* audience to understand that Ulster's loyalists were fighting the 'pan-nationalist' attempts of John Hume and Gerry Adams to reach a peace deal without them.

Joe organised the meeting for 10 a.m. on Monday morning, in the back kitchen of some sort of clubhouse in Rathcoole. The introductions were brief, the back story familiar: the UFF would fight fire with fire, and so on. Joe English, the PR man, proudly introduced me to the various 'OCs', including Johnny Adair. 'You have half an hour. These are busy men,' said Joe. The only problem was that the busy commanders hadn't much to say, except that they were 'out-terrorising the terrorists until the grannies on the Falls Road would beg the IRA to stop.' There would be no surrender and 'all deaths are regrettable'. But Mad Dog, Ulster's most infamous hard man, didn't say a single word. He was bored with the pseudo-political chat, and stayed silent as a barman passed around sandwiches cut into triangles. Then the meeting was over.

As we left, I asked Adair for a lift back into town. I needed at least one quote. So, he took me for a drive in his silver Volvo. On the dashboard there was a photograph of Adair and Michael Stone – the loyalist paramilitary who opened fire on Catholic mourners, killing three of them, at Milltown Cemetery in March 1988. 'Stone?' I said.

'Yes,' said Adair. 'A hero, a real hero. So how did you get in touch with us then?' he asked suspiciously.

I don't think I told him the Big Peter the Crusaders Goalie story. He was driving very fast – checking the mirror all the time, never making eye contact. Never looking me directly in the eye. We pulled up at his double-fronted council house off Belfast's Shankill Road. Two huge Union Flags hung on each side of the door, which was peppered with old IRA bullets. Adair was saying that everyone believes in God; he believes in God.

'And the commandment "Thou shalt not kill"?' I asked.

'Thou shalt not be caught killing,' he said.

Across the road from his house is a bar. Johnny sent a runner to summon the man he wanted. He's about to put on a show for the *Guardian*. 'Got the piece, Jackie?' he said. 'Here's Joe, he'll have one.'

And so it went on … A man swayed out of the bar and across the road. 'He's one of us,' said Mad Dog, 'ready to go at any time.'

It was almost 1.30 on a Monday afternoon. Joe had a friendly six-pint smile in his eyes and didn't look ready for much. He looked happily into the car.

'What do we do with Taigs?' Mad Dog asked.

'We spray them,' said Joe, with a friendly grin.

We drove back towards the Shankill Road. On the way, I tried to make some small talk and address the elephant in the room. 'Did you ever have a Catholic in your car before?' I asked, thinking I would take things on directly.

'Only a dead one,' he said.

I asked him if he would drop me off on Botanic Avenue. It was nearly

3 p.m.; the tour was over, Adair's show was done. I left that night, and filed my piece from the airport as though I wanted to get it all out of me while the adrenaline and fear still carried me.

I hadn't looked at the article I wrote about meeting Johnny Adair for nearly thirty years until I dug it out in order to write this piece. When I got to the part where someone had asked, 'Is she from London?' and Johnny had replied, 'No, she's from Dublin,' I still felt a chill.

That's the chill of a twelve-year-old girl from Belfast who thought she had outgrown her town and her memories. The same chill came again when I moved to Belfast a few years later, despite a warning from Joe English to the deputy editor after the article that I'd better stay out of Belfast. It was several years on – 1997 – and my husband, John Mullin, had become the *Guardian* correspondent in Belfast. We had a baby called Billy and I had temporarily given up wars. But one night John was away and for reasons I can't quite remember, I packed a small suitcase for Billy and me and moved out of our house in Cromwell Road to the Tara Lodge hotel just across the road.

I can't remember what had spooked me – or how being across the street in the high-security Tara Lodge was going to save us – but I remember looking out of the new net curtains of the recently opened B&B and realising I was scared of Johnny Adair.

Maggie O'Kane is a former award-winning foreign correspondent with the *Guardian*. In 2014, she co-founded the Global Media Campaign to End FGM – the world's largest media campaign dedicated to ending FGM – by 2030.

'We need help to speak again'
Belfast, 1993

Seamus McKee

It's always about trying to find the right words.

I am shovelling pebbles in the garden. It is a Saturday afternoon in late October 1993. My wife calls down to me from an upstairs window. Someone from the newsroom is on the phone. Something is wrong. I'm not usually on programme duty on a Saturday. I lift the receiver and the world shrinks and fades to the sound of the urgent voice in my ear. 'There's been a bomb. You'd better get in …'

'Where? When?'

'You'd better come in, now…'

I hadn't heard the explosion. While I'd been wielding a spade on a pleasant autumn afternoon in Belfast, three miles away people had been digging frantically to find loved ones, neighbours or friends beneath the rubble of Frizzell's fish shop on the Shankill Road. I am not being sent to the scene. My job will be to present a special news bulletin on television later in the afternoon. What can prepare you to introduce a television programme that will relay the news of the horrific deaths of ten people, including two girls of thirteen and seven? By rights, words should fail you. Yet words are all you have. Later, seated in the studio, I look into the camera. I stare at the words I've written, about a litany of place names down the years: Ballykelly, Enniskillen, Ballygawley, Teebane, to which could now be added the Shankill Road. Another voice sounds urgently in my ear: 'Cue!'

'Good afternoon …'

Why would I use the word 'litany' to introduce a news bulletin? Was I striving for a solemnity that would match the content? Was I trying for a gentler word than 'list' or 'catalogue'? People also talk about a litany of complaints. May we never be forgiven if we are thinking of years of bloodshed and bereavement as a tedious recital.

*

It is a warm June afternoon in 1994. I am standing in a country lane near the village of Loughinisland in County Down. A few hundred yards away is the Heights Bar, its interior still bloodied after a UVF attack on customers who were watching the World Cup game between the Republic of Ireland and Italy. The silence in the lane is broken only by the thrum of broadcasting equipment. Shortly I'll be presenting the teatime news. Better to let the contrast between the scene around me and the shooting dead of six people, including an eighty-seven-year-old man, speak for itself. There are times when the only appropriate words are the names of the dead.

It is evening, earlier that same month. The minibus is taking us to a briefing. I am nervous. There is so little time to prepare. The following morning, the bodies of fifteen of the victims of the helicopter crash on the Mull of Kintyre will be reunited with their families at RAF Aldergrove. Those on board the Chinook included almost all the senior Northern Ireland intelligence experts. The briefing is far from extensive, for understandable reasons. I don't have the detail I feel I need for a live broadcast of the ceremonial reception of fifteen coffins. But I have enough.

The next morning I'm at Aldergrove, looking at a screen in a BBC vehicle. I describe the Hercules transport plane slowing to a stop on the runway. My greatest fear is that I will look down or look away at the wrong moment. I will fail to tally the coffins carried from the plane with the number of names in my notes. Will I have gone through the list and will there be another of the dead brought out, unnamed by me? There is no Master of Ceremonies to guide us. I am struck by the utmost delicacy with which the coffin-bearers place their burden on a trestle, in view of the families gathered close by. No coffin goes unnamed. Afterwards I chat with our team. I'm conscious the sound will carry to the relatives gathered some distance away. We fall silent. Such sadness in that huddled group. Later, the widow of one of the RUC officers writes to me: 'You spoke of us as if you knew us personally.' Words can be the strength we get from strangers.

It is very early on an August morning in 1998. In the dawn light I am walking the silent streets of Omagh two days after the Real IRA bomb that killed twenty-nine people and two unborn children. In a shop doorway, a woman is lighting a candle. Such a little thing, yet so eloquent. There are reporters from all over the world in Omagh. I wish they could be here to see this. How to express what it signifies? I think of the Camowen and the Drumragh rivers, meeting to form the Strule here in the heart of the town. And an image forms of people finding consolation in the symbol of that merger. They have come through this together and they hope to move on from it as one. I say these words later in a broadcast. And a man comes to me and puts it better than I did in the phrases I worked so hard at: 'We were struck dumb by that bomb last Saturday,' he says. 'We need help to speak again, and maybe to sing.'

The day after the bombing, Nell McCafferty writes: 'Amid the shocking images of Omagh, replayed endlessly on television this weekend, the hitherto still small voice of the forgotten people is heard faintly in the background, murmuring, "my family too".'

It is many years later, 2015, and the artist Colin Davidson's magnificent exhibition *Silent Testimony* is at the Ulster Museum. I can't take my eyes off the eighteen portraits around the walls of the room. The eyes look not outward but inward in grief and hurt. These are people who have themselves been injured, or lost mothers, fathers, husbands, sons or daughters to bomb or bullet. Wall panels give brief details. In the portraits, lips are closed, some sealed tight against repressed emotion, others shut on unspoken thoughts. In their ordinary humanity, these faces are deeply affecting, and I am overcome. I weep.

Am I weeping for these wounded people, for all the dead, or for myself? In these wordless moments I am giving way to emotion I have kept at bay for thirty years. Such is the power of mute witness. I've feared silence all of my broadcasting life, always rushing to fill it. Now it has overwhelmed me. It is not that words have failed.

Looking back, for as long as I've been looking for the right words, I've turned to the poets. As we stumble towards some kind of reckoning with the past, they have provided moments of grace along the way. In the work of painters, playwrights and the writers of stories you will find a calling to account. You will also find reason for hope.

The relatives digging through shop ruins after an explosion; the reporter at the murder scene in a country lane; the woman lighting candles in a bombed shop doorway; the families huddled in the open near the coffins of their loved ones; the framed faces of the bereaved in a dimly lit room. They are all of us – 'my family too'. We have all been struck dumb. We need help to speak again, and maybe to sing.

Seamus McKee is a broadcast journalist and presenter who previously worked for the BBC in Northern Ireland on radio and television.

Early signs of the pillars that underpinned the peace process
Belfast, 1993

Nicholas Watt

On my first weekend in Belfast as *The Times* Ireland correspondent, I decided to take the train south to cover a story far removed from the Troubles. A major development was underway on the Irish music scene: U2 had become the first of the globally famous Irish rock bands to start recording in Dublin rather than in London or the US. This symbolised the renaissance of Dublin as a cultural centre with the rejuvenation of the Temple Bar area.

So, on the balmy morning of Saturday, 23 October 1993, I caught the train to Dublin to interview the music journalist Niall Stokes. Sadly, I cannot find any record of my interview with Niall in my cuttings books. In fact I don't think I ever wrote up the piece.

In the short time that I was in Dublin, the Troubles erupted. At 1.16 p.m. the IRA detonated a bomb on the counter of Frizzell's fishmonger's shop on the Shankill Road. Ten people, including one of the bombers, died. A few hours later, in the twilight of an Indian summer's evening, I walked up the Shankill Road. All was eerily quiet around a mound of rubble – the remains of Frizzell's – piled up across the road.

I will never forget the following day, standing outside the house of Leanne Murray, aged thirteen, who had died as she sought to buy her favourite packet of whelks. In the street outside you could hear the wails of her mother, Gina, as she clutched her daughter's slippers in her front room.

The bombing was a failed attempt by the IRA to kill the local Ulster Defence Association leader Johnny Adair, known as Mad Dog. Rather than killing him, the IRA had killed the owner of the fishmonger's, his daughter, seven shoppers and one of its bombers.

A few days later, I made contact with loyalist paramilitary leaders. Beside a shopfront on the Shankill, I passed through multiple doors with buzzers and video cameras. I was asked to sit in a waiting room before being ushered into a main meeting room, decorated with flags and memorabilia.

A stern-looking man with a distinctive moustache marched into the room.

In a pretty intimidating tone he informed me that he was a representative of the Ulster Volunteer Force and then issued a warning that the IRA had invited inevitable retaliation. A year or so later, that UVF representative became an eloquent voice for peace. It was my first encounter with David Ervine.

As Ervine had predicted in our meeting, tit-for-tat violence ensued. Exactly a week after the Shankill bombing, gunmen from the Ulster Freedom Fighters opened fire on the Rising Sun pub in the small County Londonderry village of Greysteel. Eight people, from across both communities, were murdered. They had been out celebrating Halloween.

On a cold November day, I found myself standing next to John Hume, the leader of the nationalist SDLP, at the burial of some of the victims. Dressed in just a suit, he must have been shivering as relatives approached him to shake his hand. Hume broke down as they delivered a message: don't give up on your search for peace. At that point, it appeared doomed.

The moment in that graveyard was a brief glimpse into a largely unlit world that eventually developed into the successful peace process. Hume had been holding secret discussions with Gerry Adams that played a significant role in bringing Sinn Féin in from the cold.

I could sense a picture developing slowly but surely. The day-to-day violence suggested a bleak and hopeless outlook for Northern Ireland. In the background – and then a few months later in the open – there were signs of intriguing developments.

My first experience that all may not have been as it seemed came four days after the Shankill bombing, when the IRA bomber Thomas 'Bootsy' Begley was buried. I remember standing in Brompton Park in the Ardoyne area of North Belfast as Gerry Adams briefly shouldered the coffin, which was draped in an Irish tricolour, with a black beret and gloves on top to symbolise Begley's IRA membership.

'"Callous" Adams Helps Carry Bomber's Coffin', was the headline over my front-page story in *The Times* the following day. A few weeks after the funeral, a senior RUC officer told me he had breathed a sigh of relief that day. A failure by Adams to carry the coffin would have denoted a republican split. That officer had ensured that the funeral passed without incident after striking a deal with a leading member of Sinn Féin.

All was therefore not as it seemed, as we found out on Sunday, 28 November, when the *Observer* revealed a secret channel of communication between the government and the IRA. Two weeks earlier, John Major had said the idea of talking to the IRA 'would turn my stomach'.

At an excruciating press conference at Stormont Castle that Sunday afternoon, the Northern Ireland secretary of state, Sir Patrick Mayhew, insisted that the government had not misled parliament. Mayhew shifted uncomfortably as he tried to draw a distinction between the 'chain of communication' and dialogue that would not take place until the IRA ended its violence. At one point, Mayhew was told his syntax had gone to pieces. One of his ministers later told me that Mayhew had not really been bothered by the accusations of misleading parliament – what had upset him was the suggestion that he, the most particular of QCs, had mixed up his syntax.

The uncomfortable scenes at Stormont indicated that an acutely sensitive peace process was underway. On 15 December, John Major stood alongside his Irish counterpart Albert Reynolds to launch the Anglo-Irish Downing Street Declaration, which laid down the principle of consent, which would become one of the fundamental elements of the 1998 Good Friday Agreement. This offered hope to nationalists, with the confirmation that Northern Ireland's constitutional status could be changed, but reassurance to unionists that this could only be achieved with the agreement of its people.

In the seven weeks between the Shankill bomb of 23 October 1993 and the Downing Street Declaration, we glimpsed three-and-a-half of the five pillars that eventually underpinned the peace process. The first and decisive development was the talks between John Hume and Gerry Adams. Hume believed there was a far greater prize than the prosperity of his own SDLP – finding a constitutional path for the unconstitutional republican movement. The Hume–Adams talks coincided – coincidentally – with movement in the British government's talks with the IRA. This led the government to conclude that the IRA wanted a route out of the conflict and the IRA to conclude that Britain was neutral about Northern Ireland's constitutional position. The third pillar is always overlooked. That was the huge effort by John Major and Albert Reynolds to normalise Anglo-Irish relations.

The initial signs of the fourth pillar were becoming visible in late 1993: the active engagement of Washington. Unionists and London were highly sceptical, not least when Bill Clinton granted Gerry Adams a US visa in early 1994, before the IRA ceasefire. But Clinton's later nomination of the supremely diplomatic George Mitchell to chair talks, which eventually became the Good Friday Agreement negotiations, built confidence among the Ulster Unionists.

That takes us to the fifth pillar underpinning the process: the arrival of a younger and more confident generation of Ulster Unionism in the form of David Trimble. The dour and Delphic Jim Molyneaux was still leader; change would have to wait another two years.

I had a ringside seat at the rise of Trimble. I found myself a few yards away from him in July 1995 when the first Orange Order march at Drumcree of the post-ceasefire era was allowed down the nationalist Garvaghy Road in

Portadown. Trimble and Ian Paisley were only allowed to join the march at the end of the contentious stretch of the road.

As soon as the march reached this point, an iconic image played out. Trimble grabbed hold of Paisley's hand and held their arms aloft as the march continued towards Carleton Street Orange Hall, cementing his reputation as a leader who could be trusted with the union.

I later asked Trimble why he had grabbed Paisley's arm given that many moderate unionists regarded him as an inflammatory figure. Trimble said he simply could not allow Paisley to walk so much as one inch in front of him in his own constituency.

On a mild autumn day I had taken a train to Dublin to discover a story about new Ireland. A very old conflict pulled me back to Belfast. Before long I was witnessing early signs pointing to a very new Northern Ireland.

Nicholas Watt is the political editor of BBC *Newsnight*. He was *The Times* Ireland correspondent between 1993 and 1997.

My neighbour John Hume
Greysteel, 1993

Roisín Duffy

As they lowered John Hume into his grave in the City Cemetery, on a hill overlooking Derry with a spectacular view of the River Foyle below, his family, we are told, broke into song: 'We shall overcome, we shall overcome some day …' I imagined them in full voice as the familiar words rang out; the Bogside below, the Creggan estate all around, and I was transported back to a different time in the city when the path ahead, for all of us, was far from clear and riven with risk.

It must have been in my last year at primary school. Those were dark days: the Troubles had erupted, Bloody Sunday would soon blight the city, the world's press had descended and the British Army had taken up a strategic position in a factory on the edge of the Creggan estate. John Hume's house backed on to the site and our house was just across the road. IRA gunmen had taken up position in the Bogside below and gunfire was exchanged nightly. Our houses were often caught in the crossfire. Like many people during that period, we had taken to sleeping at the back of our house with mattresses up against the windows, apparently to protect us from stray gunfire. We were calmly warned by our parents never to open the curtains and look out the upstairs bedroom windows at night, for fear of the army thinking there was a sniper at work. Usually, there was a barricade across the road, too, put in place to stop army Saracens being able to gain access to the factory. There was a pattern: the army would clear the barricades with their heavy machinery in the daytime, the air heavy with CS gas, only for protesters to rebuild them in the evening.

One night, as I climbed the stairs to bed, I could hear music outside. I couldn't resist. I peered out to see a barricade blocking the road with young men sitting cross-legged in big coats – and there was John Hume, with his mad curly hair, a bottle of wine in hand and in full voice leading the song, 'We shall overcome'. That song, so redolent of the civil rights struggle in 1960s America, was being sung by the man President Clinton would decades later describe as our Martin Luther King. This is my first memory of John Hume.

© Stanley Matchett/Mirrorpix

Stanley Matchett's photograph of Father Edward Daly as he cleared the way for those carrying the body of Jackie Duddy (17) was described by *The Sunday Times* as the 'iconic image of Bloody Sunday', 30 January 1972.

Journalists work frantically to get the 'Penny Marvel' – a limited edition of the *Belfast Telegraph* – to print after the bombing of the BT building in September 1976.

Peace People co-founders Máiread Corrigan (centre) and Betty Williams (right) attend a peace rally in Trafalgar Square, London, to protest against the escalating violence in Northern Ireland, 1976.

Photographer Alan Lewis captured the moment when Sean Downes (22) was shot and killed by a rubber bullet fired at close range by an RUC officer, 12 August 1984.

© Pacemaker Press International

Michael Stone opens fire on mourners at Milltown Cemetery, Belfast, 16 March 1988. Three people were killed and more than sixty were wounded in the attack.

The aftermath of the Ballygawley bus bomb, 20 August 1988. Eight soldiers were killed and twenty-eight wounded when the bus transporting them back to base was targeted by the IRA.

Security and forensics examine the scene after the IRA detonated a 200lb car bomb on Bangor's Main Street, 22 October 1992.

Paramedics remove a body from the scene of the Omagh bombing, 15 August 1998. Twenty-nine people and two unborn children were killed in the IRA attack.

Thousands of Portadown Orangemen involved in a tense standoff with security forces at Drumcree Bridge, July 1998.

Father Gary Donegan (centre background) escorts pupils of Holy Cross Girls' School through the lines of loyalist protestors, September 2001.

During her historic visit to Ireland, Queen Elizabeth II laid a wreath at the Garden of Remembrance, Dublin, 17 May 2011.

Journalist Lyra McKee (29) was shot and killed during rioting in the Creggan area of Derry, 18 April 2019. Artist Emma Blake painted this mural in Belfast city centre in her honour.

His eldest daughter, Therese, was a friend. We caught the bus to the local Catholic grammar school (now immortalised in *Derry Girls*) together and in the evenings we did the normal teenage things. I have fond memories of staging home-written plays in somebody's garage. John, and all that he did, faded into the background, except on occasions when we would be jolted back to reality because of a threat to the family. At one stage there was a fear that one of the children might be kidnapped.

It is a bleak, dark, low-cloud day in November 1993 and I (the reporter) am in another cemetery in Greysteel. Thousands of mourners walk in silence to the Star of the Sea church, the only sound the muffled impact of shoes on tarmac. A shell-shocked County Derry community is reeling from the attack on the Rising Sun bar. 'Trick or treat,' the gunmen had shouted; no bullet missed its target, it was said, as loyalist paramilitaries shot dead eight people who had been enjoying a quiet drink in a rural pub the Sunday before Halloween. Across Northern Ireland, people – Catholic and Protestant – held their collective breath, fearing what horror would come next.

Greysteel was considered the reprisal for the Shankill bombing a week before. We had been the first camera crew to arrive on the scene of that IRA atrocity at Frizzell's fish shop on the Shankill Road, where a bomb exploded without warning on a busy Saturday. Amid the chaos, I remember turning to my cameraman and saying, 'Please God let this be a tragic accident, a gas explosion, and not a planned attack.' Ten people were killed that day, with children among the dead. Later, Gerry Adams would carry the coffin of one of the IRA bombers, who had been killed when the bomb he had planted exploded prematurely.

At that time, John Hume, behind the scenes, was talking to Adams. Seeking an end to the bloodshed, he aimed to find a way to put all arms beyond use. It was controversial; little was known about their meetings. Hume was mercilessly attacked from the pages of some elements of the southern print media. The level of vitriol was shocking – and from the political class, including elements in his own party, there was little support. He was on his own. Then the Shankill happened, followed by Greysteel, with sectarian murders most days in between. It was bleak.

Ashen-faced, John Hume walked with his wife among the mourners at Greysteel, head bowed, devastated at what had happened. At one point – captured by an ITN cameraman, if memory serves – he broke down as a woman leaned in to speak to him. A relative of one of the dead of Greysteel, she told him that the family had prayed for him and his quest for peace around the coffin of their loved one. It was all too much. His tears flowed as Pat, his wife, held him. Six of the eight people who died at Greysteel were buried that day, laid to rest one after the other. Many of the mourners stopped to salute John and Pat; a random hand placed on John's bowed back; people whispering, 'Keep going, John. Keep doing what you are doing.'

The message from the pulpit was the same. John's friend Bishop Edward Daly, the white-handkerchief-carrying priest on Bloody Sunday, was there with clergy from many denominations. 'We will not be forced to hate,' he said, and placed the responsibility on the politicians to bring about an end to the violence. That must have been some comfort to the Hume family too. Later John would say that Greysteel was a turning point; his resolve, I imagine, strengthened by the people.

I am reminded, too, of something Mark Durkan, the former MP for Foyle and John Hume's right-hand man, said to me on the phone when I called to sympathise following John's death. He said John would often say, 'It's important not to react to the reaction, because you lose judgement and perspective.' Wise words.

How thankful we are that he didn't.

Roisín Duffy is a news editor with RTÉ in Dublin. In the past she has worked as a news reporter for BBC NI and BBC *Spotlight* and from the RTÉ Belfast bureau during the Troubles.

Rule 5: tell your story
Canary Wharf, London, 1996

Jilly Beattie

On 9 February 1996, my parents, at home in County Down, received a call from a crackling mobile phone as a newsflash about a bombing in London hit their TV screen. I made that call, reaching for calm; coated in dust and out of breath after running down twenty-three floors at 1 Canada Square, Canary Wharf.

Uninjured and finding my bearings, my first thought was to spare my parents a moment's anxiety. With the background noise of wailing, panic and sirens, I dialled the old familiar number in Donaghadee and my father picked up the phone immediately.

His words: 'Tell me.' Mine: 'There's been a bomb, Dad. I'm out, I'm fine.' His response remains on a loop in my mind all these years on, the tone of his voice, forced calm: 'Go further, Jilly. Go now, get away, take whoever is with you – remember the rules.'

The rules. The rules were simple, five of them etched into our brains since early childhood. They felt instinctive, but they weren't; somehow, without me even realising it, they had been placed there by the people who loved us most:

1. Take a moment.
2. Grab the nearest hand.
3. Get out.
4. Find the widest space possible.
5. Tell your story.

The rules were intended to keep us safe as youngsters, but the fifth rule took on great importance at that moment for a young journalist in the midst of a terror attack.

The crashing boom of the 3,000lb bomb reached us in Canary Wharf from a few hundred metres away in South Quay, where the IRA had detonated it at 6.59 p.m. Our usual rowdy 7 p.m. drinks exodus had been delayed by our editor, Bridget Rowe, and one of her tense newsroom detentions; this time a life-saving, limb-preserving detention. Unwittingly, we had been sitting in our *Sunday People* offices on the twenty-third floor of the tower for ninety minutes after the IRA had called in their bomb warning. As the clock ticked closer to 7 p.m., the reporters had no idea the IRA was ticking closer to murder and mayhem.

And then it happened. The boom was huge, lifting up the ceiling tiles inside the Canary Wharf tower and throwing dust and grit on to us and our desks. The whole building seemed to move and settle. The editors and news desk staff ran to the windows and put their faces against the glass inside cupped hands, looking out into the darkness. I shouted over to them: 'Eh ... that's a bomb ... the next one will suck you out with the windows. We should probably get out.'

A sea of faces turned to me as I lifted my contacts book and mobile phone, then someone shouted, 'Beattie's from Belfast, follow her.' Their confidence in me and in my experience of bomb attacks was misplaced, for this was the first I'd experienced. We had ninety-two flights of concrete steps over twenty-three floors to negotiate, hoping all the while that there wouldn't be another blast.

Finally, out in the night air, shocked and weeping strangers walked about in a daze, many borrowing my phone to call loved ones. I ran with some of the team to the apartment of our colleagues Karen Pasquali Jones and Sarah Gibbons, a ragbag crew of reporters feeling wary and unsafe, but determined to report this atrocity. With Karen and Sarah oblivious to the terror, and travelling on a train somewhere in Scotland, we negotiated our way into their apartment and set up a makeshift office. We closed the blinds and put the settees and mattresses in front of the windows, convinced another bomb was coming. It didn't come.

The IRA planted their device in South Quay, but the world described it as the Canary Wharf bomb. It ripped the heart out of the East London docklands business and banking sector, everyone quoting the damage as costing £150 million. The price was much higher than that. The price was two lives stolen, about 150 people injured, some permanently, and many more haunted by fear for years to come.

The Friday night bomb was followed by early starts on Saturday for journalists on our Sunday paper, each of us tasked with finding people to talk. We knew that people were missing, but we'd no idea two men lay dead. Newsagent Inan Bashir, aged twenty-nine, and his assistant, John Jeffries, aged thirty-one, were literally blown to pieces, hurled through two walls by the bomb, which had been left outside their premises. The blast left a crater 32 feet across and 10 feet deep, and not a scrap of the lorry driven by County Armagh man James McArdle, remained inside the crater, with pieces of it found as far as 300 yards away.

As soon as Canada Square was reopened, every staff reporter, every freelancer and every editor landed back into the office and hit the phones, trying to find out who had been affected. Each of us took a different section of the London phone book and worked methodically through every borough of London and beyond. It was our chief reporter, Ruki Sayid, heavily pregnant and no doubt exhausted, who spoke to John W. Jeffries. Recently widowed, he was still waiting for his son John to come home from his job as a newsagent in South Quay. He hadn't heard from John or his friend Inan, and he was worried because he'd heard there'd been 'an incident' at the Docklands.

Phones were quietly clicked back on to their cradles and our huge office fell silent. We all looked to our chief reporter as she talked to Mr Jeffries with such gentleness and reassurance, tears dropping on to her desk. We didn't know then that John and Inan were dead, but we understood that if they weren't dead, they were likely trapped.

The police were given Mr Jeffries' details and as this lovely old gent was waiting for his lad to come home, officers had to call at his door and tell him he was now alone in the world. The image of Ruki sitting at her desk on that call stays with me to this day.

Now we know there was confusion as to where IRA killer James McArdle had planted his deadly device. He'd left it in South Quay but the bomb warning specifically mentioned Canary Wharf. Instead of journalists and bankers being blown up, the IRA murdered two pals, two newsagents.

Inan, who was described as a 'workaholic', and John had been working late to get ready for the weekend news shift ahead – and instead they became the subject of the news, the most innocent of victims.

There was no second bomb. Canary Wharf and the surrounding area recovered; businesses rebuilt at an astonishing rate, with insurance contracts triggered and recovery planned. But there has been no recovery for the families of the murdered men or those injured or maimed that night.

James McArdle was found guilty on 24 June 1998 of conspiracy to cause an explosion in London's Docklands. The huge lorry-bomb McArdle parked at South Quay brought an end to the first IRA ceasefire in 1996. The jury at Woolwich Crown Court were told by Mr John Bevan QC, prosecuting, that it was 'little short of a miracle' that more people had not been killed or injured in the atrocity because inadequate and misleading warnings had been given by the IRA.

McArdle, aged twenty-nine, from Crossmaglen, admitted driving the lorry but told the jury: 'I had no idea [it] contained explosives.' He claimed he was just an 'innocent dupe' who had been used by an IRA godfather he referred to only as 'The Boss'. He refused to identify the man in court, saying that it would put his family at risk. There could be little sympathy for him two years after the devastation delivered to two families in particular, who had lost loved ones and their family's livelihood, and the risk he posed to thousands of people in the Docklands. He was jailed for twenty-five years.*

My good fortune in surviving the attack that night in 1996 allowed me to tell the story of the IRA evil visited on my adopted home of London at the time, and I have told my story. For those deeply affected by their losses, there is no happy ending.

Shortly after the bomb, Inan's father suffered a fatal heart attack and his mother slipped into a nervous collapse from which she would not recover. And although they have rebuilt the family business as a deli, selling fine food to the Docklands workers, no one can return to them what they lost; no one can heal their hearts or change their history.

All I could do was play my part in telling their story, the story of good versus evil, the story of the unconscionable crime that changed their world, and remember them as the years go on. The Jeffries and Bashir families may feel the world has moved on, but some of us remember them still and do what we can to honour their pain.

Rule 5: tell your story. I was lucky to be able to.

Jilly Beattie has been a journalist for almost thirty years, specialising in investigations and news features. She trained at the *Walsall Observer* in 1992 and was headhunted by Mirror Group Newspapers, now Reach Plc, two years later.

---

* James McArdle was released after two years under the terms of the Belfast Good Friday Agreement.

'All their songs are sad'
Donegal, 1996

Colin Randall

For the great Gaels of Ireland
Are the men that God made mad,
For all their wars are merry,
And all their songs are sad.

If only. No conflict, and certainly not the Troubles, is truly merry, whatever romantic thoughts G.K. Chesterton entertained when composing this poem, 'The Ballad of the White Horse'. Since the suggestion of insanity as a national trait is best ignored, that leaves us the songs.

My love affair with Irish music and folk music generally has sometimes been described as sad. But from indisputably mournful laments to the infectious vigour of diddly-dee, that music has given me six decades of real joy.

Covering events on both sides of the border for all but the first few years of the 'irregular war' could be challenging, but there was some time to mix work and pleasure on trips I made across the Irish Sea from London for the Press Association and later the *Daily Telegraph*. Occasionally, my worlds of journalism and music would collide. As well as being a reporter, I was the *Telegraph*'s folk bloke.

At the moment the IRA bombed South Quay in London's Docklands, I was not in the *Telegraph*'s offices situated there but on a press junket in Donegal, enjoying a pint of Guinness. I had just interviewed Mairéad Ní Mhaonaigh, singer and fiddler with the traditional band, Altan, which she had formed with her Belfast-born husband, Frankie Kennedy.

Frankie was a richly talented musician and a lovely, thoughtful man with whom I had profound discussions about the Troubles. He was just thirty-eight when he died from cancer three weeks after the start of the seventeen-month ceasefire that ended with the bombing in February 1996. Though no apologist for terrorism, he would say one certainty was that whenever IRA atrocities aroused disgust in the nationalist community, the British authorities could invariably be trusted to do something crass or unjust to refuel the cause of violence.

Talking about a man we both missed was remarkably easy for Mairéad and I that evening in Donegal, and she showed plenty of optimism for the future. But then the news from London cast a cloud over the gathering.

'I remember it well,' I wrote years later for my music site, Salut! Live. 'One of the band came over and asked, "Did you know there's been a bomb at your offices in London? There's a lot of walking wounded."' [In fact, two men – a newsagent and his employee – were killed.]

Instead of flying home next morning with the rest of the press pack, I was begging a lift to Stroke City to report on the broken ceasefire. It was from Derry/Londonderry that I had previously reported modest beginnings of peace, prompting one cynical colleague to say any subsequent hole in the road caused by a bomb should be named Randall Crater.

Over pints and televised football, I talked for a couple of hours with another Frank – an accomplished and charismatic musician and producer – about music, football and politics. Frank Gallagher is an Everton fan, as Frankie Kennedy had been, and they may have been on the box that night. But the conversation was dominated by his informed analysis of the ominous development. I distinctly recall this man of peace, with ears close the ground, sharing thoughts that helped me understand the background to the IRA's return to terror.

Fast-forward to 2020; it came as no surprise to hear Frank Gallagher was so respected by John Hume's family that he was asked to be the musical director for the former SDLP leader's funeral.

Looking back, I am surprised at how often I was able to fit musical interludes into visits to Ireland. Far from being a distraction, they produced friendships and experiences that enriched my journalism.

I learned how Irish music and dance could bridge the Protestant–Catholic divide. The BBC's Wendy Austin told me about Protestants like her who had enrolled children in Irish dance classes – the colourful costumes bought in Andersonstown. Other parents cooperated and it made a pleasantly off-beat piece for the *Telegraph*. A great friend, the late Neil Johnston of the *Belfast Telegraph*, was a Protestant from Omagh who presented an excellent BBC Radio Ulster series, cleverly entitled *The Wrong Note*, that chronicled the Irish music exploits of other Protestants.

Over the years, I saw Mary Black, Sharon Shannon, the Dubliners, the Chieftains, Ron Kavana and many more during these trips, without ever feeling I was compromising my reporting obligations.

One episode, however, sticks as clearly in the mind as the Donegal jolly that turned sour. It had nothing, at first, to do with music.

I had taken a keen journalistic interest in the IRA's murder of Tom Oliver, a forty-three-year-old farmer and father of seven from the Cooley peninsula, just over the border near Dundalk, in 1991. He was tortured and killed over allegations that he had been a police informer. It eventually became clear that he had probably been falsely accused, perhaps framed to cover the tracks of a double agent whose IRA unit murdered him. Whatever the full truth, it was a squalid act of supposed revolutionary justice, meted out without the least concern for human rights, ordinary decency or due process.

Some time later, I sat in a small London hotel interviewing Christy Moore. I knew there would be no room in my story for the wretched tale of Tom Oliver but mentioned him anyway. I have known Christy since the late 1960s, when he was a brilliant, hell-raising presence at English folk clubs, including ones run by me. Our exchanges have always been frank, occasionally prickly. But I have warmly praised his work – yes, the *Telegraph* allowed that – and expressed particular admiration for the way his songwriting mellowed in tandem with the peace process. 'You've written songs about British sins,' I said. 'Why not one about Tom Oliver?' Christy's answer came quick as a flash: 'Write it with me,' he said.

I am no songwriter and never did, of course. But some years after that, in 2001, the name of Tom Oliver came up again, in an interview with the Irish magazine *Hot Press*. Christy was describing his disenchantment with a cause he once found easy to justify: 'Thinking of how Tom Oliver was killed and how a kitchen porter was used in a proxy bombing, I find I've reached a point in my life where I can't fucking take it any more,' he said. 'After Enniskillen, and now, I find I no longer can support the armed struggle … it's an armed struggle in which too many little people are blown away.'

I do not suggest anything I said first made Christy think about a despicable IRA crime. But I know from experience how he remembers the detail of conversation and would feel some satisfaction if my combined interest in Irish affairs and Irish music somehow touched a nerve.

A sad song it would have been for sure. But no, Mr Chesterton, the war that brought Tom Oliver's death was far from merry.

Colin Randall writes for the *National* (UAE). He was chief reporter, executive news editor and Paris correspondent for the *Daily Telegraph* and previously worked for the Press Association and local newspapers.

Persistence mixed with luck
London, 1996

Fearghal McKinney

I worked as a journalist through some of the worst days of violence and destruction here, and then watched the slow change from pandemonium to politics, and the eventual arrival at a sort of peace. I like to think I had a ringside seat in history, even if the work often felt like trying to make order out of chaos – and there was plenty of that. The specifics would obviously change – the bombs and the bullets coming from different directions in different locations – but what was common was the heartache and despair.

From the Enniskillen bomb in 1987, not long after the start of my career, through events too numerous to mention, hundreds of people's lives changed forever. And it was my job to reflect their story and, where possible, to challenge those responsible. This was predictable, but the heat intensified after the Enniskillen bomb, and it led to a ramping-up on all sides. Hardened hearts led to almost daily violence and murder.

It was against this backdrop that my stint with Downtown Radio began. There was a requirement for speed and accuracy in this working environment – the latest atrocity would simply take the place of the previous one in the half-hourly bulletins. It was a shocking environment to live in and work in. There was little time for debate on transparency: the time discipline of the medium dictated that most of the focus was on our brief broadcasts, which were valued across the community.

Such was the nature and scale of violence that there is scarcely a town or village that I don't recognise principally from its churches or chapels that sit beside the graveyards. Mourners stood beside many graves, caught for a moment in the public eye but trapped forever in their own grief. In quieter times, I sometimes vividly remember the horror of it all – for example, dreading going to a house in Belfast where a mother had only just been told that she had lost her son to terrorists. As soon as I arrived I wanted to drive away. Looking at the living room window, I knew the extent of grief that lay behind those curtains. But that was sometimes how swift we had to be, and I value that people trusted me to tell their story.

There's no black without white and vice versa, and slowly, very slowly, the focus changed to a political one. We, as a press corps, had front-row seats in this process, and our job was to reflect, to challenge and to test. We travelled north, south, east and west as events and dynamics took us to negotiations, at home and away, before the process brought a type of peace and a political settlement.

We had to be tenacious – I never liked taking no for an answer – and so was persistent in trying to get that interview. Once – and I love this story – John Hume and I were staying at the same hotel in Washington. I arrived back from a meeting to be told excitedly by the doorman that John Hume was in the restaurant having dinner. (Tip for anyone starting out in journalism – always talk to the door staff.) Feeling exhausted, I debated going straight to bed but I decided to go and say hello. Sometime later, the both of us are in the bar next door. John is surrounded by customers, and at one point he sang the lovely 'Danny Boy'. At the end of the night, he handed me a note and said, 'Give this man a ring for the interview you're after.' I duly followed his advice and by the next afternoon I was sitting down for an exclusive interview with the Speaker of the House of Representatives, Tom Foley, in his office in Capitol Hill. This was during the prolonged talks ahead of the Good Friday Agreement and his message was that there would be no blank cheque coming from America.

Persistence usually paid off but sometimes it was mixed with luck. The Aldwych bus bombing happened on 18 February 1996, injuring eight and killing one (the bomber, who died when the improvised explosive device he was carrying detonated prematurely in London's West End). This happened some days after the London Docklands bombing, which had brought the IRA ceasefire to an end. I was sent to London by UTV some days later to follow up on the bomb story and to find out the views of Irish people in London. I flew over to meet our ITN crew at Westminster with the plan that we would then make our way to Kilburn. I had thought we'd travel by tube but the ITN crew's usual mode of transport was the black taxi, so I put my hand out and a driver duly pulled in.

We had all the camera equipment with us and, as we drove, the driver asked us what we were filming. I explained I was from a Belfast-based TV station, following up on the Aldwych bomb. In his strong London accent he said, 'Bloody bomb! I was only driving behind the bloody thing when it went off!' Of course our jaws dropped and we didn't believe him until he tossed us a copy of the *Daily Express* with his picture in it, and his story. He explained he wouldn't be deterred by violence: because his vehicle had been damaged, he had hired out a new taxi and was back on the road.

Well, I couldn't believe it – there are around twenty thousand black taxis operating in London – and, of course, I asked him for an interview. He agreed and we filmed through the passenger door. A real scoop from our point of view – an eyewitness account of what had happened and of course his resilient perspective. What good luck for me – and he made his own luck by keeping the taxi meter running the entire time.

This was not this man's only connection with Belfast – he explained to me on the journey that, as part of his business, he'd had a bulletproof black taxi that wealthy individuals who needed extra security used to get around London. When he'd decided that he didn't need that taxi any more, he wanted to sell it. Through a circuitous route, he'd eventually got in touch with Sinn Féin. As he told it to me, that was the same black taxi that had ferried Gerry Adams about in Belfast for many years.

Following a lengthy newspaper, radio and television career, Fearghal McKinney became an MLA in the Northern Ireland Assembly. He is now head of the British Heart Foundation Northern Ireland.

'I love you ...' 'Love you right back.'
Aghagallon, Lurgan, 1996

David Blevins

'I love you both,' Michael McGoldrick said to his parents. 'Love you right back,' they replied. Those were the last words they ever spoke to him. Michael Snr and Bridie had just attended his graduation ceremony at Queen's University, Belfast. The thirty-one-year-old mature student had gained a degree in English and Politics.

Their son doted on his seven-year-old daughter, Emma. He and his wife, Sadie, were looking forward to the birth of their second child. Michael had his heart set on becoming a teacher and had funded his way through his studies by taking a part-time job as a taxi driver.

It was July 1996, the height of the loyalist marching season, and the news in Northern Ireland was dominated by one place – Drumcree. For the second consecutive year, the Orange Order was engaged in a stand-off with police over the re-routing of a march past Catholic homes in Portadown.

'We will run your report on last night's disorder, then cross to you live for the breaking news,' said the news editor in London. I had just joined Sky News, but any nervousness about my first live broadcast was soon overshadowed by the horror of the story on the wires. Reports were coming in of a murder in County Armagh, about twelve miles from Drumcree: a taxi driver had been found shot dead in his cab at Aghagallon, near Lurgan.

Michael and Bridie, who had gone to Warrenpoint for a short break after the graduation, were watching the news in their caravan that Monday morning. 'A taxi driver?' They initially dismissed it. 'He was thirty-one years old and is understood to have recently graduated,' added the newsreader. Time appeared to stop as the awful reality dawned. Their only son was dead, his hopes and dreams abruptly ended by a brutal act of terrorism. Michael stepped out of the caravan for some fresh air but his legs buckled with grief and he found himself hammering his fists off the ground in despair.

Their son had picked up a fare from a loyalist bar. He was found on a lonely road, slumped over the steering wheel, shot twice in the back of the head. Others would die that month in the tension sparked by the Drumcree march, but the McGoldricks were determined to ensure it would not be in their name. They were in grief, still attempting to process the futility of it all, when they welcomed us into their home in Lurgan.

'To those who have done this, I forgive you,' Michael said. His words hung in the air for a moment, an almost incomprehensible act of grace. Earlier, he had told reporters gathered for Michael's funeral that 'the two sides in this country need to bury their pride with my son'. Seated hand in hand, comforting one another, Michael and Bridie McGoldrick were quietly defusing tension. Their forgiveness saved countless lives that summer.

Police blamed the murder on the rogue mid-Ulster unit of the Ulster Volunteer Force, under the command of Billy Wright in Portadown. The UVF's Belfast leadership ordered the unit to disband for breaching the ceasefire and gave Wright hours to leave Northern Ireland.

I did not recognise the number calling my mobile phone that Friday evening but I knew the voice when I answered it. Having grown up and started my career in the 'murder triangle' around Portadown, I had encountered Billy Wright before. He wanted to make a statement on camera. Days earlier, I had sat with Michael McGoldrick's grieving parents. Now, I found myself face to face with the man suspected of ordering his murder. The deadline set by the UVF had already expired. Every time a car drove into the cul-de-sac, I feared shots would be fired through the window. He denied involvement in the murder, dismissed the expulsion order, looked me in the eye and said, 'I am not afraid to die.'

Eighteen months later, Billy Wright was dead, murdered by a republican gunman while on remand in the Maze prison. Expelled from the UVF, he had gone on to establish the Loyalist Volunteer Force, a breakaway terror group opposed to the peace process.

In 2003, Clifford McKeown from Craigavon, County Armagh, was convicted of murdering Michael McGoldrick. The court heard he had confessed to a journalist that the fatal shooting of the taxi driver had been a 'birthday present' for Billy Wright.

Bridie McGoldrick later revealed that she and her husband had been so overcome with grief at the loss of their son, they had made a suicide pact. 'We decided to take our own lives,' she said. 'I had a lot of medication in the house because of my arthritis and we decided to take all the tablets.' Something 'or someone' made them think twice, she explained. Suddenly, it felt like they were being given a reason to keep living.

'Michael said to me, our own child does not need us any longer but thousands of other children do and that is when we started the charity,' she recalled. United Christian Aid, the humanitarian aid project founded in their son's memory, has fed and clothed thousands in Romania and Moldova. The charity sponsors one village at a time for two years, repairing homes and teaching residents how to grow crops, before moving on to the next one. The couple devoted their lives to those in greater need, Bridie gathering donations at home, Michael travelling to Eastern Europe and back every eight weeks.

Bridie says she lives for the charity and for her granddaughter, Emma, and grandson, Andrew, 'the image of his father'. It was during one of his countless mercy missions to Moldova that her husband, Michael, fell ill and tragically died from septicaemia. When he rang his wife from his hospital bed, she never imagined it would be their last conversation, but it ended with four very poignant words.

'I love you very much,' he said. 'Love you right back,' she replied.

David Blevins is the Senior Ireland Correspondent for Sky News. He received the European Journalism Institute's Freedom of the Press Award in 2019 for his reporting from Ireland/Northern Ireland.

Lives left in despair by political failure
Drumcree, 1998

Mark Hennessy

Wearing a Glasgow Rangers McEwan's jersey, the youth stood on a mound of earth that had been left by British Army engineers as he hurled abuse at the RUC officers on the other side of the razor wire down the hill from Drumcree church.

'My father and grandfather died for you bastards. Would you catch yourself on?' he roared, as the stone in his hand left at speed and flew towards the police lines. Moments later, a visored officer winced.

In reply, a baton round was fired. The youth was just yards away. It struck him in the chest. In an instant, he bent in two, holding for a fraction of a second in the air before dropping with a vicious thud on to the muddied ground.

This was Drumcree 1998, the year of the Quinns – when brothers Richard (aged eleven), Mark (aged ten) and Jason (aged nine) died after a petrol bomb was thrown into their terraced house in Ballymoney, County Antrim.

The baton round that took down the youth was nothing unusual that year – the RUC fired scores, even hundreds during one night of confrontation that drifted into the early hours. The unusual bit came afterwards. Within an hour, perhaps less, a Range Rover appeared through a gate up the hill, to the left of the Church of the Ascension, the starting point for Orange marches when Orange marches were allowed. It slowly weaved its way down the field, carefully avoiding tents and the detritus left by days of tented inhabitation by hundreds of, mostly, men, angered that Garvaghy Road was blocked to the march.

Once at the bottom, near the trench and the razor wire, a man wearing a Pringle golf sweater emerged, while his wife, in a pleated tweed skirt, moved to open the boot. Orders were issued, and some of the youth's friends, or fellow protesters at least, lifted him none too carefully into the back of the Range Rover.

From there, it left, moving equally carefully up the field to the road. Why had it come? Other routes to help could have been found, but this youth was destined for no hospital. Instead he was taken by the middle-class, middle-aged couple to be treated privately by a supportive doctor somewhere in Northern Ireland, since he would have faced police questions if he had been admitted to a local hospital. Having spent days at the church, it was a salutary lesson for a reporter that a caste system operated throughout Portadown – that some people were useful fodder for the political ambitions of others, but nothing more.

In no other circumstance would the Pringle-wearing man and his tweed-dressed wife have entertained the company of the youth. Indeed they would have been just as likely to call the police about him as offer him help in any other place and time. A caste system existed in Portadown, but it was one magnified by the press coverage. The images of the Housing Executive houses on the left-hand side of Garvaghy Road filled TV screens night after night. The middle-class, privately-owned houses on the other side did not. Nor was there much evidence that those who lived in those houses much heeded the rallying calls of the Garvaghy Road Residents' Coalition spokesman, Breandán Mac Cionnaith.

The homes on the left-hand side provided shelter for journalists, often on the floor, but everyone was grateful. In the early hours one night, one of the sons of the house we stayed in came home late, whispering to us as he made for the stairs, 'Don't answer the phone in the morning.' By then, morning was just an hour away. When morning came, the telephone rang incessantly. It was the son's boss. 'I can't get beyond Water Street, the RUC has it blocked off,' he told his employer. Chuckling, he went back to bed, believing that he had bought a day in bed. Minutes later, the phone rang again. It was his employer. 'I'm heading down to Water Street. I have organised with the police that they will let you through,' he could be heard loudly telling the son. Putting the phone down, the son quietly cursed, before heading upstairs to put on clothes and unwillingly leave.

Two nights later, Ian Paisley arrived at Drumcree. An elderly man pushed his colleagues through the gates of the parochial hall as a sole television light marked the progress of the Democratic Unionist Party leader. 'Cheer him loudly. Give him all the support you can. He is our only hope in this our time of need,' he declared, craning his neck to get a view of Paisley standing between the stone gates and a blue tarpaulin-covered burger stand.

Paisley did as Paisley did so often. 'There are certain people who think that Ulstermen and women are just going to lie down and surrender. These people have another thing coming. We are not just in this matter to achieve some hollow victory,' he thundered.

The press who were present recorded his words, though few journalists were there because it was unsafe to be near the church some nights when darkness fell and old bitterness towards us came once again to the fore. Paisley fed the hatred of the press, particularly the BBC. The killings of the Quinn children had been 'an effort by our enemies to get a way to beat the Orange Order and discredit them'. The coverage of the killings of the children by the press, including the BBC, was part of that effort to discredit the Orange Order. This was Trump before Trump was known much beyond New York, and no more truthful.

The Paisley hagiography came later. The ascension to political power; the recrafting of his political image; the role played in that – sometimes unwittingly, sometimes not – by the press, pleased that there was a new story to tell.

Days later, I entered a small pub filled with friends in Cork. Few ever spoke to me about the job. It was politics – boring. But they did that night. They wanted to know everything about Drumcree, about being close to Paisley, about the baton rounds. But the language they used was that of those who wanted, briefly, to understand the curious exhibit, the foreign, the strange. Two decades on and more, there is little more understanding on the island, despite the language we speak of reconciliation.

Drumcree and Portadown are still as foreign as they were before, if not more so. Back then, they were, at least, briefly the subject of our eyes, both those of the public and of the press. But they were quickly forgotten, just as they were forgotten by Paisley and by those on the other side who regarded the Orange Order and Garvaghy Road as useful tools in bigger, more self-centred fights.

Today, a new generation of youths has entered on to Northern Ireland's streets, spurred by poverty, deprivation, unemployment and the lack of hope just as much, if not more, than thoughts of the Northern Ireland Protocol. The Good Friday Agreement has brought much, but local politicians of all hues have failed to do much, if anything, for the man who wore a Rangers jersey at the razor wire in 1998.

It's possible that he got a job, married well, had children and lives happily, but the odds are against. McEwan's no longer sponsor the Rangers jersey. Unibet do. From alcohol to online betting, the new disease. Nor have local politicians done much for the young man who lived back then on the left-hand side of the Garvaghy Road heading towards Water Street. Again, it may have turned out well. I hope so, but I doubt it.

We in the press have concentrated too much on the words of those politicians – often an endless recitation of old lies – rather than focusing as often as we should on the lives left in despair by political failure. The lives of those on Garvaghy Road, in Tiger's Bay or in deprived estates in Lurgan are as much of a mystery to those who stood in a bar in a rural Cork town as they ever were.

It is not the job of reporters to change the world. It is not even within our power, were we of a mind; but, too often, we have contented ourselves with the Stormont press conference, saying old things in old ways, for no great effect.

Partly because of our failings, those lives are mostly a mystery to those in power in Stormont, London, or Dublin, and they remain a mystery, too, to middle-aged comfortable men wearing Pringle sweaters, thinking of golf.

Mark Hennessy is news editor at the *Irish Times*.

Silence like no other
Omagh, 1998

Mark McFadden

It's the silence. It's always been the silence that hits me; the silence that would fall after each immense human tragedy. A silence like no other I have experienced: a dark, heavy, cloaking quiet that would fall like black velvet across the streets and houses. It almost defied speech, as if the wretched deeds visited upon one human being by another were incapable of description, beyond the capture of words and pictures.

Some silences stay with me; I can feel them decades later. I vividly recall standing in my children's bedroom in August 1998 – they were just four and two – and looking at them in the dull glow of a nightlight. I was crying. But silently. In my head I was thinking, they are safe and warm, but elsewhere other little kids have been stolen from this earth. Why?

Thirty-five miles from my home, a huge car bomb had blasted Omagh's main shopping street, killing twenty-nine people, maiming many more, and wounding hundreds. The dead included so many children.

I had spent the evening at a council sports centre in Omagh. It had been hastily designated as a control point for civic leadership. The scale of the explosion and the extraordinary numbers of casualties meant a chaotic and evolving situation. It was difficult for the police and the hospitals to know who had been caught in the blast. The sports centre was a place where anxious families could come and get information on missing loved ones.

Dozens of parents and grandparents were there, with grown-up daughters and sons, all stilled by the enormity of what had transformed an unremarkable sunny Saturday afternoon into the greatest atrocity of the Troubles in Northern Ireland. There were huge boards with long lists pinned up, giving the names of those who had been identified and the hospitals to which they had been transferred.

Despite the palpable sense of fear in that building, despite the desperate need for knowledge and solace, the silence remained almost total. It was broken only by the occasional appearance of an official holding a clipboard who would emerge from one of many side rooms and call out a name. A person or maybe a small family group would stand up with enquiring and hopeful looks on their faces. So many relatives went into those small rooms only to reappear broken, bowed down by the knowledge that their flesh and blood had been reduced to just that: flesh and blood.

In the hours that followed, it became clear that among the dead was a group of children who had travelled from Buncrana, a small town in County Donegal. It is a place I know intimately, a place I have visited throughout my life to walk the golden shores of Lough Swilly, to enjoy the easy and open warmth of its people. But the Omagh bomb had claimed three children from Buncrana and two young Spanish visitors who had been staying with host families. Five kids from one small community. I spent the next few days reporting from Buncrana. A place that had been a refuge throughout my life was now thrown into the darkness that blinded Northern Ireland.

Once again, it is a silence that dominates my memory. It was well past midnight on an August night without wind when the bodies of the children were brought to Buncrana. The streets were lined with thousands of people. Candles flickered. Some held flowers. But this bustling town had been overwhelmed. The few that spoke did so in hushed voices and whispers.

The town's main street affords a view of the hills to the south and the road from the border. In the early hours of the morning these hills show almost no illumination, but in the velvet silence that draped over us in Buncrana, we watched a gleaming trickle become a river of light. It was a convoy of hearses bringing the broken little bodies to Buncrana, accompanied by fifty or more other cars.

The thousands that stood in the town centre watched the trail of lights slowly, gently progress into Buncrana. Five innocent children that had been stolen by a moment of deafening noise and rage were being brought home to an air of stillness and serenity and dignity.

That silence left its mark on me. The following night, when I had finally returned home after days on the road, I stood in my children's bedroom. They were tiny innocent children, just like the children who had died in Omagh. As I stood by their beds and listened to their peaceful and regular breathing, I kissed them and offered a silent prayer.

Mark McFadden is a senior news correspondent with UTV and an award-winning documentary maker.

The impact of GCHQ's chokehold on the investigation into the Omagh bombing
Omagh, 1998

John Ware

My abiding memory of arriving at Belfast docks in 1974 was the colour black: black voids in bombed-out buildings, streets glossed black by rain, black capes worn by policemen with black peaked caps, nuzzling black snub-nosed Second World War sub-machine guns, pitch-black nights.

Along with a handful of reporters, I spent the first few months of my Belfast posting in the Europa Hotel. So visceral was the enmity, so tribal the loyalties, so unresolved the history that we all agreed the conflict could endure for a hundred years.

Then came the Good Friday Agreement in 1998, because everyone had had enough. Or so it was thought.

The Omagh bombing four months later was the worst single atrocity of the entire conflict, a throwback to the IRA's big car bombs of the 1970s – indiscriminate, terrifying, patches of crimson-stained rubble, burnt and torn lumps of flesh, water cascading from burst mains, mutilated souls still clinging to life, and the dead laid out in side streets.

Five hundred pounds of explosives in the high street of this bustling market town packed with shoppers left 29 people – including children and 2 unborn babies – dead, and 250 injured. An emerging dissident group pathologically opposed to the peace agreement and calling themselves the Real IRA claimed responsibility. They apologised for the deaths but blamed the police for not clearing the town centre, ignoring the fact that they'd given a misleading warning about where they'd parked their bomb car.

The desolation of the victims' relatives told through the intimacy of their loss was unbearable. It was a sparkling August day when eight-year-old Oran Doherty skipped out of his house in Buncrana to catch a bus to Omagh with his cousin and friends for a day out, his mother, Bernie, waving him goodbye. The next time she saw her son was in a morgue. 'I was just so cold,' she told me. 'I just remember his eyes wide open as if he was looking up, and whatever way his lip was, to me he was crying when he died, you know, whatever way his wee lip was, his bottom lip, to me it looked as if he was crying.'

I remember, too, Kevin Skelton telling me how, coming home to an empty house after seeing his wife, Philomena, in the morgue, he felt as though life had been sucked out of him. 'It's an awful thing to walk into your home for the first time and hear the clocks ticking. I have lost the best thing that ever happened to me. She never can be replaced and that's something I'm going to just have to live with.'

Grief was matched by official steely resolve. British and Irish prime ministers and the RUC chief constable solemnly pledged to leave no stone unturned, no effort spared to bring the culprits to justice. By the spring of 2000, as the second anniversary approached, there was still no justice. The investigation was stalled.

I asked the BBC: could we try to find out what happened to those stones that Messrs Blair, Ahern and Flanagan had spoken so eloquently about? Research on both sides of the border eventually led us to identify the prime suspects who'd been in the car carrying the bomb and in the scout car driving ahead to check the route from Castleblayney, County Monaghan, crossing the border at Aughnacloy, and on to Omagh.

The RUC had worked out that the bombers must have used mobile phones. Weeks of trawling through 6.4 million phone records had given detectives the numbers of those phones used by the occupants of the bomb and scout cars to communicate en route to Omagh. 'Cell site' analysis plotted the movement of the cell phones by reference to the location of the nearest phone mast. By November 1998 – three months after the bombing – the analysis identified twenty-two people active in the planning and execution of Omagh and four other linked bombings.

However, whilst 'cell site' analysis identified the mobile phone numbers, it didn't necessarily prove that their registered owners had also used the phones during the bomb run. On the other hand, the onus was on the owners to say who they'd lent their phones to if they hadn't been in Omagh that day. So I confronted them at their homes along the border, which resulted in their lawyers threatening to sue for defamation – but no writs ever arrived. Today, not one of the prime suspects has been convicted. Why? That question still deserves an answer. Omagh wasn't just the conflict's biggest single loss of life, it was also the biggest single failure of the criminal justice system.

As Omagh's tenth anniversary approached, I began a second *Panorama* investigation and learned that the answer seemed likely to lie in the strict protocols governing intelligence-sharing arrangements at the time.

A radical rethink in 1980 of the government's counter-insurgency strategy had led to the prioritising of intelligence-gathering over exploiting intelligence to lock up perpetrators. To be sure, intelligence-led policing saved many lives. But it also gave Special Branch a veto over who the CID should – and should not – arrest. Although many perpetrators were brought to justice, the priority was saving lives by preserving both the identity of Branch's proliferating network of informers and the rapid improvement in eavesdropping technology. 'Men's lives and delicate technical sources are at stake,' said the then chief constable Jack Hermon. In Omagh, this approach left the CID investigating the massacre completely blindsided.

Omagh was the latest in a series of reckless cross-border attacks by the Real IRA. I was told that, unknown to the CID, Special Branch had identified the key operatives in those attacks thanks to a huge telephone interception operation assisted by GCHQ, the government organisation that monitors communications.

On the day of the Omagh bombing, unknown to the CID, not only had GCHQ identified the phone numbers that detectives would spend weeks hunting for, it had also intercepted exchanges between the bombers. Yet this priceless intelligence was not shared with the CID, even though their task was to identify and charge the perpetrators. Why these precious stones were unturned has never been satisfactorily explained by any British government, even though the explanation may provide the answer to why the Omagh bombers got away with mass murder.

Special Branch was GCHQ's customer, and had Branch immediately shared GCHQ's intercept 'product' with detectives on both sides of the border, there could have been early arrests with charges to follow. Had detectives hit the homes of the registered owners within the 'golden hours' – that critical period immediately after a crime when forensic and other evidential opportunities are optimum – the phones might have been recovered and their owners would have been in cells, having to explain why they'd gone to Omagh, or to whom they'd lent their phones.

Reliable sources in a position to know told me that, based on custom and practice, in 1998 the response from GCHQ to a request from Special Branch to disseminate the contents of an intercept and its telephone number would have been a firm 'no'. There was a strict firewall, which meant that CID officers were never informed when intelligence was derived from an intercept in order to prevent information about methodology and technology from seeping into the evidential chain vulnerable to pre-trial legal disclosure. 'That was the chokehold,' explained Ray White, the former RUC/PSNI assistant chief constable in charge of both Special Branch and CID.

Within thirty-six hours of transmission of the *Panorama* programme, the prime minister, Gordon Brown, ordered the Intelligence Services

Commissioner Sir Peter Gibson to investigate. Gibson's terms of reference were to conduct a 'review of intercepted intelligence material available to the security and intelligence agencies in relation to the Omagh bombing and how it was shared'. Naturally, we assumed the phrase 'how it was shared' meant Gibson would investigate *Panorama*'s central question: what possible public interest had been served by GCHQ's 'chokehold' preventing maximum exploitation of its intercept intelligence, which had potentially sabotaged the Omagh police investigation?

We were wrong. Gibson addressed only whether the fact that the bombers' phones were being monitored meant the bombing could have been prevented. It could not, he concluded. When Gibson's report was published it became clear he had deliberately avoided investigating whether and to what extent the intercept intelligence had been shared.

The Northern Ireland Affairs Committee (NIAC) conducted its own investigation into Gibson's report, taking evidence from Gibson himself. He told the MPs that, if they wanted to know why 'any intercept material' shared between GCHQ and Special Branch hadn't been shared with the CID, they'd 'have to ask Special Branch'.

However, in his evidence, PSNI Assistant Commissioner Drew Harris pretty much confirmed that the answer to this question was the one I'd been given, namely GCHQ's 'chokehold'. Asked if GCHQ's 'explicit permission' would have been required for Branch to share its intercept intelligence with their CID colleagues, and whether this protocol 'could have affected the investigation', Harris replied, '*That is correct.* The information in effect is shared by computer monitor. Some of it would have been printed off, but only for a short time, and then would have been returned to GCHQ. In effect, the RUC did not actually own that information. It was lent to them and to use it in any form beyond a very tight group would have required permission and in a form of words to be agreed between either RUC headquarters in terms of Special Branch, or Special Branch in South Region with GCHQ. *That would have required some negotiation* [my emphases].'

Yet when the Northern Ireland Secretary Shaun Woodward was asked if he considered the protocol was wrong, he told MPs, 'No.' Then again, Woodward also said the protocol had since been 'dramatically' changed. Nick Perry, director of policing and security at the NIO also said the 'revised arrangements' for GCHQ–Branch intelligence-sharing did now 'allow for all appropriate intelligence to be passed across'. So if the protocol needed fixing, why did the secretary of state say it wasn't wrong?

So highly circumscribed was the evidence of Messrs Woodward and Gibson that it was as clear as mud. Neither witness would even concede in terms that GCHQ had actually intercepted the phones during the bombing run. Their 'repeated failure to confirm or clarify,' said NIAC, was 'exasperating'. The committee's verdict was blistering: 'We find all this obfuscation very frustrating. It is unclear to us precisely what Sir Peter Gibson did investigate.' The committee chairman, Sir Patrick Cormack, concluded: 'Far too many questions remain unanswered.' And this from a Conservative committee chairman as establishment as they come.

With the subsequent collapse of trials against three of the prime suspects, today there is no longer any realistic prospect of anyone being held to account for Omagh through the criminal courts. All governments – from Blair through to Johnson – appear to have been collectively determined to protect the intelligence-gathering services from shouldering any responsibility for the catastrophic failure of the police investigation.

In 2013, the government's refusal to hold a public inquiry was judicially reviewed. In 2021, a high court judge in Belfast, Mr Justice Mark Horner, recommended that authorities in the UK and the Republic of Ireland open an investigation into the bombing. He ruled that there was 'a real prospect the Omagh bomb could have been prevented'.

John Ware was a BBC *Panorama* reporter for twenty-five years and reported extensively on the Northern Ireland conflict and its legacy.

Familiar faces in Downing Street
London, 1998

Lance Price

The lift doors opened. Two men stepped out into the corridor. They caught my eye. Looks of recognition mixed with evident confusion: what was I doing there? 'Hello, Lance.'

I knew exactly what they were doing there. But to see Gerry Adams and Martin McGuinness walking unaccompanied in a building that not so long ago they would happily have seen blown to smithereens with everybody inside it was disorientating all the same.

The corridor leads from the famous black front door of Number 10 Downing Street towards the cabinet room, which was where the two Sinn Féin leaders were heading. I had only recently left journalism to work as a media adviser to Tony Blair, who was deeply committed to keeping the shaky peace process on the road. A process based on 'equal rights and equal respect' and – easier said than done – on mutual trust.

Any slight, real or imagined, could set back progress for months. Which meant treating Adams and McGuinness just like any other politicians. Except, of course, like all the former paramilitaries who had now turned to politics, they weren't.

As a young BBC reporter, I had interviewed both men many times during the 1980s. I'd had no more success than anybody else in getting them to acknowledge their complicity in murder and the indiscriminate violence that had devastated so many lives. It's fair to say that all three of us had been on a journey in recent years, although mine was of little or no significance compared to theirs.

My last big story as a journalist had been as part of the large BBC team covering the Good Friday Agreement. My admiration for the stoicism of the people of Northern Ireland in accepting former terrorists and their supporters as ministers has always been tinged by personal doubt. Could I have been so magnanimous if this was my home rather than a place I had come to love as an outsider?

No matter how welcoming and supportive your locally-born colleagues are – and they were, almost without exception – as an English journalist you will always be an outsider. When I arrived in Northern Ireland, it was my first real job as a reporter. I was just twenty-three. I hope I never pretended I knew more about the place or the story than I did, because really I knew nothing apart from what I had read. Learning curves don't get much steeper.

In my first week, I stopped for petrol on the A21 between Bangor and Belfast. My short back and sides for the new job, and my unmistakably southern English accent, inevitably marked me out. 'So are you a soldier, then?' asked the lad behind the till. It was probably just a friendly enquiry, but I was starting to understand what it was like to live in a society where caution and suspicion were the ever-present background to the most mundane daily activities.

I learned fairly quickly, however, not to let excessive caution get in the way of as 'normal' a life as possible, particularly as a relatively open gay man in a part of the UK where homosexuality was still illegal. Nevertheless, seeing RUC men with rifles over their shoulders pushing through the dance floor in Belfast's only gay bar was another unsettling reminder that I was a long way from home.

Politics would eventually outlaw such discrimination, and Sinn Féin would be on the right side of that particular argument. So, while I struggle to think of anything I had in common with Adams and McGuinness, there was this: we were all in that Downing Street corridor after a personal change of direction because we believed politics was the way to make meaningful reform happen. Would that they had reached that conclusion a long time earlier.

My time reporting from Northern Ireland covered the early stages of that transition, although at the time none of us knew how far it would progress. In the meantime, I encountered the threats and intimidation experienced by every journalist. Occasional brushes with danger. Caught up in riots, uncomfortably close to rubber bullets being fired over the heads of a crowd, forced out of a hire car by IRA men who promptly firebombed it. The woman at the Hertz desk was very understanding the next day: 'Yes, we saw it on the telly. We thought it was one of ours.'

Being on the local news every night offered a form of protection. Nobody asked me again if I was a soldier. Being English helped too. I don't remember ever being quizzed about my religion. The assumption seemed to be that you didn't have a team on the pitch, even while English, Scottish and Welsh service people were under repeated attack.

And to be honest, for most of us it was, above all, a job. We knew we wouldn't be there for ever. As a journalist starting out on your career, it was the best training ground imaginable. I learnt the trade of broadcast journalism by watching at close hand the likes of Brian Barron, Kate Adie, Peter Taylor and Michael Nicholson. I understood the politics better thanks to the legendary W.D. Flackes and Denis Murray. I appreciated what it meant to live through, as well as report on, the Troubles from local journalists too many to mention but including the compilers of this book.

And yet, reporting the Troubles, as contributors to this volume and the one before it have expressed more eloquently than I ever could, is never just a job. It changes you and the way you look at the world. It would be extraordinary if it didn't.

I was a reporter, not a commentator. I wasn't employed to make judgements, although we always did, of course, through our use of language. The Northern Ireland story is a complex one, but not so complicated that we should lose sight of some essential truths. For Margaret Thatcher, it was 'murder is murder'. I preferred the words of John Hume, then and now a hero of mine: 'There is not a single injustice in Northern Ireland today that justifies the taking of a single human life.'

I was one of the first journalists on the scene at the Droppin Well bar in Ballykelly, where eleven British soldiers and six civilians had been killed. I interviewed the survivors at Enniskillen and the relatives of those murdered in so many other attacks that I lost count. What I witnessed barely scratched the surface of the anguish that 'the province', as we always called it rather condescendingly back then, had gone through. I did my best, though I'm sure I often failed, to remember that each and every death wasn't a 'story'. It was a person whose life had been taken, and whose loss would touch the lives of so many others.

As the lift doors closed, Gerry Adams and Martin McGuinness walked down to whatever meeting they were going to. No, not just any other politicians. But their recognition, however belatedly, that if things were going to change for the better, politics was the best way to achieve it had, in its own way, taken courage. And, after all, the only thing I had given up was a career in daily journalism.

Lance Price was a BBC reporter in Northern Ireland from 1982 to 1986. He was special adviser to Tony Blair at 10 Downing Street from 1998 to 2000 and director of communications for the Labour Party from 2000 to 2001. He is now chief of staff to Kim Leadbeater MP.

How the Troubles caught up with me in the Florida sunshine
Fort Lauderdale, USA, 1999

Lindy McDowell

July 1999. A little over a year after the signing of the Good Friday Agreement and Northern Ireland's peace process, still in its perilous infancy, was about to be rocked by fallout from a brief court hearing thousands of miles away. I was there to cover it – but only because I was looking for a bit of peace myself.

Back then, I was working full time at the *Belfast Telegraph*. In July, the family and I had headed off on holiday to Fort Lauderdale in sunny southern Florida. My husband, Jim, also a journalist, was working at the *Sunday World*. He'd been taking considerable flak (occasionally literally) from various paramilitary outfits who'd issued death threats against him. Our house was like Fort Knox, with bullet-resistant windows, alarms and constant surveillance by the police. It wasn't a comfortable way to live – especially with two young sons – but in southern Florida we'd be able to get away from it all for a few weeks. Except we didn't get away from it all … at all.

At the time, a major issue of contention in the Northern Ireland peace process was the unresolved question of the decommissioning of paramilitary weaponry. While the Provisional IRA claimed to have put its arms 'beyond use', unionist politicians, in particular, remained highly sceptical. In Northern Ireland, we were still not walking together towards the golden dawn of trust and reconciliation that had been optimistically illustrated on the cover of the Good Friday Agreement.

In Fort Lauderdale, though, the politics of home was way down our list of priorities – as tends to be the case when you're headed to the beach for the day. Until, that is, we noticed a strange wee story on the front page of the Broward edition of the *Miami Herald*. A bail hearing was to be held later in the day for three people – two of them from Belfast – who, the report said, had been arrested for running guns to republican terrorists in Ireland. It took us all of five minutes to decide we needed to go and have a look. We organised someone to keep an eye on our boys, hunted through our holiday wardrobes for something that wouldn't look totally ridiculous in a court room, hailed a taxi and headed downtown.

Previously my only insight into American court proceedings had come from the movies and news reports on TV. The manacles, the orange jumpsuits – you're familiar with all that from what you've seen on screen. Seeing it in real life, that was surreal. With chains jangling, the three defendants came shuffling in accompanied by prison officers. They were seated side by side on chairs, a couple of feet apart, in front of us.

The one woman among them was Siobhan Browne, aged thirty-four, a naturalised American, originally from County Cork. A tall woman with glossy Irish-red hair (possibly not her natural shade), she'd previously worked as a stockbroker and real estate agent. She'd been living in the upscale area of Boca Raton, just north of Fort Lauderdale, and was in a relationship with defendant number two, Anthony Smyth, who was forty-two and originally from Belfast. Smyth was a big, stocky guy who in an attempt, perhaps, to convey his disdain for proceedings, casually rocked back and forth on his chair. For this, he was sharply chastised by a prison guard. As he now stared fixedly ahead, his erstwhile lover Siobhan Browne was trying desperately to catch his eye. Her efforts had failed to elicit any response, so she reached out to touch him. A guard whacked her arm hard with a baton. It must have hurt – although possibly not as much as Smyth totally blanking her did. The final member of the trio, Conor Claxton, aged twenty-six, also from Belfast, was by far the most animated and cocky. Glancing all around him, he seemed to be just buzzing with excitement, lapping up the attention, his moment in the limelight.

The court was told that all three had been under surveillance by the FBI following the discovery of guns hidden in a parcel of children's toys that had been posted to Cork. The guns had been spotted during a routine security check at Coventry airport in England, and had been traced back to the three defendants and another man, Martin Mullan, aged thirty and originally from County Antrim. Mullan, who was living in Philadelphia, was later to face trial alongside Smyth, Browne and Claxton. They'd all been scooped following a vital lead by America's Bureau of Alcohol, Tobacco, Firearms and Explosives, the ATF. A sharp-eyed ATF official had spotted that Browne had been purchasing an inordinate number of guns for your average real estate agent. Sometimes she'd been buying them under an alias, but almost always she'd used her first name Siobhan. Not the smartest move. Without a green card, Smyth hadn't been able to buy guns himself – for the same reason, neither had Claxton, who was both money man and ringleader. Browne, therefore, had agreed to do the purchasing, travelling to various gun fairs throughout Florida.

In total, the three had sent well over a hundred weapons, as well as armour-piercing ammunition, back to Ireland, all concealed in toys and electronics equipment. But who were the guns going to? That was the crucial question – and one with enormous ramifications for our fledgling and extremely shaky peace process. The FBI and the prosecution were adamant: the weapons were going to the Provisional IRA. The court was told that, after his arrest, Claxton had given an interview to an FBI agent, Mark Hastbacka, during which he'd boasted that he was working for the Provos, and that the arms purchased would be used to kill British soldiers, police officers and Protestant paramilitaries. He did not come across as the most uncooperative of interviewees.

They were certainly a strange little gang, the three of them. Claxton was loud-mouthed and lived a life of partying. He did not appear to have money problems, flagrantly flashing the cash – even if its source was a bit of a mystery.

Browne was still married to an older Israeli man (who, loyally, stood by her during and after the trial and her imprisonment). At the time of the offences she was living, however, with the recently divorced and hard-drinking Smyth, together with Claxton as an occasional lodger. Browne was an unlikely gunrunner. How much she was committed to the republican cause was debatable. In a later interview she was to claim, 'I'm devoted to my own cause – getting my nails and hair done. I don't give a shit about the IRA and never have.' An intelligent woman, she wouldn't have been under any illusion, though, about where the guns were going and their potential for carnage – even if, as she suggested, she'd been sucked in by the charms of burly Mr Smyth.

The bail hearing didn't last long. The trio were remanded in custody. Afterwards I had a word with the prosecution attorney, Richard Scruggs. I needed further clarification on that crucial question – for whom were the guns being acquired?

In my patronising way, I began to explain to Mr Scruggs that we had no shortage of IRAs in Northern Ireland. Was he aware of that? 'There's the Continuity IRA, the Real IRA, the–' He put a hand up: 'Ma'am. These people were working for the PIRA. As in the Provisional IRA. The IRA whose political wing is Sinn Féin, whose president is Gerry Adams.' So, no ambiguity there.

Obviously, this was going to be a major story – one with undoubted implications for the peace process. Next day, it was on page one of the *Belfast Telegraph*. From Washington to Westminster there were immediate attempts to play the case down. Unionist politicians demanded to know what was going on. The Provisional IRA leadership issued a statement saying the operation had 'not been sanctioned' which, as was pointed out at the time, was not exactly the same as a comprehensive denial of involvement. US President Bill Clinton and Secretary of State Mo Mowlam also insisted there was no evidence that the arms operation had been ordered by the IRA leadership.

Uncomfortably for the politicians, however, in a later interview, prosecutor Mr Scruggs continued to stick to his ... well ... guns.

The political fallout was immense. Obviously, even if I hadn't been at the court that day, the story would have got out anyway. But I always think that the American administration and the Blair government must have wondered, in dismay, how the provincial *Belfast Telegraph* had been so on the ball that it had managed to get a staffer immediately on the scene to cover a bail hearing in southern Florida.

Smyth, Browne, Claxton and Mullan were all found guilty at their later trial and were sentenced to time in prison for shipping arms. Had they been found guilty of the original charges, including conspiracy to murder and aiding terrorists, they faced life sentences; in the end, the terms handed down were much shorter. Claxton got four-and-a-half years, Smyth and Mullan three years each, and Browne twenty months.

The peace process had been rocked at a dangerous time. But still it held as Washington and Westminster did their best to steady the ship.

This is a story that ends with a big what if. What if those guns had got through unnoticed and had been used in some horror attack that had the potential to reignite our bloody Troubles? Those of us who lived and worked in Northern Ireland through the hellish years of conflict knew only too well what was at stake.

We grew up and raised our families in a place where violence, fear and hatred were the norm. As journalists, in our working lives we'd covered the aftermath of too many atrocities. We'd listened to the wailing grief of too many widows, witnessed the glassy-eyed incomprehension of too many children who would grow up without a parent. We'd talked to too many people whose lives and minds and bodies had been ripped apart, scarred for ever. We'd followed too many coffins.

The ATF officer involved in the Florida case was called Regina Lombardo. I often wonder if Ms Lombardo ever realised the full consequences of what, to her, was probably just another day's work. By spotting that anomaly of one woman's gun-buying spree she undoubtedly saved lives. And may well have spared the people of Northern Ireland, an ocean away, a descent back into God-knows-what bloodshed and barbarity.

Lindy McDowell is a columnist with the *Belfast Telegraph* where she worked throughout the Troubles and the peace process. She has also worked in broadcasting.

Court reporting and the murder that made me question everything
Belfast, 2000

Michael Donnelly

Sally Diver was a wife, a mother, a grandmother. We never met. Yet she and the case surrounding her brutal death were to have a profound effect on me, so devastating I considered my career as a court reporter over.

I started my career in 1979 and, over the course of twenty years, had become one of Northern Ireland's top court hacks, 'a "leg-end" in my own lunch hour'. A 'doyen of the courts' as one lord justice decreed. More a big fish in a small pond, really. The North was big news and its courts even bigger. And it was mine.

Centre of operations was a slim, box-shaped, smoke-filled enclave off the main corridor leading to Court Number One in Belfast's Crumlin Road Courthouse. The 'Press Room'. My home until June 1998, when they closed it, along with the rest of the building. The following four years saw me a nomad, moving my tent around the courts until Laganside Courts, berthed by the river. Seemingly an all-singing all-dancing courthouse. In truth, a cold, inhospitable building – the worst modernity has to offer. Now, the Crumlin Road – that 'imposing Corinthian block in stucco', as described at its 1850's opening – was the real thing. It was all you imagined a court should be: imposing, austere even, but at its centre, a beating heart of humanity.

For nearly two decades I had the privilege of working within its crumbling walls with some of the North's top journalists, surviving as we did on daily rations of tales of blood, guts, and mangled bodies and minds. And from our ringside seats we reported – in sanitised form for teatime news bulletins and breakfast morning newspapers – those horrors committed by one side or other in furtherance of some indefensible cause.

The Shankill Butchers was my first big case. Then the Supergrass trials, the Maze Escape and, before that, the M60 escape from the Crumlin Road jail opposite. In between was the La Mon bombing; later the Shankill fish shop bombing, and all interspersed with a never-ending, mind-numbing stream of murders, mindless shootings and booby-trap explosions.

For the most part, our work ran seamlessly. Well, almost, save when BBC reporter Chris Moore and I nearly ended up in jail for criminal contempt – the result of a misunderstanding between ourselves and Lord Chief Justice Sir Robert Lowry. A matter best forgotten.

Then there was the time that phenomenon Big Ivan Little and I started a full-scale riot during a supergrass trial. We'd relayed reports of fighting in the court from two pay phones – and eavesdropping relatives, already ejected from the court when trouble flared, tried to storm the courtroom. One good thing came of it: from then on I was allowed my own landline in the press room.

During one quieter moment I earned myself the coveted journo title of 'Scoop'. I was chatting and joking with a few people when over a radio came a report of a shooting. Using my newly acquired landline, I phoned in my tip-off to the newsrooms. Not wanting to appear overeager, I casually enquired if they'd heard about the downtown shooting. They had – an off-duty army officer had foiled a bank robbery. With mounting excitement, in a shrill voice, I told him the army officer had prevented not a robbery, but the near-assassination of Sinn Féin president Gerry Adams. 'Fuck me, Scoop,' came the reply.

In addition to my covering what was initially called Belfast City Commission, then Belfast Crown Court, I was asked to impart my wisdom to fledglings hoping to develop a career in journalism. Having come through the same journalism course – and been assured by the organiser that I had useful knowledge to dispense – I readily agreed. Classes usually involved explaining the courts' workings and their chief protagonists, with a sprinkling of little anecdotes and myself as the hero, of course. At the end of one class in April 2000 came a question. I remember it for two reasons: because of the question itself, which paradoxically I knew the answer to yet had never properly considered; and because the student who posed it, Ann Madden, later worked for me.

'How do you live with it?' Ms Madden asked. She explained that following a recent court visit some students couldn't face lunch, let alone eat, given the post-mortem evidence they'd heard. 'Easy,' I said. 'Humour. Black humour; the sicker the better.' Met with a sea of blank stares, I showed no mercy. My amusing little ditty about one half of a murdering paedophile team was greeted with a mixture of nervous laughter and gasps of disbelief. Straight-faced, I said that those who laughed would make it as journalists; the rest should do themselves a favour and work in PR.

My smugness lasted all of two days. Working from home my wife, Marguerite, presented me with a tea tray of ever-so-rare roast beef sandwiches.

Yummy. Hungrily taking a bite, I first tasted the blood then felt the trickles oozing from the beef before seeing them. In that instant, I saw through those student eyes, recalling every detail of forty-eight-year-old Sally Diver's stabbing by Liam 'Birdie' McBride, who was the father of her youngest, one-year-old grandson. And the sanitised story I'd written about the North Belfast granny shattered and disintegrated.

My tea tray went crashing. I was literally sick over my keyboard, tears tripping my face as my mind went to Sally's last moments; of her daughters Lynsey and Tammy Leigh hearing her dying plea, 'Don't, Birdie,' as he stabbed her twenty-six times with his butcher's knife in the chest, upper abdomen, front and right sides and back.

Over the following days and weeks, my mind was in a quandary. Memories of other cases I thought long forgotten, buried deep, surfaced unbidden. My gallows humour hung me out to dry and the very thought of listening to another case sickened me. Marguerite tried to console, reason and cajole. But her arguments, though sound, held no real comfort. I felt trapped with no exit, save giving up.

Fortunately Easter provided a break and Marguerite packed me off fishing with my friend and colleague Maurice Neill, in whom I confided. Along one quiet drift, Maurice on the oars and me attempting to cast a fly, I repeated that I thought my days as a court reporter were finished. 'Aye right. The Queen's no soldiers and the Pope's an Orangeman,' came his mocking response. 'If you can't cover a court, who can?'

In quieter moments, I often think of the many hundreds of Sally Divers I've reported on – not on how they died, but about the people they were while offering up a silent prayer in remembrance. And while Maurice may have helped to reset my compass, I still reduce almost everything to humour, to such an extent that friends, even when I tell them something serious, still look at me and ask, 'And the punchline, Scoop?'

Michael Donnelly is a Crown Court reporter.

A father's quest to find out the truth about his son's murder
Tandragee, County Armagh, 2000

Gordon Adair

On one of those crisp, cold February mornings that, to the unguarded, seems to whisper of spring, two boys were found lying in a laneway near Tandragee in County Armagh. They had been beaten and stabbed to death in an almost unimaginably savage way.

It was two months into the new millennium, two years since the signing of the Good Friday Agreement. People were daring to hope for, and talk about, peace. Yet in Armagh, violent death was circling like a hawk seeking prey; had been for the six weeks since the murder of the UVF's leader in the area, Richard Jameson, apparently at the hands of rival paramilitary group, the LVF. The 'dogs in the street' knew there would be revenge and that, when it came, it would come without mercy.

But all that had nothing to do with David McIlwaine. The eighteen-year-old graphic design student had never had any involvement with paramilitaries; the 'feud' between two equally ruthless, equally violent, equally blood-soaked factions could have been taking place on the other side of the world for all he knew or cared about it. Sometimes, though, entire lives are altered forever – or even ended – by a moment that, at the time, seems barely worth noting. In David's case, it was being part of a group of five when a taxi for four turned up. The taxi was never meant for him but, if things had worked out differently, it might have taken him home – to his parents, to bed, to safety, to the rest of his life.

The law said only four passengers could travel. The driver was not for budging. David volunteered to stay, confident as only an eighteen-year-old can be, that he'd find another lift or deal with whatever mini-adventure might come along. Another passenger, Andrew Robb, also decided to get out to keep David company. Soon, they found themselves invited to a nearby house party. They agreed to go, and unwittingly delivered themselves into the hands of their killers; another of those invisible turning points. At the party, Andrew apparently made a disparaging remark about Richard Jameson. He and David were driven from the house to the laneway where they were beaten and then stabbed repeatedly with butchers' boning knives.

I had been at the BBC five days, having moved from print journalism, and the deaths of those two boys have never left me. The images of them haunt me still. Perhaps, it was the 'up close and personal' nature of them or the sheer barbarity – David's injuries were so severe that the police initially thought he had been shot in the face with a shotgun. I would spare you the detail of what happened to those boys that night. But through that seemingly impenetrable darkness, there flickered a light of decency and humanity – in the shape of David McIlwaine's father, Paul.

For the bulk of my BBC career I was based in the area where these killings took place, so I've met and talked with Paul many times over the past two decades. He does not believe the truth about what happened that night has ever emerged, and he is relentless in his efforts to change that. It has been my privilege to know him. Paul is not a big guy, but he has a quiet strength and bright, kind eyes that make you think that, whatever tight corner you might find yourself in, this is a man you would like to have by your side. I wish I could tell you that the passage of time over the years has eased Paul's pain. I wish. But I can't. 'Every year is just worse than the last one,' he tells me. 'Every year we find out more about the boys' deaths and it always means more pain, more frustration.'

He has found himself led by his search for the truth into a world of dark secrets and darker lies; the murky half-light existence of informants, agents, handlers, the protected and the sacrificed. A few years ago, while we were chatting outside a Belfast court where the only person ever to be charged with the murder of the two boys – a man called Stephen Brown, who was subsequently convicted – was on trial, Paul mentioned that his daughter was going to Australia. 'Would you not think of doing that?' I asked. 'Turn your back on all this, try to enjoy, as best you can, whatever life is left to you.' His answer was simple and honest: 'I can't.'

I reminded him of that conversation recently and a smile flickered briefly round his lips, looked for the thought that might sustain it, and disappeared. Patiently, he explained it to me: 'This year has been the worst and – in a way – the best. Because we are getting information now that is drastic, and it's been there all the time. It's being highlighted now, by whoever, just because I kept it going. No other reason. Because I stayed and did what I did. We tried going to Spain for eleven months back in 2003 and 2004, and it was nice, just lying on the beach and all that. But sure what was I doing? I was just running away.

'People need to be doing what I'm doing or this country's not going to change. I think I've made a difference. I challenge myself. I have done nothing in my life, Gordon. And I am amazed that I've had three beautiful children who turned out the way they did. I'm amazed.

'You have to take a stand. That's what I've said to all my children; don't let anybody intimidate you, don't be afraid. I'd be afraid of how I might die, but I'm not afraid of dying. In a way I would welcome it for I am sick, sore and tired of it all. It's torture.'

That little smile that struggled to find a home is long gone. Paul's doubts about the police investigation started almost immediately. Within a month of the killings, he was already displaying the resilience and determination that I would see demonstrated again and again over the years, when he persuaded the UVF to meet him face to face.

'I travelled down with the UVF commander from Portadown who took over from Richard Jameson,' he said. 'We went to Belfast, to the UVF's headquarters, and discussed [the murders] with the ten or twelve top people. I had no sense of fear. I'm not overly brave but at the same time I'm stubborn. The simple fact is that it's my son and I'd go to the ends of the earth to get the truth. It wouldn't matter who they were or what they had been involved in. They seemed to be the right people to go to at the time.

'The top man of the UVF sat there and said very, very little. In fact, the only question he asked was "What do you want us to do? Do you want us to kill them?" And I said, "No, I don't want anybody hurt; no violence, no retaliation." In the end, they were no help at all.'

That fearlessness has never waned, despite many dead ends and slammed doors as well as several threats on his life. I don't know if Paul will ever discover the whole truth about his son's death – and that of Andrew Robb. But I do know he will never stop trying, and that he will never lose his inherent decency and humanity.

Gordon Adair has been a reporter with the BBC in Northern Ireland for more than twenty years. Before that he worked for the *Daily Mirror* and the *News Letter*, having started his journalistic career at the *Portadown Times*.

Crossing paths with Michael Stone, Northern Ireland's most notorious loyalist gunman
Belfast, 2000

Kevin Magee

Loyalist paramilitaries tried to kill me twice before I was fourteen years old, and that tally does not even include my first encounter with the infamous killer Michael Stone, whose life as Northern Ireland's most notorious loyalist gunman would bizarrely feel like it had become entwined with my own.

I first experienced Stone's actions on 21 February 1973, long before anyone else had heard of him, when I was an eleven-year-old schoolboy at St Joseph's Primary school in Ballyhackamore, East Belfast. One morning the classroom walls vibrated, the windows buckled, and the teacher's face turned ashen as a pall of black smoke rose over the school yard. A bomb had exploded across the road, and a class of thirty boys sat frozen during that terrifying moment after a bomb detonates when you do not know what trauma might follow in its wake. At break time, I ignored the teacher's warnings and went to see the damage for myself. Paddy Lamb's bar at the top of the Sandown Road looked like it had been bombed from the air, reduced to a burning pyramid of rafters and broken masonry. Firemen put out the flames as soldiers looked on aimlessly, their SLR rifles resting on their hips.

Years later, Michael Stone would tell me he had carried that bomb into the bar in a plastic bin and placed it on the counter of the Catholic-owned pub. He said it was a successful mission as it had not only established his bona fides as a paramilitary recruit, but it had also sent out a message that loyalists were developing an explosive capability to match that of the republicans.

If Stone was telling the truth, he was seventeen when he planted the bomb.

Michael Stone and I grew up in the same part of Belfast around the same time, but that is where the similarities end. While he wanted to embrace violence and make a name for himself as a loyalist paramilitary, I wanted to escape from it, so I packed myself off to university in Dublin, following my father's advice that an education was much easier carried than the heavy black box of joinery tools he had to bring with him from one job to another in Belfast city centre, after death threats forced him to leave his job in the shipyard. Finding bullets

186

in his coat pocket was a powerful incentive to look for work elsewhere.

Unfortunately, that was only the beginning of the loyalist intimidation my family faced. The youngest of five children, I was born in the back bedroom of the modest house in Carolhill Drive, East Belfast, that my parents had worked hard to buy. At first life was very normal. We were an ordinary Catholic family growing up in the sixties, doing what seemed like very ordinary things, like going to Mass on Sundays and studying at the closest Catholic grammar schools. On Saturdays, I would be lifted over the turnstiles at The Oval by some man in a flat cap to watch Glentoran.

But our world changed, and the intimidation grew like the late evening shadows cast by the vast shipyard cranes at Harland and Wolff. At first it was low-level stuff, like name-calling in the street; then it seemed to increase exponentially. Our windows were put in – I remember picking shards of glass out of my pillow in the front bedroom. Another evening, a car pulled up outside the house and three shots ricocheted off my bedroom wall. Then came the most terrifying attack of all – an attempt to burn the house down with the seven of us trapped inside. A petrol bomb exploded in the hall, turning the only escape route into a wall of blue flame. In the suffocating panic, my older siblings managed to smother the flames with coats that had been hanging over the newel post. We moved out the following week. Many years later I understood exactly what a Bosnian refugee who I interviewed in the Balkans meant when she told me, 'One of the worst things about being made a refugee and becoming homeless is that you were also made to feel that in some way it was your own fault.'

I often thought I would like to sit down with the culprits or someone who shared their view of the world and ask them how attempting to set fire to an innocent family of seven could assist any cause, never mind help save the Union. Back then I did not think I would get the chance, but that was before I got to know Michael Stone.

In 1984, I moved back to Belfast for further study at Queen's University and could only find accommodation outside the student area, in a loyalist district known as The Village. It was the first time I had lived in the city since I was evacuated sitting in an armchair wedged between other bits of furniture in the back of a box van ten years before. I remember feeling anxious and nervous and my fears were soon realised. I was there less than a fortnight when Michael Stone walked into a dairy business just around the corner and shot dead milkman and father-of-two Patrick Brady with a double-barrelled shotgun from a distance of three feet. I left The Village as soon as I could.

It would be another four years before I would set eyes on Michael Stone. Like thousands of others, the first time I saw him, I was desperately trying to get away from him when he ran amok, hurling bombs and shooting at mourners at an IRA funeral in Milltown Cemetery on 16 March 1988. He was casually lobbing exploding grenades in my direction as if he was out for some sort of a macabre Sunday stroll. By then a journalist, I was in the cemetery reporting for the *News Letter* and was standing beside other reporters close to the Sinn Féin leadership, right inside his target zone, when the shooting started. Amid the confusion and chaos, I took cover behind the same headstone as my colleague Gareth Gordon from the same newspaper as we desperately tried to make sense of what was going on. Amid the danger and panic there was comedy too.

'I think it might be a mortar attack on the Shinners and we're here, right beside them. Let's get out of here,' I suggested.

'No. No. No. Sit your ground,' replied Gareth, grabbing me by the coat to prevent my retreat. 'If it's mortars, they are notoriously inaccurate. They'll overshoot their mark. Stay where you are for fuck's sake.'

Then an American reporter who had taken up temporary residence on the grave next to mine asked me a surreal but infinitely practical question. 'Do these things shatter?' he enquired, pointing to his marble headstone. How was I supposed to know?

The first good look I got at Stone was at his trial at the Crumlin Road courthouse. From the press bench, I studied him intently and noticed that his eyes looked black and vibrated in their sockets, like those of a predator in a constant state of high alert. Listening to the evidence, I wondered what kind of thought process was going on behind those eyes that allowed someone to walk up to a stranger and shoot them from three feet away. Ever one for a dramatic gesture, as he was sent down for 684 years with a minimum 30-year recommendation for six murders, including three in the cemetery, he rose to his feet, threw his hands in the air like a preacher and shouted a prayer: 'God Save Ulster'.

With such a long sentence, I thought that would be the last the public would hear about him for a very long time. I wrote some stories describing him as the 'Milltown murderer' and in one quoted a psychiatrist who described him as a sociopath – someone devoid of a conscience, defined more formally as 'a person with a personality disorder manifesting itself in extreme antisocial attitudes and behaviour'. It sounded like a fair enough description to me, but Stone did not like it. The following week I got word sent out from the prison that he was annoyed I'd called him a murderer. By then half the world had seen him shoot people on TV. Was he delusional too, I wondered?

In 2000 he was back out on the streets being lauded as a hero by his followers after he was released under the Good Friday Agreement. By then I was a reporter on the BBC *Spotlight* current affairs programme and it fell to me to make contact with him and persuade him to take part in a new TV series in which victims and perpetrators would come face to face in the company of the late South African Nobel Peace Prize winner and anti-apartheid campaigner, Archbishop Desmond Tutu. In addition to persuading people to take part, I would then make a documentary about those involved and their experiences of the meetings.

At first we met in the County Antrim town of Carrickfergus; then we started to meet in a fast-food restaurant in Dundonald, where he'd ensure he was unrecognisable by wearing a blue, bell-shaped hat pulled down to his eyebrows. The only thing that set his appearance apart from anyone else's in the restaurant was the bulge of his flak jacket. We got on well and, after a while, he invited me back to his home territory of the Braniel estate, a large loyalist housing development on the edge of East Belfast. I would meet someone at a designated place, follow them on foot down a series of back entries and be shown into a house where he'd then make a theatrical entrance like Zorro, wielding not a sword but his paintbrush. I filmed him painting in his makeshift studio, and getting some new body art of his own as he lay bare chested on a bench in a tattoo parlour, and wondered, too, how much the camera was massaging his ego.

He agreed to take part in the filming of an encounter with the family of bread server Dermot Hackett, thirty-seven, one of his victims, although he told me he had not killed him. I picked him up alone one morning in my car and we drove to the meeting in the sunshine. From a journalistic point of view, I was delighted he had turned up to our meeting place as the Hackett family and Desmond Tutu were all waiting for him, but an inner voice was also asking, 'Are you half wise? You are alone with a mass murderer in your car. What happens if he goes off on one?' Thankfully, he didn't. Not then anyway.

Sylvia Hackett's world ended when her husband, Dermot, was murdered for no reason on 23 May 1987. She was terrified of Stone, who was convicted of his murder, but wanted to look the man who robbed her of her happiness straight in the eye. Walking with the aid of a stick, Stone limped into the room and met Sylvia, daughter Sabrina and Dermot's brother Roddy, three of the kindest souls on earth in the company of another, Archbishop Desmond Tutu. Afterwards, Sylvia said, 'After all this time, all this hurt, I was able to face my demons and look him straight in the eye – yet he didn't have the guts to return my gaze.' Driven by the power of her love for her murdered husband, she'd finally faced down his killer.

That same day, Stone told Archbishop Tutu he had embraced a peaceful life – but just six months later he got stuck in the revolving doors at Stormont armed to the teeth with explosives, knives and an axe as he prepared to launch another kamikaze attack on republicans.

Like Sylvia, I was having my own catharsis. During my time spent with Michael Stone, I searched – as you often do – for a commonality to help make conversation. We discussed growing up in the same part of the city and Tartan gangs. That was when he told me he had blown up Paddy Lamb's pub. After his release from jail, he had become such an iconic figure within strands of loyalism that I expected the import of his answers to match the weight of his status. I asked him why loyalist paramilitaries had targeted so many innocent Catholics – omitting to say 'including my own family' – but as ever there was a banality and superficiality to his answers. His standard response was to make a vague connection between the actions of loyalists and the exertion of pressure on the IRA to abandon its armed campaign.

I held back from asking him a hypothetical question – would he have thrown a petrol bomb into the home of his neighbours, an innocent family with five children inside? I didn't ask because I sensed I already knew the answer.

Kevin Magee was a correspondent and news reporter with BBC Northern Ireland for twenty-nine years. He is now a documentary filmmaker.

Clandestine meetings with the 'park walker'
Belfast, 2001

Barry McCaffrey

'I believe you want to speak to me,' said the soft-spoken voice on the other end of the telephone. The caller made no attempt to identify himself. He didn't have to. The sixth sense that all reporters are born with immediately told me who this was and what this call was about.

There were two ways this conversation could now go. He would either agree to meet me, or, alternatively, I would be told in no uncertain terms never to contact him again; if I did, I would live to regret it. It wouldn't be an idle threat. The voice on the other end of the line was not only awaiting trial, charged with the murder of Pat Finucane, one of the most notorious killings of the Troubles, but he had also been exposed to the world as a Special Branch informer. His life expectancy had been seriously reduced as a result, and we both knew it. A number of years earlier he had been shot five times in the back and left for dead by an infamous loyalist gunman, who suspected my caller was working as a police agent. Now everyone knew his dark secret and he was a man with a target on his back.

'Yes, that's no problem,' my caller calmly continued. 'I'll meet you today if you want.' In that split second, my reporter's brain started to race with a euphoria that I could be on to the biggest scoop of my journalistic career. But at the back of my head a little voice questioned whether I was being set up for a catastrophic, career-ending fall.

The suggested location for our first meeting came as a surprise. The caller insisted we meet in a public park in a predominantly nationalist area of North Belfast. Normally encounters with such individuals are clandestine and take place well away from prying eyes. The fact that this man's grisly police mugshot had been splashed across every newspaper front page for weeks on end meant his presence in a Catholic area, just a short walk from the murder scene, was unlikely to go unnoticed. The park was also overlooked by a heavily fortified police station with dozens of surveillance cameras watching every possible angle. Our 'quiet' chat would surely not be missed.

It's a popular misconception that the motivation of every informer, Special

191

Branch agent or whistle-blower is the same. In my experience, each individual has their own reasons for doing what they do. Some have been sickened by violence and are desperate to escape the trap they find themselves caught in. Others are driven by a desire for revenge against former colleagues for a particular wrong they perceive as having been done to them. For some it's simply the lure of cash promised by police. Others need the thrill of the chase, to be their own James Bond, convinced they can control who lives and dies. The majority of agents I encountered were ordinary, nondescript individuals, who found themselves inescapably ensnared between a paramilitary rock and a Special Branch hard place. Most, if not all, realised that their fate was already sealed and that their lives would never again be their own. The life of an informer rarely has a fairy-tale ending.

The newspaper images of the man I was about to meet portrayed him as a shaven-headed, tattooed loyalist thug who had supplied the guns used to shoot dead a Catholic solicitor as he sat down to Sunday dinner with his wife and children. But walking towards me in the park was a middle-aged, pot-bellied, granddad-type figure with a little black dog. There was little hint of menace or threat. Instead, I was looking at an individual facing a life sentence for a murder that he had twice warned police was about to take place. When he challenged his Special Branch handlers as to why they hadn't stopped the killing, he was told there hadn't been enough time to act. Days after the attack he again tipped off police that the gang leader was about to move the murder weapons. He had become increasingly concerned when his information was ignored.

Now, twelve years later, the man walking towards me was a sacrificial scapegoat in a deadly game of cat and mouse between police intelligence and loyalist paramilitaries. When I asked why we were meeting in a nationalist area, he smiled and admitted he felt safer in Catholic parts of town. Why he had chosen to meet under the watchful eyes of police surveillance cameras was never explained. He would only speak to me – and agree to fill in vital missing details of the killing – on condition of anonymity. Strangely though, through either recklessness or naivety, he agreed to be photographed. This should have been a warning that he either didn't understand or didn't care about the added danger he now could find himself in.

The park became a regular meeting point for us over the next eighteen months. On one occasion, as we walked along the path, he stopped mid-sentence. 'There's Ken in his taxi,' he said. If I'd been in a typical conversation, this statement would have been nothing more than the speaker recognising a neighbour or work colleague. In this instance, it was my contact identifying the gunman who had actually fired the fatal shots into the Catholic victim, who was now within touching distance of us. Was this a chance encounter? Or was this the final confirmation the killer needed that my walking companion was continuing to talk to the 'wrong' people. After a number of days of worrying – in which nothing happened – we reassured ourselves we hadn't been seen. Were we fooling ourselves?

As part of his bail conditions, the 'park walker' was obliged to attend court once every few months for a judge to be updated on progress in the forthcoming murder trial. At those hearings he would be placed in the dock, flanked by two prison officers. On each occasion I attended court and sat alongside fellow journalists to report on the latest developments in the case. My clandestine meetings with the park walker should have remained our secret, but as I sat waiting for the case to begin a journalist colleague nudged me: 'He's pointing at you. He wants to speak to you.' From the dock, the park walker was beckoning to me to come and speak to him. The more I pretended to ignore his gesturing, the more pronounced it became. Finally, sheepishly, I scuttled to the dock. I felt the eyes of every police officer, journalist and lawyer in the courtroom on my back as I approached the dock. 'Are you okay to meet later?' he asked, as casually as if he were asking about the weather. As if the guards on either side had temporarily gone deaf. Embarrassed and amazed, I quickly agreed and sneaked back to the safety of the press bench. My sixth sense shouted danger.

Later that evening, I pleaded with the park walker to be more careful. The bullet scars on his back should have been a reminder to him that his life was expendable to those who wouldn't appreciate him talking to reporters. He tried to reassure me, explaining that a well-known loyalist had sat in this same living room days before and promised him faithfully that he wouldn't come to any harm – as long as he agreed not to implicate any former paramilitary colleagues in his forthcoming trial. He recounted that the two men had hugged like long lost brothers reunited. The fact that this visitor was the same individual who had previously shot him five times in the back and left him for dead seemed to be a distant memory. My sixth sense again shouted danger.

In November 2001, the case against the park walker unexpectedly collapsed when a key witness was unable to testify. That should have been the end of the story, for the park walker at least. In his euphoria that the case against him was now over, he made it publicly known that he supported calls for an inquiry into why RUC Special Branch had failed to prevent the solicitor's murder. It was an incredibly brave but dangerous statement to make. I – and others – urged him to leave Belfast and find another life, far away from those dangerous individuals with long and vengeful memories. He assured me that he planned to find another park to walk in on the other side of the world.

Two weeks later, shortly before 7 a.m. on Wednesday, 12 December 2001, a journalist colleague called to tell me that there had been a shooting and that the park walker was dead. Some said he had been a dead man walking from the beginning. I make no judgement. People make their own choices for their own reasons. Twenty years later, I still think about Billy Stobie and wonder what that faraway park might have looked like, if he had escaped Belfast in time.

In September 2004, Ken Barrett pleaded guilty to murdering Pat Finucane. It emerged during Barrett's trial that he had also been a Special Branch agent.

Barry McCaffrey was a reporter with the *North Belfast News*, *Irish News* and the Detail.tv investigations website.

Holy Cross – why was it allowed to happen?
Belfast, 2001

Allison Morris

No one really knew how the new school term would begin. The Catholic Holy Cross Girls' Primary School in Ardoyne in North Belfast had been forced to close a week early for the summer holidays after loyalist residents held a protest outside the school gates.

On that Monday morning, 3 September 2001, it was to become the centre of an international news story when hundreds of loyalist protesters tried to block the main route to school taken by the children and their parents. It had been a long hot summer of discontent at the interface. In North Belfast, loyalist and nationalist homes can be less than a hundred yards apart and yet huge walls divide them, ensuring neighbours remain separated and segregated.

I was new to the reporting game but no stranger to a riot, having grown up in West Belfast during the worst years of the conflict. By 2001, just three years after the Good Friday Agreement, the west of the city was already starting to see the benefits of peace, whilst for those living in Ardoyne – well, their peace process had yet to begin. That summer I had covered quite a few violent street disturbances in my role as a rookie reporter; riots linked to the annual and predictably volatile Orange Order marching season.

But nothing could prepare me for what was about to happen on the Ardoyne Road that first week in September. The Holy Cross uniform is distinctive with its little bright red pullovers, and lots of the girls had pigtails and huge bows almost the size of their heads, and shiny patent leather shoes, brand new and unscuffed, for what should have been a happy return to their classrooms. Instead, the school run had become a war zone, and life for those children would never be the same again.

Thousands of loyalist protesters gathered, lining the Ardoyne Road, their numbers equalled only by the uniforms of the British Army and the RUC (the historic change to the Police Service of Northern Ireland would not happen for another two months).

The local media captured the scenes of children with tear-stained faces running the gauntlet of adult protesters – they were ugly images that were soon being flashed around the world and, within twenty-four hours, the travelling global press pack landed on the streets of Belfast. Veteran journalists who had moved on several years previously, thinking our 'war' was over, returned in the most disturbing of circumstances.

Almost twenty years on, I cannot remember if I offered to, or it was decided that I should, on the second day, walk up the road with one of the mothers and her daughter. To write a 'colour piece' about what it was like to walk through the protest.

Heart racing, I started my walk. The wall of sound came first; so loud the road beneath my feet felt like it was vibrating. The first thing I noticed was that the heavily armed British soldiers stood with their backs to the protesters, their guns pointing inwards towards the parents and children – the pictures of rifles just inches from screaming primary school children's heads made for striking front-page images.

In the early days of the blockade, the protesters were permitted to get very close to the parents and children – they would later be pushed back behind a line of police Land Rovers.

As I walked up the road, the protesters must have assumed I was one of the Holy Cross mothers and directed sectarian and occasionally sexual slurs at me. I could hear the blood pumping in my ears. I focused on one face in the crowd, an elderly lady who looked to be in her mid- to late-seventies. I thought, at first, that she looked kind but as we passed by her, she leaned forward and shouted, 'You look like a monkey, ya ugly fucker.' The child at my right-hand side showed no emotion. She was eight years old and, amid the deafening noise, I assumed – and hoped – that she hadn't heard. Minutes later we were in the quiet sanctuary of Holy Cross. I still remember that lovely chalky smell of the warm and welcoming school. I breathed slowly to slow my heart rate. The little girl beside me looked up at her mother and said, 'Am I ugly?' And then I cried.

It is one of only two times I have ever cried while doing my job. 'Write the story, don't be the story' was the mantra of my news editor. I was ashamed of myself – I was only a visitor to this world who could leave at any time. What had I to cry about?

On one of the days a blast bomb was thrown in the direction of the children. It landed just yards from the screaming pupils; a number of police officers and a police dog were injured by shrapnel. Passionist priests Father Aidan Troy and Father Gary Donegan, of Holy Cross Church, became the public faces of the inter-community conflict, giving regular media interviews and calling for dialogue to end the dispute.

They also received death threats. Father Gary told me later that, during that time, he would wear a Fermanagh GAA jersey under his priestly robes so that if he was killed, he'd at least be in his county colours.

The global press pack were fascinated. Scenes from Ardoyne were top of the hour in America, France and Italy – and then two planes hit the Twin Towers in New York and, just like that, a week into the protest, the foreign reporters packed up their cameras and left. Of course the local press remained and continued to cover the seemingly never-ending story.

I spent a night visiting homes along the interface, which made for an eye-opening experience. North Belfast was ripping itself apart. The nightly violence on interfaces between Ardoyne and the loyalist Shankill and Twaddell, and between the nationalist New Lodge and loyalist Tigers Bay, seemed like a cycle of sectarian conflict that would be impossible to resolve.

In the homes along the interfaces, I met families living in one room, the rest of their houses in darkness, with windows boarded up, to prevent petrol bombs being lobbed through them. It meant there was no night or day, just a constant depressing gloom. A mother showed me the kettle she used to make bottles for her baby on the windowless landing of her home. She had been forced to do that after being showered with glass when the windows of her kitchen came smashing in around her and a brick landed at her feet. So many of the men, women and even children I spoke to were on antidepressants, clearly suffering from what we would now recognise as PTSD. The loud hum of a low-flying police helicopter was a constant. The young mother, with dark circles under her eyes from lack of sleep, joked that her baby woke up if it ever stopped, so used were they to the constant noise.

I left for home shortly before dawn, driving across North Circular Road, heading for my home in West Belfast so I'd be back in time to take my own primary-school-aged children to school. I got into bed for a quick hour's sleep before getting my own daughters dressed for a very different school run and noticed immediately the silence. We were just a few miles across town but a world away in terms of how families similar to mine were living.

It would be January of the following year before the dispute could be resolved and the protests finally ended. It was a weary, distrustful peace, and community relations were irreparably damaged.

Ten years later, I tracked down some of the Holy Cross pupils, now teenagers and young women. Some were even mothers themselves. They spoke of that time, of the trauma, and the lasting impact on their lives and their own mental health and that of their families. Any time I drive past the school I wonder about those young women and how they are doing now. Are their lives happy? Have they able to put that time behind them?

And I wonder why it was allowed to happen. Why no one stepped in sooner and stopped it. Why a little girls' primary school was allowed to become a war zone.

Allison Morris is a journalist specialising in crime and the legacy of Northern Ireland's conflict.

Still agonising about a front-page story
Rathcoole, County Antrim, 2002

Jonny McCambridge

For the generation of journalists who entered the trade after the Troubles were supposed to have finished, the shadow of what had gone before could be difficult to escape. Conversations with peers were usually dominated by what those older colleagues had seen and reported on. There often seemed to be a twisted moral framework to these exchanges. What was implied, but never explicitly stated, was that seasoned reporters had for years built their reputations on the back of the conflict, and that would no longer be the case. To be blunt, journalists were and are drawn to big news, and the likelihood was that there would be a lot less of it about now the guns were quietened.

At the beginning of this millennium, I was a cub reporter at a weekly paper, the *Newtownabbey Times*, eager to find my way in the industry and perhaps not always as careful or considered as I should have been about how I set about doing it. I was ferociously territorial about 'my patch' and would have believed it to be a personal affront if another journalist broke a story in Newtownabbey that I did not know about.

One week, I heard about what seemed to be a significant scoop. I had been quietly told that the PSNI were to set up a mobile police clinic in the Rathcoole estate on the outskirts of North Belfast, one of Northern Ireland's largest housing estates. The significance of this was that the police had never before had a physical presence there. Even though the ceasefires had been declared several years before, those streets were still considered a no-go area. Most of the estate was under the control of loyalist paramilitaries, particularly the fearsome UDA brigadier John 'Grug' Gregg. His men dealt drugs freely there. I phoned the local police commander with my nugget of information. I recall that, although he confirmed it was correct, he seemed to want to play the story down, not draw attention to it.

My idea was rather different. Needing some tougher quotes, I phoned a local socialist councillor, Mark Langhammer, who I knew had been involved in the initiative to establish the police clinic, and who was often outspoken. Mark gave me the tough quotes I needed and I splashed the story on the front page of the *Newtownabbey Times* that week with a banner headline 'Police Move into Rathcoole' imposed over a photograph of the estate's four iconic tower blocks.

My satisfaction with my scoop was increased when the story was picked up by some of the daily newspapers and even the broadcast media. My profile had been significantly raised on the strength of the exclusive.

The following week was a quieter one for news. On deadline day, I was driving to the office when I received a phone call. It was from the manager of the Dunanney Centre, the local community centre where the police clinic was to be established. She told me that the building had been attacked. I changed course and drove straight there. There was minor damage and the word 'tout' had been daubed several times on the walls. While I was interviewing the centre manager she received a phone call that visibly upset her. She told me that there had been a bomb attack at Mark Langhammer's house. I pressed her for further details but she knew nothing more. I dashed back to my car.

It was a short drive to Mark's house, but one that seemed to take a long time that morning. As I worked my way through the rush-hour traffic, I was forced to confront an uncomfortable truth – that perhaps this man had been hurt, or worse, because of a headline that I had written. My previous pride in my story was now replaced by a low, sickly feeling in my stomach.

I arrived at Mark's house just as a police officer was sealing off the drive-way with tape. I rushed to him and breathlessly asked for details of what had happened. The officer kept his poker-face as he fobbed me off with the usual line that I would have to phone the press office. I persisted, my enquiries becoming more urgent. I didn't want the information for a story, I told him – I just needed to know that nobody had been hurt. The officer's face softened and then he quietly told me that a device had exploded underneath the householder's car. There were no injuries, but the resident had discovered the damage to his car as he was about to take his children to school.

After that I just hung around the scene while police conducted their interviews. I didn't really know what else to do. Eventually Mark spotted me lurking outside his home and invited me in. Even though he had been the subject of the attack, he noticed how shaken I was and took time to reassure me. He made me tea and toast and repeatedly told me that it was not my fault and that he knew what he was doing in speaking out. He said that the UDA were sending out a clear message. Then I went back to my office and wrote up what had happened as the front-page story in that week's paper.

The plans for the police clinic were quietly shelved after that. Over time, I came to understand better exactly what had happened. The Rathcoole police clinic concept came about due to quiet negotiations between police, politicians and community representatives. The paramilitaries were aware of the plan and were prepared to tolerate it as long as it was low-key and did not threaten their activities. In the bluntest terms, the police needed the permission of the UDA to operate in the estate. After my story drew unwanted attention to the proposal – especially with the undoubted hint of triumphalism in the headline – that permission was very publicly and directly withdrawn.

My career continued to progress. Within a couple of years I had been appointed to the position of crime correspondent at the *Belfast Telegraph*. The use of the word 'crime' in the title – 'security correspondent' had been the previous one – was significant; we were trying to establish a new direction of travel, away from the paramilitary news which had dominated the pages for years.

But it was not quite that simple. The past had a persistent habit of continuing to catch up with us. More and more of my time was taken up with writing about crimes committed by terror groups – loyalist feud murders, republican drug dealing and fuel laundering, a seemingly never-ending series of punishment beatings and shootings. Perhaps the busiest week of my career occurred when the IRA robbed the Northern Bank in Belfast city centre, just days before Robert McCartney was killed by republicans while drinking in a bar.

Working on high-profile paramilitary stories meant that I was occasionally asked to go on TV or radio as a commentator. Once, I was asked to give a talk about reporting on crime to a group of mature media students at the University of Ulster. The participants had been asked to bring along something that they considered to be an 'example of a bad piece of journalism' for us to chat about as a group after I had given my presentation.

One of the students produced an old, tattered newspaper front page that I recognised. It was my *Newtownabbey Times* story about the police clinic. He was a former police officer who had been involved in the ill-fated Rathcoole plan. He clearly blamed me and, even though years had elapsed, he decided to take the chance to confront me about it. We had a robust exchange.

It did force me once again to consider my decision-making at the time. On one side of the argument was the undermining of the quiet work that had gone into trying to give people access to a police service that had previously been denied to them, and the sinister consequences for those who spoke out. On the other was the right of the public to know the truth, to be aware of the true extent of the control of a paramilitary group within a community.

Which argument carried more weight than the other? Looking back now, many years on, I'm still not sure that I'm any closer to knowing the answer. As with many aspects of reporting on the Troubles, the answers are seldom black and white.

Jonny McCambridge is a journalist, author and columnist. He has previously worked at the *Belfast Telegraph* and *News Letter* and is currently a reporter with PA Ireland.

Face to face with Freddie Scappaticci
Belfast, 2003

Robin Livingstone

The late William Goldman coined the phrase 'Nobody knows anything'. The screenwriter, whose most notable works are *Butch Cassidy and the Sundance Kid* and *All the President's Men*, was referencing the fact that, behind the Hollywood facade of glamour, brash confidence and bluster, there's a rolling sea of insecurity and fear. 'Not one person in the entire motion picture field knows for a certainty what's going to work,' he observed.

Bit like that with newspapers. Don't get me wrong – if an A-list celebrity walked into the *Andersonstown News* office one day and agreed to give me a few quotes and pictures, it's going to shift a few papers, and the copy and pics are going to be in big demand, no matter what William Goldman says. But what's the likelihood of that happening? You'd be surprised.

So, I'm in my car in the summer of 2017 when the phone goes. It's Deirdre from reception and she's whispering so low that I have to ask her to speak up. I hear her moving, a door opening and closing. 'Coleen Rooney's sitting here getting passport pictures taken on her way to the airport.' (We offer a passport-photo service out front.) I laugh through my nose. 'There's two bouncers with her standing at the door,' Deirdre adds. I'm suddenly and coldly aware she's being quite serious. I tell her to put whichever photographer is at his desk on.

It's Thomas. I tell him to get out to reception and get pictures. Don't start snapping. She's availing of our service in a private setting. Ask nicely. I tell him to call me back and hang up. Two minutes later Thomas is back on the phone. Not a chance. The bouncers were straight over as soon as they saw the cameras. Coleen had raised a gently admonishing hand.

'I'm gonna go outside and get her in the car park,' Thomas tells me.

I picture our car park – surrounded by trees, invisible from the road. Maybe that's why they stopped there. 'Don't do that,' I tell Thomas.

He's not happy. He's not happy at all.

We didn't get the pictures. I got somebody to write a half-arsed, apologetic news-in-brief piece.

I still don't know if I was right or wrong. If that was one story with pictures that I knew for a fact would have been a big hit, with apologies to William Goldman, our actual, provable most-popular-ever story was a ringing endorsement of Goldman's maxim.

At an unremarkable morning news conference in 2003, a reporter told me that a married couple of Manchester United fanatics had changed their names by deed poll to Posh and Becks. I'm going to be completely honest here and say I never batted an eyelid. Victoria and David Beckham in Andytown? Worth a visit and a pic – I put it in the 'soft' page two slot, if memory serves me correctly. To say the thing exploded would be to underestimate the detonation that took place on the Thursday morning. It got picked up all over the place – emails and phone calls from media outlets asking for quotes and pics, especially the pics, flew in. Up to that point, I barely knew about the existence of, never mind the importance of, the *Chat*, *Bella* and *Take a Break* journalism sector. And I was still shaking my head when somebody pointed at the TV on Tuesday morning, and there were Andytown's Posh and Becks in full Man Utd home kit on a breakfast TV sofa in London. 'Nobody knows anything.'

Indeed. And we'll pull a quick and kindly veil of silence over my failure in 2015 to anticipate the crazy appeal of a story we did about cops in a Land Rover in Twinbrook playing ice-cream-van music over the Tannoy to placate a crowd of unruly kids. Tip of the hat to Mr Goldman.

I remember that when I first became aware of the Freddie Scappaticci informer story in 2003 two things occurred to me. The first: nobody seems to be sure whether he's 'Stakeknife' or 'Steak Knife' (it settled into Stakeknife over time, of course). The second: that I needed to put 'Scappaticci' on the commonly misspelled words and names list on the wall behind me. Before the story broke, I'd known of Scap – I used to live round the corner from him in Riverdale – but I didn't know him. I'm pretty sure I came up against him on the five-a-side court once or twice. As the story gathered pace and the intrigue deepened, Scap went to ground (which he seems good at as he's off the grid again at the moment). Where's Stakeknife? Find Stakeknife. Who's got Stakeknife? We sent a reporter to his house a couple of times, an extremely tidy semi in Riverdale Park North (I lived in South). No sign of life – if he'd gone (and he had), he'd taken his family with him. I was on the settee at home on the Saturday evening in May after the story broke, watching a live soccer match and having a beer, when I got a call from a senior colleague. Scappaticci was ready to talk – and he wanted to talk to me. Whether he really wanted to talk to me or whether my colleague had volunteered me, I still couldn't tell you. It was set up for a house in Andytown the next morning. I got a notebook and we chatted for twenty minutes or a half-hour about what I might want to ask him. And then I went back to my beer and my match.

On Sunday morning, the West Belfast monsoon season began. A Sinn Féin guy who I knew well called for me in a car, and as I walked down the path towards him, the rain was bouncing up to my waist off the tarmac. We chatted on the drive, but not about Stakeknife. Another, much more senior, Sinn Féin guy was waiting for me at the door of the house where the interview was to take place. If somebody was to give me a pin and tell me to stick it right where I imagine the very centre of Andersonstown to be, I'd stick it in this house. I was brought into the living room and, as I wiped the rain from my forehead and eyes with my palm, Scap got up from his chair to greet me. He let out an anguished groan as he rose. We shook hands and he explained that his back was playing up. A chronic condition. 'Wouldn't surprise me if it was this weather,' he said. I could hardly hear him, the rain was beating so loudly on the windows – it left a constant background hiss on the tape-recording, which – when I came to transcribe the interview – made it sound like it was a dodgy cassette.

He was short and if the word stocky didn't exist I'd have had to invent it. Unbelievably solid. Dark-eyed, but not as swarthy as in the newspaper pictures I'd seen. Short, salt-and-pepper hair, heavily stubbled face, grey polo shirt with black collar and a logo I couldn't read beneath an open blue Berghaus fleece. Scap sat down again, with another groan. He told me the history of his back travails while I set up my recorder and got out my notebook and pen. He shifted constantly in his chair, trying and failing to find a position that would give him relief, or at least less pain. Every time he moved, he groaned and winced.

Scap moved on to my family. He knew two of my older brothers well, he'd met my father a few times. He told me a few funny stories about my eldest brother, who, when I asked him later, shrugged and wasn't able to stand them up or knock them down. My lorry driver father sang in clubs in the evenings and Scap told me what a lovely voice Archie had. He then started calling me 'Livvy', a family nickname that has been bestowed on some of my brothers, but which I've never been called.

And to tell you the truth, I can't tell you eighteen years on if I knew that morning he was playing me like a fiddle, or if it has just occurred to me as I write this. His back; his groans; my brothers; my father's singing; 'Livvy'. But I'm thinking about it now, and I'm thinking that maybe that was his IRA shtick – the trait that got him promoted from foot soldier to interrogator.

Our story – in which he categorically denied the accusations made in the press – took off, as we knew it would. The *Irish Times* ran with it and headlined their story with the quote, 'Jesus, What Are My Family Going to Think When They See This?', which I wish I'd done. But it was the pictures that our photographer took later that day at our offices that everyone wanted. Listen, civilians, quotes are great, but it's always about the pictures. I'm looking at them now. Scap looks dishevelled, his eyes are narrowed, querying and uncertain, as if it's just occurred to him for the first time that things are never going to be the same again.

'Nobody knows anything.' Fair enough, as far as it goes in the movies, but in the newspaper business, people usually know enough. And as far as Scap was concerned in his dark business, everybody knew something.

Robin Livingstone is Group Editor, Belfast Media Group.

Thomas Devlin: his family's fight for justice and the trust that keeps his memory alive
North Belfast, 2005

Stephen Breen

Gary Taylor and Nigel Brown had never met the three teenagers who walked just a few yards in front of them. Although it would later emerge that Taylor held 'deeply sectarian views' and had attacked Catholics in the past, he had no way of knowing the religion of Thomas Devlin, or that of Jonathan McKee or Fintan Maguire.

That didn't stop Taylor and his accomplice from initiating what Justice McLaughlin – the judge who presided over Taylor and Brown's subsequent trial in 2010 – described as a 'horrifying and brutal attack upon utterly defenceless and harmless boys' as they made their way along Belfast's Somerton Road on the night of Wednesday, 10 August 2005.

Taylor's deep-rooted hatred of all things Catholic was in stark contrast to the views shared by the teenagers, who were simply making their way home after a visit to the shop. The trio had never encountered sectarianism and were just children when the Good Friday Agreement was signed in 1998. Thomas may have been brought up in the Catholic faith, but he had been a member of the Boys' Brigade and also a student at Belfast Royal Academy. Religion didn't matter to him. His friends were drawn from all backgrounds. The mayhem and misery of the Troubles had never touched his young life. The teenager's interests were music and friendship. And when fifteen-year-old Thomas, who was preparing to sit his GCSE exams that year, and his two friends set out that night to buy a snack after an evening of playing video games, little did they know it would be their last ever outing together.

Within twenty minutes of leaving the Ross House flats in the loyalist Mount Vernon Estate, Taylor and Brown had identified their targets. Approaching the trio from behind, Brown used a baton to beat Jonathan around the head and shoulders as Thomas and Fintan attempted to flee their attackers. Fintan managed to escape, but Thomas was dragged from the wall of a nearby school by Taylor as he ran for his life. Once caught, the schoolboy was stabbed nine times in the chest and back in a frenzied knife attack. As Thomas lay dying, Taylor turned his attention to Jonathan, stabbing him in the stomach. His efforts to stab Jonathan in the back only failed because the boy had been wearing Thomas's backpack.

When Thomas was pronounced dead at Belfast's Mater Hospital, his parents, Penny Holloway and Jim Devlin, along with his brother and sister, James and Megan, their wider family and the teenager's large circle of friends, were thrust into a world of darkness. Condemnation for the senseless and completely unprovoked murder of a schoolboy quickly followed from all sections of society. It was no surprise to Thomas's family to see almost one hundred of his schoolfriends gather in the garden of his home ahead of his funeral.

As with many other horrific murders over the years, I remember where I was when news of the senseless killing emerged. The murder carried particular significance for me as it had occurred on the exact same day my father, also called Thomas, had lost his life to knife crime in London just three years previously. At the time of Thomas's killing, I was working as the crime correspondent for the *Sunday Life* newspaper. Thomas's killing would dominate the news in the coming months.

A few months after the incident, and as Thomas's family continued to grieve, I was welcomed into the Devlin family home. The purpose of my visit was to assist his parents in making an appeal for anyone with information to come forward. When I arrived, a beautiful black Great Dane was looking out the window. Rosie was Thomas's pet and I could see that she too missed him desperately. As Rosie waited anxiously for the teenager's return, Thomas's parents eloquently described the raw trauma that had consumed them since the loss of their son. After Rosie passed in 2013, there would be no other pet.

I returned to the family home a week before Christmas 2005 as the teenager's parents made another heartfelt appeal for anyone with information to come forward. I will never forget Penny and Jim, who had received dozens of letters of support from around the world, describing their son as a 'gift'. They told me, 'Our pain is very real and very deep and anyone who has lost a child will tell you this. Thomas was a gift to us, but an evil killer has taken this away from us.' Despite the impending trauma of spending their first ever Christmas without their youngest son, I could also see there was determination that their son's killers would one day be brought to justice, and also a determination from Thomas's family that some good would come out of his killing. Even in their own grief, they still wished my own family a peaceful Christmas.

In February 2006, they launched the Thomas Devlin Fund, with the aim of raising funding for scholarships for students. Launching the trust, Eamonn Holmes called for an end to knife crime when he said, 'The fund is dedicated to promoting the futility of violence against young people. It will support young people involved in music and the creative arts, commission a sculpture on the theme and make representations to the government on appropriate actions and responses. Over a hundred young people have been killed in North Belfast since 1970 and we must ensure that, in future, our children live without the fear of violence.' Since its inception, the fund has helped change the lives of students across Northern Ireland by providing ninety bursaries in the areas of art, craft, fashion, design and music. Alongside the fund, Thomas's parents also spearheaded a campaign in local schools to raise awareness of the dangers of knife crime.

With Thomas's legacy secured, the PSNI investigation into the murder continued. The family were dealt a crushing blow in July 2008 when the Public Prosecution Service in Northern Ireland decided there wasn't enough evidence to bring charges against the chief suspects in the case. The PPS then undertook an internal review of their decision, with the family only being notified about the PPS decision after it was confirmed to the *Sunday Life* in a statement. In November 2008, the PPS again confirmed there would be no prosecution.

The family requested an independent review of the decision. The exact same evidence and documents were then presented to an independent lawyer in England, who concluded there was a 'compelling circumstantial case'. In March 2009 – and at the third time of asking – the PPS brought charges of murder against the prime suspects in the case. At the same time, the family were also insistent that the prosecution be led by a barrister from outside Northern Ireland due to the PPS's earlier decisions.

Although I was working in Dublin at the time, I contacted Thomas's mum at the time of the trial to wish her the very best, to which she replied, 'We have been waiting for this day for a long time, but we have a long way to go.' Just over a year later, the Devlin family's extraordinary resilience and determination in pursuit of justice was finally rewarded when both men were found guilty of the teenager's murder. Following the verdicts, which vindicated the family's determination to pursue the joint enterprise method of prosecution, I had another call with Thomas's mum. Though relieved justice for her son had been secured, the PPS, which later apologised to the Devlin family, came in for harsh criticism for compounding the family's grief.

Speaking to the family again in 2021 for this book, Thomas's mum reminded me of her family's loss when she said, 'We will never forget Thomas and we have had to find a way to live with our loss. Looking back, if we hadn't been so determined, I don't think the two of them would have been convicted. It shouldn't have been such a fight and we know the PPS has initiated changes in how it operates since Thomas's case. It was a very difficult time for our family and we take comfort from the fact that our son's memory is very much alive thanks to the ongoing work of the fund.'

Stephen Breen is the crime editor with the *Irish Sun*. He was previously crime correspondent with the *Sunday Life*.

'We don't want to go back to this'
Massereene Barracks, Antrim, 2009

David Young

It was the lack of sound that made the footage feel almost unreal. The grainy quality of the CCTV images also helped dull the brutality. But while the cracks of the assault rifles were not audible, and the pictures were blurry and unclear, those thirty-four seconds of footage still left an indelible imprint on me. In little over half a minute, two Real IRA gunmen had sprayed sixty-three rounds at a group of soldiers who had emerged from the gates of Massereene Barracks in Antrim town to collect a pizza delivery. One of the killers stopped to reload. Both shooters then walked forward and, unflinching, fired down at their prone victims who lay on the ground.

The footage was played to a silent courtroom during the 2011 trial of two men accused of murdering Royal Engineer sappers Patrick Azimkar, aged twenty-one, and Mark Quinsey, aged twenty-three. Two other soldiers and two pizza delivery drivers were seriously injured in the hail of gunfire. The soldiers from 38 Engineer Regiment were hours from deploying to Afghanistan. Already dressed in desert fatigues, the sappers from the regiment's 25 Field Squadron had ordered pizza as they awaited transportation.

Before the chilling security camera footage was played to Antrim Crown Court, the soldiers' grieving mothers left the room. Other bereaved relations remained to bear witness to their loved ones' final moments. It was early November, and they were wearing poppies.

Two-and-half years earlier, a late-night call from my editor had alerted me to what had happened outside the barracks shortly after 9 p.m. on Saturday, 7 March 2009.

Such calls were commonplace for reporters at the height of the Troubles. A decade on from the Good Friday Agreement, and with no security force members killed in the years since, this one was a stark bolt from a past Northern Ireland was supposed to have left behind.

By the time I arrived in Antrim, a wide police cordon was already in place. The Randalstown Road where the base was situated was closed to traffic. It was wet and bitterly cold. As the hours passed and news of the shootings spread, local people started to arrive to pay their respects. An old stone wall adjacent to the police tape became a temporary memorial, with flowers and sympathy cards buffeted by the icy winds. Some who stopped at the cordon had clearly not yet heard. Dog walkers and joggers appeared stunned when officers told them why they would need to find another route.

But the confusion of early morning soon gave way to resolution, and as lunch approached on that bleak Sunday, a remarkable act of solidarity played out in the face of evil. They came from every corner of the town. And in their hundreds. From St Comgall's Catholic chapel close to the murder scene, from First Antrim Presbyterian church in the town centre. From Antrim's Church of Ireland and Methodist churches too. Cutting short their traditional Sunday morning services, worshippers of every denomination walked in silence to the police line and stood together amid the growing floral tributes. They bowed their heads and prayed. Together. 'Everyone will hug each other a little tighter tonight after this,' Father Tony Devlin told the crowd, his voice choked with emotion. 'We don't want to go back to this. Nobody wants to go back to this in any way at all. We don't want those years of the past; they were horrible years for everyone.' People from different churches hugged one another, some weeping openly, as the short service came to an end.

There was a striking contrast between that show of unity and the scenes that awaited up at the barracks gates when the cordon was finally lifted the following day.

Two days of rain had failed to wash away the blood stains on the tarmac. They were visible among shards of glass and chalk outlines of spent bullet cases. There was also scattered bandage packaging, discarded by the medics who fought to save the lives of those gunned down. Bullet holes pockmarked the security watch tower, one having pierced a 'Stop' sign on the main gates. Flowers placed by the old stone wall the previous day had by then been moved to the front of the base. They lay among dozens of other bouquets left by locals. The accompanying messages conveyed the deep sorrow and great anger that had consumed this close-knit county town.

At one point, the army's then commander in Northern Ireland, Brigadier George Norton, arrived to view the floral tributes and read some of the sympathy cards: 'You never stood a chance,' stated one. Another needed only one word: 'Why?'

Brigadier Norton added his own thoughts as he addressed a sizeable gathering of news reporters. 'They were magnificent individuals, and we mourn their loss,' he said.

Patrick Azimkar was a sports-mad Londoner who had joined the Engineers to develop his carpentry skills. He had grown to love Northern Ireland in the short time he had been based there and had told his family of his hopes of eventually settling in the region. Mark Quinsey, from the Birmingham suburb of Warstock, was described as a fun, popular young man with a love of life and a brilliant sense of humour. His family said he was looking forward to proving himself in Afghanistan and had been cheated of the opportunity to serve his country. His mother, Pamela Brankin, who left court that day in November 2011 before the CCTV was played, died two years later – her daughter Jaime attributing her death to a heart broken by Mark's killing.

Lurgan republican Colin Duffy and Brian Shivers, from Magherafelt, were ultimately acquitted of the young sappers' murders, the latter after a retrial.

As the TV cameras focused on Brigadier Norton as he spoke on the Monday after the attack, an unassuming lady from the nearby town of Crumlin attracted less media attention as she quietly approached the barracks gates to leave flowers. 'I thought we had left all those pointless days behind us,' she said, tears welling in her eyes. 'I just feel so sorry for those poor boys' mothers.'

Within hours of those words, dissident republican gunfire had rung out again, this time in Craigavon, County Armagh. Constable Stephen Carroll, aged forty-eight, had been shot dead by the Continuity IRA while responding to a 999 call-out. He was the first police officer murdered in Northern Ireland since 1998. Sappers Quinsey and Azimkar were the first soldiers murdered since 1997.

In those two days in March 2009, Northern Ireland lurched backwards. But amid the darkness, on that cold Sunday beside the police cordon, there was a glimmer of hope that a brighter future was still within reach: 'In our churches today, many people were crying because of the experiences they remembered from the past,' Father Devlin told the impromptu cross-community vigil. 'They do not want it to come back again.'

David Young is the Ireland Editor at PA Media – the UK and Ireland's national newswire service. He was previously PA's chief reporter on the island of Ireland. Prior to joining the Press Association, he worked at the *News Letter*.

I'll never forget the Queen's visit to the Garden of Remembrance
Dublin, 2011

Charlie Bird

Even today, all these years after the historic moment when I witnessed Queen Elizabeth II enter the Garden of Remembrance in Dublin, I still pinch myself and recall it as one of the most spine-tingling moments of my almost forty years as a journalist with RTÉ News. I had covered many major news events, at home and abroad, but those relating to the developing peace process in the North of Ireland were the stand-out parts of my long career.

There was a huge anticipation about the Queen's historic state visit to the Republic in 2011. It had been many years in the planning and was clearly linked to the success of the peace process and the Good Friday Agreement. I was assigned to cover the visit to the Garden of Remembrance. It was one of the highlights of her groundbreaking trip. But for me, it had an added significance, which made that day even more memorable.

Back in the early 1990s, as the stirrings of the peace process in the North were beginning, I was asked by my boss, Joe Mulholland, to become RTÉ's link person with the IRA. With the help of my colleague and pal Tommie Gorman, I established a line of communication with the IRA. My first contact was a man called Brendan. And yes, occasionally I would meet him near or in the Garden of Remembrance, which is located at Parnell Square at the top of O'Connell Street in Dublin city centre.

On 30 August 1994, I got a phone call from Brendan and was told to be at a location not far from the Garden of Remembrance the following morning. It turned out that I was one of three journalists who were given the IRA's ceasefire statement – the first significant move in the developing peace process that began to unfold. That day, just after 11 a.m., I read the opening lines of the IRA statement live on RTÉ Radio One:

Recognising the potential of the current situation and in order to enhance the democratic peace process and underline our definite commitment to its success, the leadership of Óglaigh na hÉireann have decided that, as of midnight, Wednesday, 31 August, there will be a complete cessation of military operations.

And now almost seventeen years later, not far from where I had made my broadcast, I was witnessing the Queen arriving at the garden that was dedicated to the memory of all those who gave their lives in the cause of Irish freedom. She was accompanied by President Mary McAleese and escorted around the memorial by the minister for justice, Alan Shatter. Not far from where once I had met my IRA contact, I was now watching the familiar figure of the British monarch laying a wreath at the memorial and then observing a minute's silence with her head bowed – an amazing symbolic gesture. Something even more remarkable happened that day too – during the ceremony, the Irish Army band played 'God Save The Queen'. Not so many years earlier, it would have seemed unbelievable that 'God Save The Queen' would boom out across one of the most revered places that commemorates the fight for Irish freedom. This historic state visit was yet another powerful symbol of the success of the peace process and the hard-won rewards of the Good Friday Agreement.

In June 1995, little less than a year after the IRA announced its first ceasefire, Prince Charles made the first official visit to Dublin by a member of the British Royal family since Irish independence. I was at Baldonnel military aerodrome to witness the Prince of Wales arrive for this significant visit, paving the way for the Queen's arrival in 2011.

During the evolving peace process, I was to witness other memorable events. Perhaps one of the most controversial was President Robinson's visit to West Belfast in the summer of 1993, almost a year before the first IRA ceasefire. The media was focused on just one thing: would the president shake the hand of Gerry Adams?

It would be an understatement to say that neither the government in London nor the Labour Party element of the coalition government in Dublin were pleased with this visit. But to Mary Robinson's credit, she went ahead with the trip – and the handshake happened. As part of the balancing act, earlier that day she'd visited a woman's centre in a loyalist area where someone shouted at her, 'You're not welcome here.'

Back then, even as an RTÉ journalist, one couldn't interview any member of Sinn Féin – under Section 31 of the Broadcasting Act, interviews with members of Sinn Féin were proscribed – but the president was prepared to shake Gerry Adams' hand.

In January 1994, the ban was lifted by the minister for communications, Michael D. Higgins.

If the Queen's 2011 visit was a stand-out moment, the other time I got goosebumps on a story was during President Mary Robinson's visit to London in June 1996. There was huge sensitivity at the time about how she would be announced at the various functions – in a careful balancing act, the diplomats settled on President Mary Robinson, with no reference to where she was president of. The high point of the visit came when she travelled to Buckingham Palace to meet the Queen. It was such a powerful symbol of the developing relationship between Britain and Ireland. On arrival, Mary Robinson, accompanied by Prince Edward, set off to inspect the guard of honour and, at that moment, the military band played 'Amhrán na bhFiann'. Yes, the Irish national anthem was booming out across that inner square at the centre of Buckingham Palace. I looked across at Dick Spring, the minister for foreign affairs – with a nod, we acknowledged the significance of the moment.

Just two years later, the key moment in the Northern peace process finally arrived with the signing of the Belfast/Good Friday Agreement in April 1998. But the real moment for me came when Queen Elizabeth visited the Garden of Remembrance in Dublin and 'God Save The Queen' rang out across the centre of Dublin. Today, sitting in front of my work desk at home, is a photograph taken by the *Irish Times* on the day of a huge media scrum peering at the British monarch as she walked into this hallowed ground. I'm in the middle of this photograph, and I can remember one of the things that flashed into my head at the time. What would Brendan, my first IRA contact, have thought of this moment?

Just a couple of years ago, I travelled to Belfast to take part in a discussion about my memory of the first IRA ceasefire. I stopped off to visit the new Titanic visitor centre. I was totally gobsmacked by what I saw. An enormous parking area full of hundreds of cars, and almost all of them had southern number plates. Not that I ever doubted it, but this was more clear evidence that the peace process was working and that we are all living on a shared island.

Charlie Bird was chief news correspondent for RTÉ News for many years. He was also RTÉ's contact person with the IRA for twelve years as the peace process unfolded.

The night my luck ran out
Belfast, 2011, and Derry, 2019

Niall Carson

It was the night my luck ran out. As a press photographer, I'd had a huge number of close encounters with danger during the Troubles. But that night in June 2011, the violence finally caught up with me.

I was covering sectarian clashes in Belfast at the Newtownards Road/ Short Strand interface, and had stationed myself with a group of television cameramen and newspaper photographers on the Protestant side of the peace wall, on the lower Newtownards Road. Further up the road, there was rioting, and as members of the media had had their equipment taken by the rioters in recent days, we opted to stay at a safer distance and use long lenses. We'd gathered beside an armoured PSNI Land Rover, hoping to use it for cover in the event of an emergency, as we had all done many times before. What happened that night changed my opinion about the wisdom of standing beside police vehicles on darkened streets.

The first warning signs came when I heard voices coming from the Short Strand side of the peace wall, followed by the sound of the clanking of ladders. I knew a gunman would appear sooner or later but, naively, I believed he would aim his weapon up the street at the loyalist rioters, so I pointed my camera up at the spot on the peace wall where I believed he would emerge. Then, just ten feet away from me, I saw a pair of hands in blue surgical gloves appear at the top of the wall, followed by a face covered in a Celtic football scarf and a baseball hat. For what seemed like a lifetime, I stared straight at him. I could see his eyes, I could clearly see a revolver – I could even see the bullets in the cylinder of the gun. The penny dropped. The reason I could see right down the barrel was because the weapon was pointed straight at me. I turned on my heels and shouted 'Gun, gun,' to my colleagues before five or six shots rang out, followed by the awful, unmistakeable smell of gun powder.

I felt a very hard slapping sensation in the back of my right leg. My first impression was that the police had fired a plastic bullet at the gunman but had hit me by mistake. My leg muscles began to contract and my leg started

217

to tense up. Then I felt the horrible sensation of cold blood running down the back of my calf. I felt the back of my leg with my hand – my jeans were soaked with blood. When I looked down I could see blood trickling out the front of my jeans. A shiver went down my spine and the blood drained from my face as it dawned on me what had actually happened. I had been shot through and through. The bullet had entered the back of my right thigh and come out of the front. The strange thing is that I was in absolutely no pain. The body's shock mechanism, I now know, really is amazing in a situation like that. It would be a good hour before I felt anything except numbness where I'd been shot.

I put my hand up like a child in school and told the police officers in the Land Rover that I'd been shot. I knew that from their years of training and experience they would be able to stabilise me before an ambulance could come. I felt quite safe in their hands. A water cannon was reversed down the Newtownards Road towards us and used as a blockade to protect us from further shots. My colleagues could see I was not seriously injured and to take my mind off the blood we exchanged some good-natured banter as a female police officer expertly applied wadding and bandages to my leg. I'm indebted to my friend Colm Lenihan from the Pacemaker Press news agency who kept my car and gear safely at the *Irish News* car park until I'd recovered.

All the medics who treated me were amazing. I was looked after by a great many people in the NHS over the next three months and gained a great appreciation for the work that paramedics, nurses, surgeons, GPs, pharmacists and physios do.

I was in awe of the seamless organisation of the NHS and it made me see just how fortunate we are to have it.

It would be a long time before I would be in such dangerous position again.

Just in case, I've had extensive training in hostile environments and conflict resolution from my employers, the Press Association. However, during an Easter visit to my in-laws in Derry in 2019, I was to witness another tragic chapter in the history of Northern Ireland.

I was checking Twitter on my phone on the Thursday before Easter and saw some reports of police searches in the Creggan area of the city, which is a hotbed of dissident republicanism. I was sure it was the police trying to shut down any Easter Sunday attacks or shows of strength by dissidents. At first, because I was off work, I didn't think what was happening was serious enough to warrant my presence. But then I saw videos by local reporter Leona O'Neill, which showed several burning vehicles. I decided to take a run up and shoot a few frames. When I arrived at the scene, it was very confusing. There were two crowds of people at the top and bottom of a street called Fanad Drive.

The burning vehicles were at the bottom of the street, and there were about a hundred youths filming the chaos on their mobile phones.

At the top of the street, where I was, there were a couple of police jeeps with around a hundred people behind them. A mix of residents, including young children in their pyjamas, watched as men ran up the street and threw petrol bombs at the police vehicles. No police officers got out to give chase. Instead they opted to use CCTV cameras on top of the jeeps to gather evidence. I immediately saw that as a bad sign. It meant that the PSNI were going for what's known as 'hard cover', which is usually a sign that a gunman has been spotted nearby. I met Leona at the top of the street and she told me there were rumours of shots having been fired. She and I took refuge behind a brick wall, as we had been trained to do.

Unbeknownst to me, a number of people – including an up-and-coming young journalist called Lyra McKee – were taking cover by a police jeep, just as I had done in 2011. It was very hard to distinguish live rounds from the sounds around us that night. All the time there were bangs from fireworks, fire crackers, exploding petrol tanks and even exploding car tyres.

My phone battery was dead because I'd filmed a lot of videos of the scene so I made my way to my car during a lull in the violence to get a portable battery pack to charge it. Just then, a number of shots rang out among the cacophony of noises. As I returned to the top of Fanad Drive there was a scene of absolute pandemonium as someone was carried into the back of the armoured Land Rover.

The jeep sped off in the direction of Altnagelvin Hospital. Initially I wasn't sure what had just gone on. Judging by the angry reaction of the crowd I thought someone had been arrested by a police snatch squad. But then I saw a woman with blood on her hands and heard someone scream, 'Lyra's been shot.' A group of very nervous-looking police officers began to roll out crime scene tape before more heavily armed officers started to seal off the area for a proper forensic examination. Things very quickly quietened down as word spread about what had happened. Lyra McKee, who was just twenty-nine years old, had been killed.

In the coming days and weeks, we all learned of Lyra's life and work, and of how a promising career had been cut short. At her funeral in St Anne's Cathedral, Belfast, Father Martin Magill – a priest well known for his cross-community and mental health work – delivered a hard-hitting sermon about restoring power-sharing at Stormont, with First Minister Arlene Foster and deputy First Minister Michelle O'Neill sitting in the pews in front of him. It was not long after that Northern Ireland's Stormont Assembly did get back up and running as public outrage at the stalemate and political vacuum increased.

I hope there will be no more Lyra McKees. But in Northern Ireland the peace process is regularly at a tipping point, with reporters and photographers like me called on to chronicle its dangerous path.

Niall Carson is a multi-award-winning press photographer with over twenty years experience. Born in Belfast, he has travelled the globe covering everything from conflict to entertainment. He is currently based in Dublin, working for the PA Media Group

Continuing violence, north and south of the border
Dublin, 2013

Paul Reynolds

It's been a while since the infamous IRA slogan '*Tiocfaidh ár lá*' has been proclaimed in an Irish courtroom. The last time I heard it was in April 2013, when a fifty-year-old Limerick woman gave a clenched-fist salute and shouted it in defiance at the Special Criminal Court in Dublin before she was led away to begin a life sentence for murder.

The assassination of David Darcy two years earlier was reminiscent of so many other murders of innocent victims of the Troubles, north and south. The thirty-nine-year-old father of two lived in the west Dublin suburb of Ballyfermot and worked as a delivery driver for a local butcher. David Darcy got up early to go to work on the morning of 28 November 2011, but was shot dead in the company van in the driveway of his home as he was about to leave at 6.55 a.m.

Rose Lynch told gardaí that she was 'an IRA volunteer' and had 'executed' David Darcy. The mother of four was a community worker and suicide counsellor, and also an unrepentant killer. She showed no remorse for what she had done. The Continuity IRA issued a statement describing the murder as a 'military operation' on the house of a 'criminal drugs gang'. The Garda officer in charge of the case, Detective Inspector Colm O'Malley, described that statement as 'total lies'. He pointed out that David Darcy had never been involved in any criminal or subversive activity; he was a hard-working man who was 'totally blameless' and 'wholly innocent'. 'The pseudo paramilitary organisation was mistaken,' said O'Malley.

The dignity and courage of the Darcy family outside the court as they spoke to us – the waiting media – that day was striking. They were determined that the truth about their father, brother, partner and son should be known. 'For these people to come along and salute, with their hands up in the air and say it's for Ireland? It can't be. They're just cowards,' David's father, Henry Darcy, said. 'We do not want to see this happening to another mother, father, partner, son, daughter or grandchild.'

221

How many times have we all heard that?

It was common practice over the years for IRA prisoners – before they were taken down the winding stairs from the dock to the cells in the old Special Criminal Court in Dublin – to shout out in the Irish language that their day would come. They saw themselves as part of a continuing violent revolutionary tradition in a court that was first opened by the British in 1797, and from where the voices of republican history, the United Irishmen, the Young Irelanders and the Fenians, resonated. They, too, had stood in the same historical dock from where Robert Emmet made his famous 'when my country takes her place among the nations of the earth' speech before his execution in 1803.

The Georgian courthouse building in Green Street in Dublin became the Special Criminal Court in May 1972. The IRA refused to recognise it; as did Martin McGuinness when he was convicted there of IRA membership in 1973. Sinn Féin still has issues with it today. Initially, the court dealt solely with subversive cases, but now it also tries gangsters, gunmen and drug dealers. The murders in June 1996 of Detective Garda Jerry McCabe by the IRA in County Limerick and the journalist Veronica Guerin by a criminal gang in Dublin were the catalyst for this.

The state took the view then that organised crime south of the border had become as big a threat to the state as terrorism. It's a view it still holds today. The connection between subversives and gangland criminals is now firmly rooted in the Republic of Ireland's criminal justice system.

The Gilligan drugs gang, which was responsible for the murder of Veronica Guerin, was the first organised crime group to be targeted by the new approach. These trials also marked the first time the witness-protection programme was used south of the border. The Gilligan gang's quartermaster, former soldier Charlie Bowden, turned state witness and gave evidence against his fellow gang members.

The court was also used to try the late Michael McKevitt, founder of the Real IRA and one of four men found civilly liable for the Omagh bombing. McKevitt was sentenced to twenty years in prison after FBI and MI5 spy David Rupert infiltrated his organisation and testified against him in Dublin.

The actions of Bowden and Rupert were in stark contrast to those of Patrick Harty, a bachelor farmer from Tipperary who was to be a witness against the IRA in the Special Criminal Court in 1999. Harty refused to testify against Pearse McAuley, Kevin English, Jeremiah Sheehy and Michael O' Neill, the four IRA members charged with the murder of Detective Garda Jerry McCabe. The state had to abandon the prosecution for capital murder because of IRA intimidation and was forced to accept a plea of manslaughter from the four garda killers. The reaction to the murder of a garda is always one of shock, anger and disgust. The four IRA men were seen to have been involved in an organised crime – the robbery of a post office cash van – when they shot and killed Jerry McCabe and seriously injured his colleague Ben O'Sullivan. For many people south of the border, the case enshrined the links between violent republicanism and organised crime and the reality of witness intimidation.

The IRA in whatever incarnation – Official, Provisional, Continuity, Real, New, or ONH (Óglaigh na hÉireann) – has always been involved in criminal activity in the Republic of Ireland. Subversive organisations have in the past funded, and continue to fund, their activities through various crimes, such as cross-border smuggling, diesel laundering, extortion and armed robbery. They invariably claim these crimes are committed for 'the cause', but there are also several examples where key figures have lined their own pockets. Involvement in criminality has also therefore inevitably led to cooperation as well as conflict between subversives and criminals.

The Provisional IRA always claimed to abhor drug dealing and clamp down hard on it. It made very public shows of carrying out punishment beatings and kneecappings, and exiling drug dealers, particularly in disadvantaged communities in Dublin. It also, however, funded its activities by 'licensing' selected criminals to operate in these areas. Once the Provisional IRA disbanded, the dissident republicans tried to carry on that tradition but did not engender the same level of fear or respect among the criminal fraternity. One of the most prominent examples of this was the murder in Dublin of the Real IRA member Alan Ryan.

Ryan was a senior figure in the dissident republican group who, along with five others, including the late Real IRA leader Seamus McGrane, had been jailed after the Gardaí found their underground training camp in Stamullen in County Meath in 1999. When released from prison, Ryan became the head of the Real IRA in Dublin, and the group began extorting money from criminals and legitimate businesses. It violently punished those who did not pay up and in one year, 2010, it shot dead three criminals in Dublin and Cork. However when the dissidents shot dead Michael 'Mika' Kelly the following year, the criminal gangs decided they had gone too far. Kelly was a senior figure in organised crime in Dublin, with links to the Kinahan Organised Crime Group, and the gangsters were by now as well armed and as ruthless as the dissidents. On 3 September 2012, they shot Alan Ryan dead, sending a clear message to the dissidents that they were no longer prepared to allow them to cream off the profits of their multi-million-euro criminal enterprises.

Four years later, the Kinahan Organised Crime Group blamed the dissidents for supplying the rival Hutch Organised Crime Group with the guns used to murder the Kinahan gang member David Byrne in the Regency Hotel in Dublin in February 2016. Its retaliation was swift and brutal. It shot dead two dissidents in the next two months, including Alan Ryan's brother Vincent, and targeted a third, who died in custody before he could be extradited from the North to face trial in Dublin.

Rose Lynch was groomed into violent republicanism by her father, Joe 'Tiny' Lynch from Limerick, who was at one time third in the hierarchy of the Continuity IRA. She remains in prison and has vowed to die 'an IRA volunteer'. Her father said he was proud of her on the day she was jailed for life. He has since changed his views. Joe Lynch was one of seven men caught in an MI5 operation targeting the dissident group and was jailed in Belfast in 2020 for three years and three months. At over eighty years of age, the court was satisfied he no longer posed a danger to society and that he had cut his ties with dissident republican activity. 'It's all over for me,' he said.

That may be true for one man. However almost a quarter of a century after the Good Friday Agreement, the violence and the accompanying pain and sorrow for the victims of the Troubles and their families continues, north and south of the border.

Paul Reynolds is the crime correspondent for RTÉ and has reported extensively on organised crime, terrorism and subversive activity in Ireland for over twenty-five years.

Ready to tell their story: survivors revisit the horror of the Ballygawley bus bombing
Ballygawley, 2013

Peter Cardwell

The media's interest in tragedy is often fleeting. If someone caught up in terrorism said 'no' to the microphone thrust in their face in the immediate aftermath of probably their most traumatic life event, their moment to speak on camera was usually lost. Having conversed with countless victims and survivors of the Troubles during my time both as a journalist at BBC Northern Ireland and UTV, and as a UK government special adviser to two Northern Ireland secretaries, it's clear that many people affected by the Troubles eventually reach a time when they are, in fact, ready to tell their stories. But by that stage, the cameras are usually long gone.

I grew up during the tail end of the Troubles, cosseted from most of the horrendous terrorism gripping Northern Ireland in the late 1980s and early 1990s because we lived in the largely peaceful, middle-class village of Richhill in County Armagh. I had a particularly unthinking teacher at the local primary school who once asked each of the thirty children in her class what their dad did for a living. Twenty-four of the thirty replied, 'My dad is a civil servant,' and even as children we knew what that was code for: Richhill was a village heavily populated by members of the security forces.

One of them was thirty-year-old Private Paul Blakely of the Ulster Defence Regiment, who was murdered in an IRA bomb attack at the Glenanne Barracks in south Armagh in 1991. Two other soldiers were murdered alongside Private Blakely in that appalling and unjustifiable terrorist act, with a further fourteen people injured. I remember the facts very clearly, because his seven-year-old daughter, Natasha – the eldest of four children left fatherless by the senseless attack – sat beside me in primary three. Her single day off school that year was to mourn her father. A year and a half before, the Blakely family had been made homeless over the Christmas period by an IRA car bomb.

So, like the vast majority of journalists – and, indeed, people in Northern Ireland – I was merely an observer of the effects of the Troubles and, personally, suffered nothing. But what I was privileged to experience during my journalistic and political careers – and will remember for a lifetime – is the dignity, resilience and quiet determination of most of those who did.

Kenny Donaldson is an indefatigable campaigner who runs the victims' group, the South East Fermanagh Foundation. I first met Kenny when I was an eighteen-year-old on work experience at Stormont; he was working for a Fermanagh and South Tyrone assembly member. A journalism and politics graduate of Leeds University, Kenny knows the media well, and, over the years, many reporters have benefitted from his pointing them in the direction of a story, or facilitating access to a victim who hadn't spoken before, perhaps on an anniversary. In 2013, Kenny rang to ask whether I would like to interview retired troops returning for the first time in twenty-five years to Ballygawley, where eight soldiers from 1st Battalion The Light Infantry were murdered in 1988.

On the night of 20 August 1988, thirty-six soldiers were travelling from Belfast to a base in Omagh. When a bomb loaded with 200lb of Semtex exploded, eight of the soldiers were killed, and the remaining twenty-eight sustained injuries. The bus wasn't supposed to be on that road between Ballygawley and Omagh: earlier in the journey, diversion signs had rerouted it. No one knows who put the signs on the road.

In August 2013, when I arrived at the memorial service at the roadside in County Tyrone in a UTV car driven by cameraman Brian Newman, it was striking to be told that this was the first time in a quarter of a century that many of those bonded by the tragedy had even seen one another, let alone conversed. Despite the length of time, memories were understandably still raw, as James Leatherbarrow, one of the soldiers who had been on the bus that night, told us on camera: 'I remember the smell of cordite, the smell of burning rubber and the diesel, and when I came round I knew that we'd been blown up because I was trapped underneath the back of the wreckage.' James injured his back and his eardrum was perforated in the attack, but the real scars he bears are unseen. In the coming years, he started drinking heavily and developed anger issues. 'A lot of people wouldn't speak to me. They got scared of me, just in case they upset me,' he said. 'You have the nightmares, you have the flashbacks. It was just a lot to cope with at a young age.'

Benny Jutsum, another soldier on the bus, recounted his memories of that night: 'My first experience was coming round, lying in the field over there and scrambling up the bank. It was just very, very dark. People who attended the scene said there was a lot of noise and I just have no recollection of any sound whatsoever. Just the intense darkness and just the overwhelming sense of not being able to cope.'

Immediately behind the soldiers' bus on the road was a second bus carrying the Omagh Protestant Boys' band. One of its members, Gordon Burnside, rushed to the carnage in front of him to help. 'We just went out, we used our uniforms, we tore up our shirts and t-shirts as bandages and helped as much as we could. There were guys trapped underneath the bus and we got down, we all got in a line and lifted the bus up. And guys, including myself, crawled underneath the bus and got the guys out.'

Allan Rainey, a local man driving in the line of traffic, also rushed to help. His recollection of the evening is also undimmed: 'There's not a day that goes past, or a time that you pass over it, that you don't get that scene of the carnage, the result of the evening, the body bags laid out in a row across the road,' he said. 'And that's still with me, and I suppose will remain with me for as long as I live.'

'Today was very, very emotional,' James Leatherbarrow continued. 'I was scared to come over. I've always wanted to come over, always, but I've never had the courage to come over. When we landed I was nervous, anxious, scared.'

'It's been really good because I've met people who helped us on that night,' Benny Jutsum continued. 'We didn't know their names; we just knew them as faces, really. It's been so rewarding to be able to thank them, to see them and thank them for their help. Sometimes it was just an arm round the shoulders or a blanket to keep warm, but it's been really rewarding to be able to thank them.'

Most wreaths were laid at the roadside memorial as planned, but one was left at an outbuilding across the road. It was where Blair Bishop, one of the soldiers, had crawled for refuge after the bomb. His body was found slumped over a bale of straw.

The Ballygawley bus bombing was one of the worst terrorist attacks on the army during the Troubles. Only two took more soldiers' lives – Narrow Water near Warrenpoint in 1979, when eighteen soldiers were murdered and a civilian killed in the confusion that followed; and the INLA Droppin' Well bombing at Ballykelly in 1982, when eleven soldiers and six civilians were killed. The fact that so many survivors came back to Ballygawley in 2013 was not just an act of remembrance, but also about dealing with their present.

Resolving the legacy of the Troubles is a nearly impossible task. Some victims want truth, some want justice, and some want to move on with their lives. And for many – in all three of those sometimes overlapping categories – there is simply a desire to be listened to, even once; to remember and to commemorate. Because that can help the healing that is needed in Northern Ireland. And that is how, sometimes, even in a very small way, journalism can contribute. Thanks to Kenny Donaldson, the survivors of the Ballygawley bus bombing were given a second chance to tell their story. The anniversary and the exclusivity was the 'hook' for our extended report on *UTV Live Tonight* in 2013.

But I strongly believe the ad hoc nature of reporting anniversaries is not enough. The recounting of such tragedies should have a better outlet, and one with a more consistent and defined purpose. That's why I strongly believe a permanent, impartial, historically rigorous and properly funded oral history archive should be set up at either Queen's University or the University of Ulster to allow those who are ready to do so to tell their story. The University of Ulster already has the outstanding CAIN archive, and an oral history archive would be a logical extension of this project. This would allow victims and survivors to tell their own stories, in their own way, and at their own pace. And it would be a much more enduring record than any piece of journalism ever really can be.

Peter Cardwell was a reporter for *UTV Live* and *UTV Live Tonight* between 2012 and 2014, and special adviser to the Northern Ireland Secretary from 2016 to 2018.

Lyra
Derry, 2019

Donna Deeney

Waking up on my last working day before a week in the sun, all I was hoping for was a quiet day. I soon realised that 19 April 2019 was going to be anything but. House searches in Derry are nothing out of the ordinary, and the occasional ensuing riot with stones and petrol bombs is common enough too, but the early morning news reports on Good Friday 2019 stopped me in my tracks. They said that a journalist had been shot the previous night in Creggan.

My first thought was: who? In Derry, the pool of reporters isn't all that big so we're a close bunch. I rushed out the door and jumped into my car with real dread. En route I learned that the journalist killed was called Lyra McKee. Lyra's was a name that I hadn't heard before and from talking to my colleagues in Derry, this young woman was not familiar to any of us – not that it mattered. From the moment I arrived in Creggan, there was a sense that Lyra McKee's death had had impacted hugely on people living in the area. Speaking to Father Joe Gormley – the parish priest who administered the Last Rites to Lyra as she lay on the ground – it was clear to see how deeply he was affected by her death. Still emotional and visibly shaking, Father Gormley first voiced a phrase I would hear repeatedly in the hours I spent talking to residents: 'This was not done in our name.'

I should perhaps say something about Creggan people. They are a resilient bunch, used to hard knocks. This is one of the most socially deprived areas in the UK or Ireland. Unemployment is high and hope is low but the compassion for Lyra McKee and the loss of her life was beyond doubt. It was real and genuine. It was written on the faces of the men and women I spoke to on the pavements – men and women of a similar age to myself who had grown up through the worst of the Troubles. They had seen and experienced it all, and a lot of it right on their own doorsteps. They did not expect a young woman who had lived her life in a different world to the one they had lived through to die on their streets at the hands of a gunman from their own community so many years after we had all signed up to peace. There was shame, embarrassment and anger at the portrayal of their Creggan, but without doubt the overarching emotions were sorrow and compassion for Lyra McKee's family and friends. One after another they told me, 'This was not in our name.'

As one hour followed another, it became clear that Lyra McKee's death had struck a chord not just within Northern Ireland but across the globe, in every country that had ever shown an interest in Northern Ireland. The death of this young woman touched not just the political and religious leaders in Northern Ireland, but also drew words from the British prime minister, Theresa May; former US president, Bill Clinton; the president of Ireland, Michael D. Higgins; the taoiseach, Leo Varadkar; and leader of the Fianna Fáil, Micheál Martin.

She was an innocent bystander, observing a riot when she was shot. What also became clear was how much of a rising star Lyra McKee had been. While her name was not familiar to those of us who work the news desks across the North West, she was recognised as a gifted writer with a bright future ahead of her.

Given that she was twenty-nine years of age, Lyra McKee was a child of the Good Friday Agreement era, aged just eight when it was signed. The sad irony that I was in Creggan covering her brutal death at the hands of terrorists on Good Friday was not lost on me, or indeed on any of the reporters who had arrived from news outlets far and wide. There was a thirst to know what had happened. Would her death impact on the fragile peace process? Was it connected to Brexit? As I finished a report for one radio station, another one was standing by and all the while, I was compiling my own interviews into a piece for the *Belfast Telegraph*.

As the day went on, we found out so much about the young woman. Although Lyra was not from Derry, her life partner, Sara Canning, was and the couple had planned a life together in the city. Sara, supported by a group of her friends, came to speak to the assembled press and residents of Creggan. She bore testament to the love she and Lyra had shared and spoke of her deep personal loss. She also shared what a loss to the world Lyra was, and how her killer was the antithesis of everything Lyra held dear and represented.

Significant stories don't stand still for very long and this was certainly the case with the killing of Lyra McKee. A hastily arranged press conference to take place in Creggan with all the political leaders was announced. A significant influx of police preceded the arrival of Arlene Foster, Michelle O'Neill, Mary Lou McDonald, Colum Eastwood, Robin Swann and Naomi Long, who all took their place on a platform and delivered a message of political unity and fierce opposition to the violence that claimed the life of Lyra McKee.

Never before had I reported on such a sight on the streets of Creggan. Seeing high-profile members of the DUP who had never, until that day, set foot in that part of the city was something to behold. Politics in Northern Ireland had been stagnating for almost three years; the feeling that day, which continued in the days to follow, was that this was a pivotal moment. If Arlene Foster and Michelle O'Neill could stand side by side on a platform in the middle of Creggan, then why were they not both in Stormont?

This question gathered momentum. As the political leaders from the British, Irish and Stormont governments sat in the pews of St Anne's Cathedral for Lyra's funeral, it was Father Martin Magill who put the question directly to them, saying, 'Why in God's name does it take the death of a twenty-nine-year-old woman with her whole life in front of her to get to this point?' He also challenged the terrorists to put down their weapons, telling them that 'the pen is mightier that the sword' – something else that resonated amongst the people of Derry, where there appeared to be a greater withdrawal of support for dissident republican groups than I had seen at any other time.

Derry felt different in the immediate aftermath of the death of Lyra McKee, and that feeling grew in the days that followed. There was a strange optimism that perhaps the death of this bright, talented young woman would be the catalyst that would at last silence the guns and stop the violence. Sadly, this was not to be.

Donna Deeney was the North West correspondent for the *Belfast Telegraph* from 2010 to 2021, when she retired from journalism.

'I want the world to know my Philip's name': remembering the children who were killed in the Troubles

Northern Ireland, 2019

Freya McClements

I am ashamed to admit that until a few years ago, I had never heard of Philip Rafferty. 'Nobody knows my Philip's name,' his mother, Maureen, would later tell me. 'They took a child off the road, put his hood over his head and murdered him. I think the world should know these things.' She was right.

In 2017, I was working on what was initially a documentary about the children who were killed during the Troubles. My job was to identify children who might feature in the programme and to interview their families – a task that brought me to Relatives for Justice (RFJ) in Belfast, one of the many victims' and survivors' groups whose support would be crucial to what eventually became my book, *Children of the Troubles*. It was here that I met Mrs Rafferty, at the insistence of Mary Kate Quinn from RFJ, who devoted many months to helping my co-author, Joe Duffy, and I with our research. From the off, Mary Kate had been adamant I needed to talk to Mrs Rafferty; Philip, she said, was one of the forgotten victims of the Troubles, and with his mother now elderly, it was important their story be told before it was too late. Philip's is one of the many tragic and senseless losses that litter the history of the Troubles. In January 1973, he had just turned fourteen; he was walking home from band practice in West Belfast when he was snatched from the street by loyalist killers. They took him to the Giant's Ring, a Stonehenge-like monument outside Belfast, where they beat him and then murdered him. Philip was wearing his new coat; his mother had bought it to keep him warm when he was walking home. The next time she saw it, it was in a plastic bag, saturated with blood.

I can still picture her in the RFJ office, her eyes shining and her face lit with love as she described the delicate, sensitive boy who played the violin and the flute, and filled their home with music; who asked her to buy him wellies so he could clear the snow from the pathways outside the neighbouring pensioners' houses; who wanted to be an architect and promised his mother he would build her a house.

'Nobody knows my Philip's name,' she said. 'I want the world to know my Philip's name.'

In the two years or so I spent travelling the country meeting and interviewing the parents, siblings, cousins and friends of the lost children, her words travelled with me; they were my constant companion, my inspiration and my guide. In the lexicon of the Troubles, the reality is that there are some victims, fairly or unfairly, whose names are instantly recognisable, just as there are some place names that will be forever associated with the atrocity that took place there. From our very first meeting with our publisher, Joe and I knew instinctively that we had to try and make contact with the families of all of the children – not just some, or those whose names were better known, or whose families were easy to contact, but all of them. The children, we felt, should be equal; there should be no 'hierarchy of victims', to use that awful phrase; our only criteria was their age – sixteen or under – and that their death should have been as a result of the Troubles.

Eventually, our research left us with a list of 186 children, though details of others have since emerged. Sadly, some children had no family left to speak for them; some we were unable to track down; and others did not want to be interviewed – mostly because they found what had happened too difficult to talk about. In the end, we conducted interviews with around a hundred families. This meant that we met probably several hundred people, in offices, cafes and sitting rooms all over Ireland.

It is no exaggeration to say that every one of those meetings has stayed with me.

The walk around Mullaghmore, County Sligo, with the sisters of Paul Maxwell, the fifteen-year-old boat boy who was one of two children killed in the explosion on Lord Mountbatten's boat. The tour of Milltown Cemetery with Gary Roberts – the cousin of thirteen-year-old Jimmy Cromie, one of two children killed in the bombing of McGurk's bar – who showed Joe and I where many of the children were buried.

On the wall of the Nicholls' living room there is a picture of baby Colin on his first summer holiday to Portrush; a chubby baby boy with blond hair sits in the sand beside a giant sandcastle, a spade in his hand. He was only seventeen months old when he was killed, one of two young children to die in the Balmoral Furniture Company bombing on the Shankill Road in 1971. His father, Jackie, shows me baby Colin's rattle and lets me hold it. As I run my finger over the marks his teeth have left in the wood, the space of fifty years vanishes and Colin is there with us.

In the family home of Annette McGavigan in Derry, her brother Martin brings her things down from the attic. The fourteen-year-old was watching a riot – she and her friends had gone to see 'the talent' – and was still wearing her school uniform when she was shot. Martin hands me her copybooks, then the plimsolls she had been wearing, then her school skirt. He points out the window to the back wall. 'Annette used to sit there,' he says. 'When I look out, I still see her sitting there.' In that moment, we both see her, a laughing teenager swinging her legs on the wall.

The ghosts of these children still walk among us. For a time, they walked with me.

Driving along the Falls Road one day, exploring filming locations for the documentary, every street corner was transformed into a place where children had lived and died. At what was once Watterson's shop – still a newsagent – I saw not only the pavement outside where fourteen-year-old Peter Watterson was killed, but also Peter and his younger brother Johnny, lying on their beds in the room above, reading *Batman* comics as their very own Gotham City disintegrated outside.

One evening, after a day of interviews with families, I was unable to stop crying; I drove home with tears falling silently down my cheeks. I sought help when I found myself watching the pedestrians on a busy road and seeing them not as people, but as bundles of trauma that had somehow been given legs and feet and were walking about. I wanted to know what each of their stories was, and what had happened to them and their family.

I have often wondered what it is that leads me to write about the Troubles. Of course, it is stating the obvious that for any journalist in Northern Ireland it is impossible to avoid, even more than twenty years after their supposed end. To paraphrase the father of fifteen-year-old James Kennedy – a victim of the Ormeau Road bookmakers massacre – bullets travel in time as well as distance. Some of them have never stopped travelling and, so far, neither have their consequences.

Yet there is something that draws me back. Nobody in my family was killed, as people from this place will often say, and of course all of us for whom that is true are lucky that we can say so. Nevertheless, I have come to believe that in Northern Ireland we are all, to a greater or lesser extent, traumatised by the Troubles, whether or not we believe this to be the case. How could we not, when our land, our people, our society was brutalised to such an extent? When something on this scale happens around us, and to us, I believe we have a duty to write about it. The best thing we can do – sometimes all we can do – is to acknowledge those ghosts of the past, and try to answer them.

Of all that I learnt from *Children of the Troubles*, the greatest lesson was that the past must be tackled. Of course, as our history has shown time and time again, this is easier said than done, and I would not presume to know how we might do so. But at its most basic level, *Children of the Troubles* was an acknowledgement – in some cases, of children who had never before been recognised as victims of the Troubles – that their family member lived, and was loved, and should not have been lost.

I do believe that, in some small way, this made a difference. At the launches – in Belfast, Derry and Dublin in October 2019 – the vast majority of those present were relatives of the children remembered in the book. I remember looking down at the crowd in Belfast, several hundred people all packed into the room, and seeing a man whose sixteen-year-old sister had been shot dead hugging the book tightly to his chest. Some later told us they had bought the book but could not look at it; others had hidden it away. But all wanted to know it was there, in the house, and that it would be there for their children and grandchildren in the years to come. One man who had worked in peacebuilding and reconciliation for a lifetime later told us, 'I've been at hundreds of these things, and it's always the same people. But most of those people I had never seen before.'

When Joe and I were interviewed about *Children of the Troubles* on *The Late Late Show* on RTÉ, Mrs Rafferty came with us and spoke Philip's name on air. The next day she got a phone call from a former neighbour who had watched the programme on the other side of the world. 'They even know Philip's name in Australia,' she said.

Afterwards, I went back to talk to Mrs Rafferty again and told her how her words had stayed with me. 'All those years I've been saying that,' she said. 'Sometimes you never know who's listening.'

Freya McClements is Northern Editor with the *Irish Times* and co-author (with Joe Duffy) of *Children of the Troubles: The Untold Story of the Children Killed in the Northern Ireland Conflict.*

Terrorist threats
Belfast, November 2020

Patricia Devlin

I had just returned from South America with a scoop – the first interview with drug trafficker Michaella McCollum. But it wasn't long before I was accused on Twitter of making a drug smuggler a celebrity and of 'glamourising' drugs, and told that the piece was 'gutter journalism'. I was personally attacked and belittled by numerous tweeters who hadn't even read the story, and I was made to feel unscrupulous for doing my job, and doing it well. When I look back to that experience now, I realise how insignificant it is. If only I knew what was to come.

In the space of the last two years, I've had multiple paramilitary death threats delivered to my door by police; my name has been spray-painted on walls with a threat to shoot me dead; and my infant son has been threatened with rape, twice.

I've been subjected to relentless online abuse, harassment and smears in an orchestrated effort to silence my reporting on gangsters who still exert control over communities. And social media has played a significant role in it all.

In November 2020, hours after a malicious post appeared on a loyalist Facebook page, accusing me of 'working hand in glove' with criminals, I was informed by police of two threats to my life. The first threat, I was told, emanated from a loyalist gang connected to the West Belfast UDA. The threat message, which was handed to me on a piece of paper by a senior PSNI officer, said those who planned to carry out 'some form of attack' on me were in 'possession of firearms and explosives'. It also warned I could be entrapped in some way – asked to cover a story and attacked. Within twelve hours, police were back at my home to inform me that they'd received intelligence that the West Belfast UDA planned to 'shoot me in the next day or two' at a precise location. On the same day, a *Sunday World* colleague, who had also been reporting on the criminal activities of these very same gangsters, was also formally warned by police that his safety was at risk.

In Northern Ireland, threats to the lives of journalists are seen as coming with the territory. Over the years, I have watched other journalists deal with these sinister attempts at silencing them and so I almost expected that I would be on the receiving end at some stage. What I did not expect, and what I could never have prepared myself for, was my children becoming targets.

It was early 2019 when I was first targeted in an orchestrated smear campaign, which began after I'd written articles on a paramilitary-related murder. Ian Ogle, a father of two, was butchered in the street, yards from his East Belfast home, by members of the outlawed Ulster Volunteer Force (UVF). In the months prior to his January 2019 killing, Mr Ogle and his family had been subjected to frightening levels of intimidation. He had been forced from his job, threatened numerous times and was even ordered to surrender himself for a so-called punishment beating at the hands of paramilitary bosses. His crime was defending two of his children who had been attacked in a bar. His refusal to bow down to gangsters led to his murder, which caused revulsion in the loyalist community where he was loved and respected.

In the days and weeks following his killing, hundreds took to the streets calling for justice. Many in that community followed in the footsteps of his brave daughter Toni, who spoke out about the harm the gang had been inflicting on those living in the area for many years. Drug dealing, attacks and extortion were – and still are – rife, and those who had been suffering far too much, for far too long, decided enough was enough.

Each and every time I wrote a story about this gang's criminal activities, I was subjected to relentless online abuse, smears and hate. My personal details, including a link to my private Facebook page, were published on social media sites with invitations for others to join in with the trolling. One woman said that she hoped I would have to 'bury' my children. Another account told me I had a target on my back, and it had been there 'for a while'. Even at the height of the relentless abuse, which played out whilst I was heavily pregnant, I did not go to police because I believed it was something that came with being a crime reporter in Northern Ireland. I just had to deal with it. That view changed a few months later when I received a message to my personal Facebook account in which the sender threatened my newborn son, who had been born in June 2019. On 28 October 2019, I logged in to my Facebook account to find a new message in my inbox. It read: 'Don't go near your granny's house in Maghera Tricia or you'll watch your new-born son get raped COMBAT 18!'

The moment I read those words will never leave me. I felt physically sick with a nausea that did not leave for many, many months. I did not sleep; I could not eat. I contemplated my future in journalism, and I questioned my own part in exposing my son, and all my children, to the sinister elements I had never once been afraid of confronting in my work. Then there was the anxiety, the never-ending worry that this person – who had quite clearly pored over my Facebook profile with pictures of me holding a tiny baby in my arms – would attempt to carry out their sick threats. Did they know where I lived? Would they find out? Were my children safe in their own home? At just three months old, my son Tiarnan couldn't roll over, crawl or even hold his head up, yet he was seen as a legitimate target by someone who did not like his mother, simply on the basis of her job. The sender of that horrendous message intended to intimidate and terrorise. They did.

That's the thing about social media – a phone or a computer screen does not stop the monsters from getting inside your life. It brings them right into your living room, your kitchen, your bedroom. Worst of all, they get inside your head. You can log out, but erasing the effects of poisonous words is not as simple as hitting delete. Today we are living in a virtual society where the internet is now intrinsically linked with our 'real' lives.

I reported the message to the Police Service of Northern Ireland with the hope the sender could be traced and arrested. Although it has been confirmed to me that the individual who sent the sickening threat is a dangerous criminal with links to loyalist paramilitaries, he has yet to be arrested. I was told he fled the country not long after sending that message and is now living on the continent. I believe police did not treat my complaint as seriously as they should have and, as a result, I made a formal complaint to the Police Ombudsman for Northern Ireland. I was later informed that the watchdog upheld my complaint.

Although police are able tell me which gang plans to carry out an attack and when, they don't seem able to arrest anybody. I know who is behind the threats. Through my own criminal contacts, I'm able to get names and locations of where they hold their meetings, where these cowardly acts of intimidation are discussed. But it's apparently not enough for the PSNI. In February 2020, when my name was spray-painted on three walls in East Belfast alongside gun crosshairs, I was told how a senior UVF man rang a business the day before the graffiti appeared. He asked the businessman if there was CCTV covering the wall where my name would appear less than 24 hours later. The PSNI are aware of this, but still, it's not enough.

The brazen levels that these gangs go to to silence the media here were very much in evidence in May 2020. A day after placing a blanket threat on all reporters at two Northern Ireland newspapers, the South-East Antrim UDA then threatened the lives of a number of politicians who had publicly supported those journalists.

Meanwhile, my family and I continue to live in fear of what is coming next. I've been asked many times why I continue to do my job under such intimidation. If I were to give in to these bullies, life would not only be much harder for the ordinary, decent, hardworking people terrorised by these thugs on a daily basis, but also for all journalists under threat. And there are many.

Patricia Devlin is a crime and investigative journalist. She has previously worked for the *Sunday World*, *Irish Daily Star* and *Sunday Life* newspapers.

How the storming of the Capitol reminded me of Drumcree
Washington DC, 2021

Mark Davey

> Don't tread on me!
> No surrender!
> Hold the line!
> Not an inch!
> What we have, we hold.
> Whose country? Our country!
> Whose House? Our House!
> Remember 1690! Stretch their necks like it's 1776!

Are these the rallying cries of the Capitol Hill mob or of the loyal sons of Ulster? Proud Boys or Billy Boys? They are a mix of both.

On 6 January 2021, I was inside the US Capitol with those storming it, and there was a ring of the familiar. These emerging militants, blooding themselves in insurrection, seemed cut from the same cloth as the angry loyalists I had encountered in Northern Ireland. Both bemoan the erosion of their culture and complain of being silenced. Their country and way of life is being stolen by an establishment that is selling them down the river. Rallying around their revered flags, they espouse an unshakeable belief in the rule of law, until they end up on the wrong side of it. Then they declare 'their only crime was loyalty', a slogan I remember seeing on the T-shirts of Johnny Adair and his cohort at a Drumcree rally. No wonder the 'stop the steal' message resonates so loudly. It taps into a deep vein of grievance dating back more than four centuries to when these seeds of dissent were planted, in Ireland's unruly North.

King William of Orange, affectionately known as King Billy, was and remains a hero to the Ulster-Scots folk transplanted to Ulster in the early 1600s. The phrase 'last ditch' has its origins in a speech of his, in which he said, 'There is one way never to see my country lost and that is to die in the last ditch.' Craving the religious liberty denied them by their English overlords in Ireland, hundreds of thousands struck out for the New World, settling in Appalachia and beyond. These hillbillies, as they became known, played a crucial part in the Revolutionary War. 'Call it not an American rebellion,' declared one observer. 'It is nothing more or less than a Scotch Irish Presbyterian rebellion.'

Ulster people later signed the Declaration of Independence, produced eighteen presidents, designed the Great Seal of America and wrote 'The Star-Spangled Banner'. Bluegrass music begat country and western. Artists from the Carter family and Johnny Cash to Elvis Presley can all lay claim to Scots-Irish roots. How odd then that people so central to the young nation's formation should feel so utterly abandoned.

During Donald Trump's term I encountered his supporters everywhere, from Appalachia in the north-east, to Florida and Texas in the south. I found heavily armed militias, Proud Boys, Boogaloos and Angry Vikings in places like Louisville, Kentucky. I got on okay with them, often asking about their roots and marvelling at the numerous Ulster-Scots connections. Paranoid folk, they needed constant reassurance that their voices would be heard; that our news was not Fake News. 'Whose news are youse?' – the perennial query from home – has a razor-sharp edge here. Could we be the loathed NBC, the despised CNN? In the dying days of Trump, the biggest enemy was Fox News: in an echo of the Northern Irish street view of the BBC, they had betrayed their own.

In the run up to 6 January, I jokingly referred to the planned pro-Trump rally as Bluster's Last Stand, a nod to General Custer's Ulster-Scots heritage. I should not have joked. In his 'Save America' speech, the president lavished praise on the loyalists who had come to stake their claim to a stolen election. 'They try and demean everybody having to do with us, and you're the real people. You're the people that built this nation.'

At the rally I encountered plenty of folk who hailed from Appalachia (or within a beagle's gowl of it). None present viewed Trump as a claim jumper. West Virginian Scott Matheny had made his own sign: 'Stretch their necks like it's 1776.' He told us, 'Trump is our man. He's brought the damn jobs back … he's closed the friggin' borders. This man has done nothing but good for this nation and all this damn media has done is tear him down.' He mocked his president's detractors: '"Orange-man bad." Orange-man ain't bad, Orange-man is the only man sticking up for us. I'm friggin' mad. I'm pissed. Everybody here is mad. And I tell you what, you unleash this damned bunch when the time comes, it's going to be ugly. Democracy is busted. It's done and it's time – we're taking this country back. These people have sold us out and we know it.' The surname Matheny is French Huguenot, which chimes with another man whose family married into Ulster-Scots stock before being drawn to wilder frontiers – Davy Crockett.

President Trump exhorted his followers to march to the Capitol. 'If you don't fight like hell, you're not going to have a country anymore.' To the west of the building, a noose hung from a recently erected gallows. I wanted to climb up to get a picture, but I couldn't because too many folk wanted to mount the rickety steps, grab the noose and denounce those deserving a lynching: 'Biden!' 'Pelosi!' 'Pence!' Others wrote their hanging requests on the timbers of the makeshift scaffold. Their comrades-in-anger filmed them on their smartphones.

Shortly afterwards, as part of the long-simmering Brexit border row, loyalist graffiti in Belfast threatened Irish tánaiste, Leo Varadkar. 'We have a noose, we have a tree …' – language unmistakably borrowed from another militant American Protestant group, the Ku Klux Klan.

A month after the Capitol storming, I travelled south to a conservative conference, where Trump was given top billing. But my search was for David Medina, the Oregonian who had ripped down Speaker Nancy Pelosi's nameplate on 6 January and smashed it with extreme prejudice. I was fascinated that he remained free after this flagrant act. I trawled the hundreds of arrest records to see if he had been lifted yet. We tracked him down. 'ITV News, my biggest fans,' he said, but offered no explanation for his continued liberty.

He had been more forthcoming on the day. He looked up after smashing the sign and saw me filming. He began pointing and shouting, 'You! Who are you? Who are you with?' 'British TV,' my correspondent, Robert Moore, told him. He raged at us: 'You want to know the difference between people like us and Antifa and BLM? We respect the law.' Then turning directly to camera, his voice almost breaking with rage, he said, 'The government did this to us. We were normal, good, law-abiding citizens and you guys did this to us! We want our country back.'

Suspicion and distrust were heightened in this frenzied tumult. During another interview, the mob intervened: 'What news crew?' 'Who do you represent?' Not for the first time, our outsider status spared us the worst of it, though many of the rioters remained angered by our presence. An older military veteran, with the most magnificent mountain-man beard, was inflamed with rage, livid at being pepper-sprayed by the police as he was breaching the Capitol. He hit my camera with his flagpole and let out a guttural roar straight into the lens. He looked like he had come straight off Walton's Mountain just for the occasion. We were the only TV news crew inside, but, outside, other camera teams were viciously attacked and had their equipment destroyed. This transported me back to a Drumcree field, circa 1996, and a Channel 4 News crew leaping over a barbed wire fence with angry Orangemen in pursuit. Ironically, that news crew had been seeking voices that might explain the Orangemen's protest.

Other than being foreign, I'm not sure what saved me on 6 January, but I did catch myself in the mirror when cleaning up back at the office later: middle-aged, with a crew cut, a Covid-diet belly, a hat in Trumpian red and a work ensemble most charitably described as army surplus. I felt I had my answer – I looked like a Proud Boy.

Many have tried to understand these incensed people, but does the lie they believe – that the election was stolen – belong to them or to those who sold it to them? Egging them on are dangerous folk, and these willing followers are no less dangerous. It would be unwise to dismiss this as their Alamo, their last-ditch effort. They have not gone away; rather they have been radicalised in alarming numbers – and in Northern Ireland we know all too well that the consequences will likely last for generations. As over a thousand enraged people stormed the Capitol, I thought of home once again and the hordes outside Belfast City Hall who proclaimed that Ulster Says No, with Ian Paisley declaring, 'Never, never, never!'

Hundreds are facing trial in Washington DC for what are serious federal offences. They had tried to overturn the result of a national election after all; one described by officials as the 'most secure in history'. As I read more of their pleas of innocence, ranging from 'I wasn't there' to 'The president told me to do it', I am transported back to a scene from a quarter of a century ago, viewed from my camera position just inside Ormeau Park. The police line below was taking an endless battering from angry bandsmen, including having a trophy riot shield thrown back at them, just as I had seen happen on Capitol Hill. One young lad had been giving it loads for hours on end, but finally decided it was time to walk quietly through the line and up the road home for his tea. But the Peelers who had endured his earlier rioting grabbed him by the scruff and trailed him away as he screeched high above the melee, 'I ne'er done nathin'!'

Mark Davey is a senior camera operator/editor with ITV News. On leaving Belfast, he spent ten years in Asia before moving to Washington DC shortly after Donald Trump's election. He got his start with Ulster Television in 1984 as their newsroom runner.

Too close
Belfast, 2021

David Lynas

Baring your soul is not easy. All of us who have reported on the terrible events of our past carry scar tissue. Some talk about it, some don't and won't. Some deal with the harshest memories differently. Some of us drink. Some of us take medication. Others want to talk, to somehow try to make sense of it all. There is no cure. There is no panacea.

So many deaths. So many funerals. So much grief. Shamefully, it all became so routine. Go to work. Go to a shooting or a bombing. If not that, then there's a funeral to watch over. A family to track down and talk to. It all became much too calculated and cold. Almost formulaic. It'll harden you, they said. It did not. It wore me down.

At work, there was no time to talk about worries or concerns or how any of this was beginning to eat away at your sense of well-being. Every hour there were deadlines to meet, scripts to write, programmes to fill. Self-doubt was ever-present, lurking in the background, but weakness was failure.

Over time, some of the horrific memories fade or at least become blurred around the edges. Many incidents are gone from me now. Others somehow segue into each other with such ease that they remain vivid and crystal clear.

BELFAST 1
He was face down. Lying where they'd dumped him behind a gable wall. Someone had brought a blanket. It covered his head and stretched down to his waist. His legs were crossed. Left over right at the ankles. One shoe had almost fallen off. His shoes were almost like my own. Slip-ons for ease – no cumbersome laces to tie. Strange what you remember about a murder scene. You can get too close.

ARMAGH
The crater was massive. It stretched all the way across the road from hawthorn hedge to hawthorn hedge. The landmine in a culvert had gone off prematurely. Winston McConville – photographer with the *Armagh Guardian* – and I, then

a junior reporter, went to see it. Winston couldn't get a decent shot at ground level, so we climbed the hedge and walked to the top of a field. Winston was snapping away when we both heard the voice: 'Can I shoot him, sarge?' It came again, this time louder: 'Sarge, can I shoot him?' Then another voice, this time shouting, 'Stand where you are, do not move. Do not move.' We froze. Several figures emerged from the hedgerow all in camouflage gear and all with weapons. Two knelt with weapons trained on us while we were questioned, again and again and again. We didn't see them search our car, but it had been well turned over when we were finally told to go and not come back. We drove back to the office in silence. It could all have been so different. Too close again.

BELFAST 2

The police and ambulance teams were already there. It was late and dark. The body had been removed and there was little left to see. A small gathering of locals clearly knew who had been murdered but were unwilling to tell us. Fear of retribution. Some of them were in shock, arms around each other. As the evening grew colder they drifted away one by one. Soon there was no one left but us, the media. Us and the detritus of a death that would soon be another grim statistic. The wrappings from sterilised bandages littered the ground beside a pool of blood in which the blue lights of the ambulance were reflected. Too close.

> Circles and Squares
>
> The driver's door is open
> The lights flash blue in
> The black, black blood.
> And everywhere
> The markings
> The circles and
> The squares
> The tell-tale signs of
> Slaughter
> The chalk marks of despair.

A reporter from London came with me once to a murder. He was a vastly experienced BBC journalist who had reported on events all over the world. We spent the day on the story and duly compared notes and scripts. Next day he came to me and asked, 'Can I talk to you privately? Have you been offered counselling?'

245

'Counselling for what?' I asked.

'For yesterday – they've asked me if I want counselling about that killing.'

'No one has offered me anything,' I said, 'but if you really want comforted, we meet on Friday in the BBC Club and we get counselled there.'

'Who by?' he asked.

'Brian,' I told him.

'Is he a psychiatrist?'

'No, he's a barman,' I replied.

And that's how it was then. If you really wanted to talk, confess, confront, sound off or just get pissed and let it all go, that's where it was done. The old BBC Club in Linenhall Street, Belfast. The safety valve.

There have been many sleepless nights and bad days. Getting off the road and behind a desk helped. Talking with friends who have had similar experiences keeps things in perspective.

Writing about it can be difficult because it's all too easy to hurt someone unintentionally. Someone who has already been hurt beyond words. If that has happened here, I apologise.

The Worst Time

When you're all alone and thinking,
That's the worst time.
When you realise
There's really only you
When there's nothing on your mind
And there's no one there to help
You see it through.

When you're all alone and thinking,
That's the worst time.
With no friends there to
Help you raise the roof
When a single helping hand
Would make everything so grand
And a drink would only
Blur and veil the truth.

When you're all alone and thinking,
That's the worst time.
When you realise
Self-pity's called again.

246

When you want what you once had
Because it doesn't seem so bad
Then daylight comes
And takes you by the hand.

Whether we know it or not, at one time or another over the past forty years we've all been 'too close'.

David Lynas worked as a reporter in Northern Ireland for fifty years – thirty-nine of them with the BBC.

Keeping the peace in the TV studio
Belfast, 2021

Mark Carruthers

Things have come a long way from the days – not so very long ago, if you think about it – when many of Northern Ireland's politicians wouldn't, or couldn't, be seen to be engaging with their long-time political opponents. For some of them, at one time, it was even too much to be seen in the same room, breathing the same air, and so – especially given the UK government's broadcast restrictions, which were in place from 1988 to 1994 – what was to follow was remarkable.

In August 1997, *Newsnight* presenter Gavin Esler found himself doing something no other television anchor had done before. It fell to him to chair that memorable, mould-breaking encounter between Ken Maginnis and Martin McGuinness; the first live debate between a senior Ulster Unionist and a leading Irish republican on British television, one the UUP's security spokesman, the other Sinn Féin's chief negotiator. It's worth watching the encounter back if you get the chance. The two men are broadly respectful of each other, but their lived experiences are clearly poles apart and the common ground between them appears almost non-existent.

Mr Maginnis had, of course, already confronted the Sinn Féin president, Gerry Adams, on American television in October 1994 on CNN's *Larry King Live*, but the people in Northern Ireland who gave these politicians their mandates in the first place did not routinely get to see them engaging face to face on home soil in the way they do today. For years, certain politicians were spirited around the labyrinthine corridors of Broadcasting House in Belfast from studio to studio by production assistants tasked with ensuring they didn't meet certain other politicians in the make-up room or at the lift doors. They used the stairs instead – one set for this MP, another set for that MP. That was the rigmarole that was required – especially at election times – and, in the main, it worked very well. We became very good at the ritual.

Today, with the very odd exception, our politicians do engage with each other in council chambers, at Stormont, at Westminster – those who go there, anyway – and across the table in familiar television and radio studios. When I was starting to present live editions of BBC Northern Ireland's *Spotlight* programme in the early 2000s, I remember the challenge of facilitating debates between politicians who still weren't prepared to sit down with their opponents. I'd take up my place on the main set with two or three guests seated around the same table, but, in turn, I'd have to bring in to the conversation another politician who refused to be in the same studio as the rest of us. The refusenik would appear on a small television screen set off to one side, despite being seated just a matter of yards down the corridor in a separate studio. My questions would be answered – but there would be strictly no engagement on his or her part with whichever other participant was seen as *persona non grata*. Broadly speaking, these days that kind of semi-detachment is gone – though there are those who still refuse to acknowledge some of their opponents in the corridors at Stormont, and who would certainly never agree to shake their hands or take part in polite small talk. It's certainly not widespread, but I do know it still happens.

I count myself fortunate to have been around long enough to have learned from some of the best in the business. The list of accomplished reporters who covered the worst of the Troubles is a lengthy one – though in my memory David Capper, Paddy O'Flaherty and Austin Hunter stand tall among the best of them. Their beat was that seemingly endless procession of bodies dumped on deserted border roads, bomb blasts in market towns, doorstep killings, riots and car bombs, book-ended with relentless political failure. Of the studio-based presenters, David Dunseith and Barry Cowan already enjoyed legendary status in my eyes when I was a politics student at Queen's in the mid-1980s, and both went on to become colleagues from whom I learned a lot. Tackling the big beasts of Northern Ireland politics didn't unduly bother David and Barry; for me it was a steep learning curve. I established pretty quickly that it was better not to try to be clever with the Paisleys and the Humes of this world – but only after I'd made the kind of rookie mistakes aspiring journalists perhaps need to make.

I remember all too well – and with some embarrassment to this day – the occasion a very long time ago that I engaged an Ian Paisley in attack mode before the assembled media pack on the steps of Parliament Buildings. Foolishly, I chose that moment to accuse him of grandstanding – and he gave me the full Paisley comeback with both barrels. That's not a mistake you rush to make twice. Lesson learned.

Reporting on the tragedy of what happened here in the last five decades was never easy. It took a certain kind of journalist to head off into the night to report from the scene of the latest murder, to listen to the heartbreaking stories of the lives destroyed by the conflict, and to try to make sense of it all. Holding politicians to account for initiatives they were supporting – or destroying – in warm, well-lit studios perhaps seems straightforward by comparison. In reality, though, it was part of a much more complex ecosystem – because what politicians or community leaders said in studios had consequences on the streets. How Seamus McKee, Wendy Austin and Noel Thompson handled themselves and their guests in studio discussions and debates programme after programme, week after week, really mattered too.

Journalism, at its simplest, should be about the search for the truth. It's about generating light – not heat – and sadly, as a profession, it is now more open to misuse and abuse than ever with the rise of social media, which in a few short years has entirely altered the journalistic landscape. All too often now, opinions are confused with facts on social media outlets – whereas proper journalism always has to be about dealing in facts without fear or favour. It's about holding the people who have power over the rest of us to account for their words and actions – on behalf of the voters who agreed to hand over that authority as part of the democratic process. Perhaps the old adage about the correct relationship between a journalist and a politician being the same as that between a dog and a lamp post is at the extreme end of cynicism – but it is certainly part of any self-respecting journalist's job description to be sceptical.

There is one straightforward solution to this challenge, of course. *Newsnight's* former chief interrogator, Jeremy Paxman, was asked about it by the *Guardian* back in 2005, when the programme was celebrating its twenty-fifth birthday. His response was prescient: 'It seems to me that the way to remove people's cynicism is, when asked a straight question, to give a straight answer. The cure for cynicism is simply to engage honestly.'

In a society emerging from decades of conflict, where politics can be divisive and where existing and emerging issues remain unresolved – constitutional status, Brexit and the Protocol, legacy, culture and not to mention a raft of social issues – journalism has a critical role to play. But that role needs to be a finely balanced one. As journalists, our job is not to make a bad situation worse, but nor should we make the mistake of believing we are here to paper over the cracks; we don't work in PR. And, critically, we should never fall into the trap of allowing ourselves to become the story. Journalism is not entertainment.

So, today's crop of political leaders shouldn't be surprised to be asked challenging questions when they sit down to be interviewed, just as their predecessors were before them. I don't imagine David Trimble and Martin McGuinness and Seamus Mallon liked it any more than Jeffrey Donaldson and Michelle O'Neill and Naomi Long do – but it's part of a long-established practice and, as I've suggested, for very good reason. In fact, it's an even more important part of the democratic process in a society like ours where there's still no mechanism in place for a conventional opposition to operate. And here's one final thought to help allay the fears of those who don't like journalists shining a light into some of society's dark corners: we're invested in this place just the same as everyone else. Those journalists who've been reporting on horrors and upheavals here for the past fifty years were and are themselves citizens of this place – and maybe that's worth bearing in mind the next time you find yourself shouting at your TV screen.

Mark Carruthers presents *The View*, *Sunday Politics* and the *Red Lines* podcast for BBC Northern Ireland.

The Ballymurphy Inquest – and the meaning of legacy
Belfast, 2021

Will Leitch

Northern Ireland is a small place. If you are regularly on the road reporting the news here for any length of time, you will inevitably start to run into the same people over and over again, often on quite different stories. One summer's evening, a story about the IRA abduction and murder of a teenage boy called Bernard Teggart led me and a cameraman to a caravan site in Newcastle, County Down. Bernard's brother John was there on holiday, but he took time to tell me how the IRA had finally apologised for killing Bernard, accepting that he never was 'a tout', as he had been branded.

As we spoke, I realised I had met John before, on a suburban street called Springfield Park. On that day, he and his friends had been explaining their campaign to clear the names of the ten people killed in the Ballymurphy Massacre. Among the victims had been John and Bernard's father, Danny. Here was a family who knew great grief, and great pain, having lost two members to men with guns on opposite sides of the conflict.

Some years later, the attorney general called for new Ballymurphy inquests, which started in November 2018, and the pain felt by the Teggart family was to become known to many more people.

In Northern Ireland there is a word for dealing with the past. It is a word for the killings during the Troubles, the murders, assassinations, the abductions, the bombings, the dreadful mistakes, the people who were simply in the wrong place at the wrong time. We call it legacy. But legacy is difficult, because legacy lasts a lifetime.

Sitting on the press benches in Courtroom 12 in Laganside Courts during the one hundred days of hearings in the Ballymurphy inquests, it was easy to wonder just how much legacy, how much grief and pain ordinary families can bear. Several dozen of the witnesses were former soldiers in British Army regiments, and the vast majority opted for anonymity, granted by the coroner. Their names were not used. These men in their seventies and eighties were given 'ciphers', such as witness M3 or M506. Hidden by a curtain, no one on the press benches or in the public gallery could see who they were.

The families of the victims could. With the coroner's permission, they sat directly opposite the witness box on the jury benches, and when a soldier gave evidence about the death of their loved one, they could look him full in the face. Kathleen McCarry looked full in the face of a man known to the court simply as 'M3'. In 1971, he had been a sapper, using a military bulldozer to try and clear a barricade. He told the Royal Military Police that he fired his Sterling sub-machine gun at a petrol bomber, watching him fall back. But the man who died was standing some distance behind the barricade and many witnesses, including the state pathologist at the time, testified that he had not been, and could not have been, handling or throwing a petrol bomb.

Under cross-examination decades later, M3 admitted that he might well have fired at a petrol bomber and missed, instead hitting thirty-one-year-old Edward Doherty, Kathleen's brother. Eddie was a husband and father, a former Territorial Army soldier who was passing through the area, simply trying to get home. 'I just can't believe … I just can't understand how … for a mad thirty seconds to last a legacy like this,' M3 told the court, as he looked over at Kathleen and the Doherty family. Outside later, Kathleen told me she had not sensed any real compassion for her family, or sorrow for Eddie's death, in M3's words.

'My mother went to her grave seven years later,' she explained. 'The priest that buried her said he should have buried her the day Eddie was buried, for she died when he died.' Kathleen's legacy. M3's legacy.

One of the most telling moments in court came on day thirty-three of the hearings, when an elderly woman, a civilian, was describing the aftermath of the death of forty-four-year-old grandmother Joan Connolly. Margaret Elmore, then Margaret O'Hare, had lived in a house next door to a field where four of the Ballymurphy victims were shot. She had tried to help Mrs Connolly after she had been shot in the face, urging her to come to safety in her home. But Joan Connolly had already lost her sight. She later fell, and died slowly and in agony. Later, soldiers came with an armoured vehicle, and lifted her and other victims into the back, taking them to a nearby army base.

Answering questions in the witness box in 2019, Margaret described how the next day she had shown the scene to an overseas news crew, pointing out the obvious signs of where someone had been shot and had bled to death. Margaret told the court that on the wall of her home that day, you could see bloodstains, and what she took to be brain matter. At that moment came a cry of horror. A sharp cry of pain, of grief and of sorrow. A visceral cry that rippled out across the courtroom and struck everyone in the chest and pierced them to the heart. On those jury benches, Joan Connolly's daughters reached out and comforted their sister. As waves of emotion raced back and forth across a room of more than eighty people, the coroner very wisely halted proceedings for a few minutes.

Joan Connolly's family had come to find out the truth of her death. For them this was the reality of legacy, and nothing could have prepared them for it. During thirty years as a news reporter, I had covered many sad and upsetting stories. But nothing had prepared me for the cries of a woman who had just heard how her mother's face had been shot off. Nothing could have prepared anyone for much of what they heard in those hundred days.

One day Bobby Clarke, a man in his eighties, grabbed at his shirt as he rose unsteadily to his feet in the witness box. He was explaining how he had been shot by soldiers, the bullet passing across his back, cutting a deep groove which is still there. Now he was offering to show the scar to a startled coroner. Mrs Justice Keegan assured him that would not be necessary. Bobby had been shot after taking a neighbour's child to safety across a field. He told the court that, as he returned, he glanced up and saw two soldiers tracking him with their rifles. He was hit and went down. Among those who ran to help him were a local priest, Father Hugh Mullan, and a nineteen-year-old father, Frank Quinn. In the next few minutes after they tried to help, both men were shot and killed. Bobby lay and listened to them die.

After he had given evidence, I approached Bobby outside court. 'I hold myself responsible for two people losing their lives,' he told me. Bobby's legacy.

There were other victims. The families of Noel Phillips, Joseph Murphy, John Laverty, Joseph Corr and John McKerr are all still living with their own legacy.

It seems certain that for all the Ballymurphy families, the pain and the grief will never go away. Each of them has a slightly different idea of how they might find justice. But through fifty years of waiting, and a hundred days of inquest, the world now knows that their loved ones were 'entirely innocent'.

Perhaps that is the best legacy they can hope for.

Will Leitch is a senior journalist at BBC Northern Ireland, having worked for more than thirty years as a reporter and presenter in TV and radio news.

Acknowledgements

Our joint thanks go to:

All the journalists and photographers who have so expertly and willingly shared their painful stories with us for volume two of this book.

Patsy Horton, Helen Wright, Michelle Griffin and all the team at Blackstaff Press, who went the extra mile in very trying circumstances to get this book to print.

Mandy Johnston in Dublin and Julie Crowley in London.

Robin Walsh, a giant of Northern Irish journalism, whose sage advice was invaluable.

Deric Henderson Jnr for his innovative thinking at every turn.

From Ivan Little, thanks to:

My wife, Siofra O'Reilly, for helping to guide me through the technological maze.

Emma and Kevin Lawless for their unstinting support and their relentless research.

My siblings, Norman, Raymond and Caroline, for their encouragement.

From Deric Henderson, thanks to:

My wife, Clare; son, Deric Jnr; daughter-in-law, Ursula; son, Edward and his fiancée, Amy, for all their support.

And to my lifetime friend Kieran Campbell, a BT9 legend, who was always there for the Henderson family.

Index

257

258

McCaffrey, Barry, 191–4
McCambridge, Jonny, 199–202
McCann, Danny, 110
McCarry, Kathleen, 253
McCarthy, John, 78
McCartney, Robert, 113, 201
McCartney sisters, 112–13
McCaughey, Francie, 100
MacCionnaith, Breandán, 163
McClements, Freya, 232–5. *See also*
    Children of the Troubles
McCollum, Michaella, 236
McConville, Winston, 244–5
McDonald, Billy, 73
McDonald, Frank, 66
McDonald, Mary Lou, 230
McDonald, Sir Trevor, 5–7
McDowell, Jim, xiv, 8, 9, 11, 176
McDowell, Lindy, 176–9
McElwain, Séamus, 76
McElwain family, 76
McEwan's (jersey), 162, 164
McFadden, Mark, 166–7
McGavigan, Annette, 234
McGavigan, Martin, 234
McGirl, Francis, 54–5
McGlade's pub, Belfast, 1
McGoldrick, Andrew, 161
McGoldrick, Bridie, 159–61
McGoldrick, Emma, 159, 161
McGoldrick, Michael (Jr), 159, 160
McGoldrick, Michael (Sr), 159–61
McGoldrick, Sadie, 159
McGrane, Seamus, 223
McGrattan, Hugh, 30–33
McGuinness, Dermot, 133
McGuinness, Martin, 7, 72, 76, 77, 87, 112,
    120, 173, 174, 175, 222, 248, 250
McGurk's bar, Belfast, 233
McIlwaine, David, 183–4, 185
McIlwaine, Paul, 184–5
McIntyre, Chris, 79
MacIntyre, Darragh, 124–7
McIntyre, Emily, 79
McIntyre, John, 79, 80
McKeag, Stevie, 131, 132, 133
McKee, Alan, 80
McKee, Jonathan, 207, 208
McKee, Lyra, xiv, 219–20, 229–31

McKee, Seamus, 139–41
McKeown, Ciaran, 39, 40, 41
McKeown, Clifford, 160
McKevitt, Michael, 222
McKinney, Fearghal, 156–8
McKittrick, David, 23
McLaughlin, Justice, 207
McLaughlin's bar, Belfast, 38
McMahon, Thomas, 54–5
McManus, Billy, 124
McManus, Willie, 124
Macmillan, Dick, 34–5
Macmillan, Michael, 121–3
MacNeill, Hugo, 89
'Mad Dog'. *See* Adair, Johnny
Madden, Ann, 181
Madonna, 89
Magee, Hugh, 133
Magee, Kevin, 186–90
Maghera, County Londonderry, 48–51,
    237
Maghera Presbyterian Church, 50, 51
Maghera Primary School, 49
Magherafelt, County Londonderry, 50,
    213
Magill, Father Martin, 219, 231
Maginnis, Ken, 93, 248
Maguire, Anne, 39, 40
Maguire, Canon Bernard, 76
Maguire, Fintan, 207
Maguire, Jackie, 40
Maguire family, 39, 62
Mahoney, John, 123
Maidstone prison ship, 23
Major, John, 143, 144
Mallon, Seamus, 41, 250
Manchester United, 28, 204
Manor Street, Belfast, 132
Marita Ann, 78–80
Markets, Belfast, 24
Marley, Larry, 74–5
Martin, Micheál, 230
Mary Peters Trust, 60
Massachusetts, USA, 79
Massereene Barracks, Antrim, 211–13
Matchett, Stanley, 16–18
Mater Hospital, Belfast, 208
Matheny, Scott, 241
Mawn, Barry, 79